Decisionmaking
on War and Peace

Decisionmaking on War and Peace

The Cognitive-Rational Debate

edited by
Nehemia Geva
and Alex Mintz

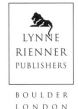

LYNNE
RIENNER
PUBLISHERS

BOULDER
LONDON

JX
1395
D42
1997

Published in the United States of America in 1997 by
Lynne Rienner Publishers, Inc.
1800 30th Street, Boulder, Colorado 80301

and in the United Kingdom by
Lynne Rienner Publishers, Inc.
3 Henrietta Street, Covent Garden, London WC2E 8LU

Library of Congress Cataloging-in-Publication Data
Decisionmaking on war and peace : the cognitive-rational debate /
    edited by Nehemia Geva and Alex Mintz.
        p.   cm.
    Includes bibliographical references and index.
    ISBN 1-55587-721-4 (hc)
    1. International relations—Decision making. 2. International
relations—Psychological aspects. I. Geva, Nehemia, 1946–   .
II. Mintz, Alex, 1953–   .
Jx1395.D42   1997
353.1'3234'019—dc21   97-44
                                                                  CIP

British Cataloguing in Publication Data
A Cataloguing in Publication record for this book
is available from the British Library.

Printed and bound in the United States of America

The paper used in this publication meets the requirements
of the American National Standard for Permanence of
Paper for Printed Library Materials Z39.48-1984.

5 4 3 2 1

Contents

List of Tables and Figures vii

Acknowledgments ix

1 Foreign Policy Decisionmaking: Bridging the Gap Between
the Cognitive Psychology and Rational Actor "Schools" 1
Alex Mintz

Part 1 Rational and Cognitive Approaches to International Conflict

2 A Rational Choice Approach to International Conflict 11
James D. Morrow

3 Prospect Theory and the Cognitive-Rational Debate 33
Jack S. Levy

4 Rational and Psychological Approaches to the Study of
International Conflict: Comparative Strengths and Weaknesses 51
Janice Gross Stein & David A. Welch

Part 2 Alternatives to Rational Choice and Prospect Theory

5 The Poliheuristic Theory of Foreign Policy Decisionmaking 81
Alex Mintz & Nehemia Geva

6 The Rationality of Surprise: Unstable Nash Equilibria
and the Theory of Moves 103
Steven J. Brams

7 A Two-Level Analysis of War and Revolution:
A Dynamic Simulation of Response to Threat 131
Marc V. Simon & Harvey Starr

Part 3 The Cognitive-Rational Discourse: An Appraisal

8 Decisional Stress, Individual Choice, and
Policy Outcomes: The Arab-Israeli Conflict 163
Zeev Maoz

9 Prospect Theory Versus Expected Utility Theory:
   A Dispute Sequence Appraisal   183
   Dina A. Zinnes & Robert G. Muncaster

Part 4   Conclusion

10 Decisionmaking on War and Peace:
    Challenges for Future Research   215
    Nehemia Geva, Steven B. Redd & Alex Mintz

References   223
About the Contributors   247
Index   251
About the Book   257

Tables and Figures

TABLES

5.1	Number of Items Viewed on Chosen and Nonchosen Alternatives Under Conditions of "Justification" and "No Justification"	96
5.2	Proportion of Subjects Exhibiting an EBA Search Pattern as a Function of the Experimental Conditions	98
5.3	The Choice of the "Target Alternative" as a Function of the Experimental Conditions	99
7.1	Baseline Values for Simulation Parameters	138
7.2	Average Effect of System Size on Security Gains	145
8.1	Individual Decisionmakers and Their Decision Performances	173
8.2	Effects of Threat, Opportunity, Time Pressure, and Stress Levels on Decisional Paths	175
8.3	Analysis of Variance of Decision Performance Indices by Threat, Opportunity, Time Pressure, and Stress	176
9.1	Summary Results of the Simulations	209

FIGURES

5.1	Choice of Alternatives on a Given Decision Board as a Function of the Decision Model	91
5.2	The Decision Matrix as Displayed on the Monitor	94
6.1a	Surprise Game (Simultaneous Play)	106
6.1b	Surprise Game (R Moves First)	106
6.2	Six 2 x 2 Strict Ordinal Games Subsumed by Surprise Game (Simultaneous Play)	108
6.3	The Pearl Harbor Game (Game 56)	119
6.4	The Sadat Initiative Game (Game 27)	121
7.1	Basic C, R, S, T Framework	133
7.2	Summary of Functional Relationships in the Model	135
7.3	Simulation Flowchart	144
7.4	Security Gain by System Polarity	146

7.5	Security and Resource Changes in Systems with One Hawk or One Dove	148
7.6	The International Hawk/Domestic Dove Strategy	150
7.7	The Effect Legitimacy Has on Security and Resources	152
7.8	The Effect Willingness of Other States to Go to War Has on Security and Resources	152
7.9	Relative Impact of Variables on Security and Resource Gains	154
7.10	Security and Resources over Time for Weak Dovish State	155
9.1	General Structure of the Dispute Sequence Model	186
9.2	General Structure of the Dispute Involvement Submodel	188
9.3	Substructure of the Model of Dispute Involvement and Subsequent Relationship Updatings	189
9.4	The Utility Function and Its Inverse	198
9.5	The Value Function and Its Inverse	199
9.6	The Probability Weight Function	201
9.7	A Prospect Theorist in an Expected Utility World	203
9.8	An Expected Utility Maximizer in a Prospect Theory World	205
9.9	A Prospect Theorist in a True World	206
9.10	An Expected Utility Maximizer in a True World	207

Acknowledgments

This volume, the first in a new series on "Advances in Foreign Policy Analysis," grew out of a conference organized by the Military Studies Institute at Texas A&M University and cosponsored by the university's Program in Foreign Policy Decision Making and Department of Political Science. We thank Professor Joseph G. Dawson III, the director of the Military Studies Institute, for his support for the conference and the development of this volume, and we extend our appreciation to the participants and contributors to the endeavor. We also thank Lyn Reitmeyer Mack, the coordinator of the Program in Foreign Policy Decision Making at Texas A&M University, for her input and assistance in organizing the conference and in helping prepare the manuscript for publication. Finally, we thank Lynne Rienner and her staff for a first-rate job.

1

Foreign Policy Decisionmaking: Bridging the Gap Between the Cognitive Psychology and Rational Actor "Schools"

Alex Mintz

The debate over whether rational or cognitive decision rules explain decisions about war and peace has received considerable attention in recent years.[1] At the core of the debate are questions about the actual decision-making behavior of political leaders: whether they maximize or satisfy utility, whether they are engaged in a holistic or nonholistic search, whether they are capable of making detailed calculations or are limited to simplifying heuristics, and whether they are influenced by framing effects. These issues are important, as they affect the ultimate decision:

- No decision is possible without a decision rule.
- Decision rules and strategies affect choice; the use of different decision rules (analytic, cybernetic, or cognitive) or "mixed" strategies (such as analytic-cybernetic) is likely to influence the outcome.
- The way issues are "framed" and "counterframed" and the situation represented (e.g., to the political leader, to the opposition, and/or to the public) are likely to affect the choice.
- Rules of aggregation (of individual preferences into collective opinion) affect choice.
- The comprehensiveness of the decisionmaking process and the exhaustiveness of the information base are likely to affect the choice.
- The order in which information is processed typically affects the outcome.

The rational actor model assumes global optimization. It can be traced back to the work of Von Neumann and Morgenstern in the early 1940s. According to their subjective, expected utility theory, decisionmakers attempt to think about the outcomes "that could result from the available choices as well as the chances of those outcomes occurring, and then choose the alternative that seems in some rough way to offer the best potential" (Beach and Mitchell 1978, p. 441).

Support for and challenges to the rational actor paradigm are widespread and come from a variety of disciplines, each viewing the debate through its own (disciplinary) lens: Cognitive psychologists tend to focus on the decisionmaking process; sociologists on social structures, values, and norms; political scientists on the predominance of political factors and political institutions in decisionmaking; economists on the maximization of wealth subject to varying constraints; finance theorists on the imperfect behavior of markets; marketing experts on the "framing" of consumer choices as leading to quasi-rational behavior.

Defenders of the rational, expected utility model point to at least three qualities of the model. Milton Friedman has observed that individuals behave "as if" they maximize utility. Friedman also argues that theories should be judged "not on the basis of their assumptions but rather on the validity of their predictions" (cited in De Bondt and Thaler 1994, p. 2). Predictive power (outcome validity) is what counts; expected utility is not about the process but about the choice. Arrow (1982, p. 1) adds that the expected utility model offers "an important starting point . . . in the sense that it provides a refutable hypothesis and indeed one for which the testing of implications is rather straightforward." There is also agreement that models that build on the maximizing principle may be useful as benchmarks to evaluate the quality of actual decisionmaking and that they lead to more accurate and more desirable outcomes (Herek, Janis, and Huth 1987). Grofman (1993, p. 242), however, thinks that thus far the main contributions of rational choice theory have been more "in the questions it asks than in the answers it has given."

In cognitive psychology, where experimental work is common, the challenge to the rational, expected utility model of behavior under uncertainty is strong, with evidence from the laboratory usually showing that people just don't make decisions as prescribed by the classical model. As numerous articles in influential journals such as *Organizational Behavior and Human Decision Making* show, people seldom maximize utility (Simon 1957); they frequently violate the invariance assumption while being sensitive to framing effects (Tversky and Kahneman 1986; Frisch 1993); they seldom engage in holistic search (see Ford et al. 1989); and they refrain from complex calculations because of cognitive limitations (Simon 1957; Jones 1994). Many cognitivists therefore see expected utility theory as normative and prescriptive, but not as describing the actual process of decision; another model, prospect theory, has emerged as an alternative. It is almost fashionable in cognitive psychology to engage in rational choice "bashing" and to (almost) automatically accept as given its limited applicability. But as numerous scholars have pointed out (Beach and Mitchell 1978), expected utility theory does not aim at dealing with such issues as how to frame the problem or to develop alternatives (Zey 1992, p. 3); instead, the consensus is that people choose schemata "which are most available rather than the most fruitful" (Wittman 1991, p. 405). The Cognitive Psychology "School" is also not without its own limitations, however.

In economics and related fields (finance, marketing) the concept of rationality is central, of course. And whereas the behavioral challenge to the classical model is gaining some market share, quasi-rational behavior is still perceived as explaining the deviant (anomalous) case rather than the common phenomena. Important contributions to the behavioral orientation come from Lichtenstein and Slovic (1971) on "preference reversal" (see also Tversky, Slovic, and Kahneman 1990), Thaler (1980) on quasi rationality in economics, De Bondt and Thaler (1985; 1990) on systematic deviations from the classical model in financial decisions— for example, the equity premium puzzle (see also Mehra and Prescott 1985), the dividend policy puzzle (see De Bondt and Thaler 1994)—and more recent work in the area of consumer choice and marketing strategies (see examples in De Bondt and Thaler 1994, p. 2). The rational actor-maximizing model still dominates in these fields, however, even though such prominent economists as Nobel laureate Kenneth Arrow caution that although people typically maximize utility subject to certain constraints, important anomalies in economic behavior cannot be explained by the maximizing principle and deserve a different model of choice (1982).

Notable sociologists such as James Coleman (1992) and Amitai Etzioni (1992) argue that cultural and structural factors account for variations in decisionmaking. According to Etzioni, decisionmaking is not an individualistic event that takes place in isolation. Decisionmaking models need to recognize the broader context of decisionmaking: The impact of social factors, social structures, moral commitments, emotions, and values has a profound effect on decisionmaking. Furthermore, Etzioni believes that individuals have multiple utility functions because they have multiple goals, and these functions "are not tied together into some overreaching utility function" (Uslaner 1993, p. 72).

The optimality assumption has also been challenged in political science. A well-known study by Quattrone and Tversky (1988) shows that political men and women often violate the invariance assumption by being affected by framing effects. And the voter turnout paradox, which predicts low turnout in elections due to a low or negative expected utility, almost kills the approach (but see Grofman 1993 and Uslaner 1993). The Downsian model of turnout is fundamentally at variance with the empirical facts. Important books by Green and Shapiro (1994) and Sniderman, Brody, and Tetlock (1991) show that these phenomena are not just deviations from individual rational behavior but more common patterns of political behavior.

Rational choice work in the field of international relations and foreign policy decisionmaking has been dominated by the very important contributions of Bueno de Mesquita (1981, 1985) and Bueno de Mesquita and Lalman (1990, 1992). Game theoretic models of deterrence, the arms race, war initiation, war termination, trade, bargaining, and negotiation are also widespread (see Brams 1985 and Chapter 6 of this volume; Kilgour and Zagare 1993; Morrow 1995 and Chapter 2; and Zagare and Kilgour 1993). But authors such as George (1980), Jervis (1976), Lebow (1981), Stein and Welch (1995 and Chapter 4), Vertzberger (1990), and others often point to shortcuts to rationality in the foreign policy behavior of leaders. Despite several attempts, however, no dominant model of quasi-rational behavior has emerged as an alternative to the expected utility model of war and peace decisionmaking (see Mintz 1993).

Critics of the alternative, cognitive "school" of decisionmaking claim that it does not offer a unified theory but a set of ad hoc descriptive hypotheses "tending to claim . . . a new explanation for every observation" (cited in Jones 1994). Herek, Janis, and Huth (1987) argue that deviations from the analytic, classical model often produce defective procedures. Authors also point to the shortcomings of laboratory research that too often ignores learning, experience, feedback, repetition, and adequate incentives and, most important, lacks external validity/generalizability (see Wittman 1991 for a critique of the relevance of cognitive psychology for other fields of inquiry). According to Wittman (1991, pp. 408–409), "almost all of the [cognitivists'] experiments are plagued by the problem that errors in judgment are not costly and there is no chance for long-run learning and survival." Moreover, Wittman claims that whereas cognitive psychology can explain some anomalies, "standard behavior becomes anomalous from the viewpoint of cognitive psychology" (p. 416). According to Wittman, economic theory explains the typical case, even though it may not be able to predict anomalous behavior. And according to Grofman (1993, p. 240), "you can't beat something with nothing"—it is not enough to show that some given rational choice model does not fit the data; it is necessary to show that some other perspective leads to a model with a better fit and predictive power. How can the debate on rational versus cognitive decisionmaking be resolved?

BRIDGING THE GAP BETWEEN THE "COGNITIVE" AND THE "RATIONAL"

Foreign policy decisions have typically been explained by either the rational actor or cognitive psychology models. It is my contention that it is not the rational model or the cognitive model that best explains political behavior in the realm of national security and foreign policy, but that people/leaders/decisionmakers use a mixture of choice strategies (analytic, cybernetic, cognitive) on route to a decision and that they often switch strategies during the decision process itself (see Mintz, Geva, Redd, and Carnes 1997 for experimental evidence). As Brecher (1995) points out, the rational actor and cognitive psychology models are not as incompatible as they may seem at first glance. Moreover, neither approach "has a monopoly of the truth; both explain part of the totality of foreign policy behavior; and an attempt to achieve integration is essential." According to Brecher (p. 17), to explain a decision to initiate war "solely in terms of a subjective expected utility calculus may satisfy a penchant for parsimony, but does such a model do justice to the complex process attending a decision to go to war? . . . Similarly, to focus exclusively on the cognitive dispositions of decision-makers to fight or not to fight and to imply that a calculus of utility is either not made or plays a marginal role in the choice process" may also be misguided. Together, the cognitive and rational actor models explain much, perhaps most, but not all about the foreign policy decisionmaking process.

My point is that political decisionmakers often use more than one decision strategy in reaching a particular decision. They may start the decision process by using one strategy (e.g., Elimination by Aspect [EBA]) and switch to another (e.g., expected utility strategy). Moreover, rational choice models can, of course, include psychological, cognitive factors. The cognitive approach is also rational in most situations, since leaders, as cognitive managers, are motivated to select the decision strategy that requires the least investment for a satisfactory solution. The important questions pertinent to the cognitive-rational debate, therefore, do not concern which of these models provides the "best" description or explanation of the phenomenon under study, but are rather

1. Under what conditions do decisionmakers use one decision strategy or another?
2. Under what conditions do they switch strategies during the decision process?

Process models and outcome models of choice highlight different aspects of decisionmaking and have different strengths and weaknesses.

With process models the strategies that people use in arriving at a decision are the main focus of inquiry (see Ford et al. 1989, p. 76). In contrast, with outcome models what counts is the accuracy of the prediction. And indeed rational choice models of international relations have been rather successful in predicting foreign policy choice even though they pay scant attention to the cognitive processes of decision. They thus emphasize outcome validity, while paying less attention to process validity. Cognitive models in international relations typically do better at explaining the process of decisionmaking but need to develop predictive models of foreign policy choice. The challenge, then, is to develop models of decisionmaking that have strong predictive power *and* are more descriptively valid. Expected and subjective expected utility models differ from cognitive models in the amount of resources each requires. After all, strategy selection is a compromise between "the press for more decision accuracy as the demands of the decision task increase and the decision maker's resistance to the expenditure of his or her personal resources. [Thus,] the tendency toward selecting strategies of ever increasing probability of being correct is checked by the disutility for increased resource expenditure" (Beach and Mitchell 1978, pp. 447–448).

New computer technologies that enable both process tracing and structural analyses may allow scholars to advance the state of knowledge on both the process and the outcome of important foreign policy decisions (see Ford et al. 1989; Mintz and Geva 1996). The use of models that utilize "cognitive algebra" and computational process tracing can also enhance process and outcome validity (Taber and Steenbergen 1995). Elements of the (descriptive) cognitive psychology model and components of the (normative) rational actor model should be integrated.

The chapters in this volume take us a long way in describing the leading cognitive and rational models, introducing alternative models of foreign policy choice, and identifying the conditions under which one strategy is more appropriate than another. The first part introduces several theoretical approaches to foreign policy decisionmaking: the rational choice model (James D. Morrow), prospect theory (Jack S. Levy), and several cognitive approaches to international relations (Janice Gross Stein and David A. Welch). Part 2 includes chapters that offer alternative models to the rational, prospect, and cognitive models of decision: the poliheuristic theory of decisionmaking (Alex Mintz and Nehemia Geva), the theory of moves (Steven J. Brams), and "two-level" game models (Marc V. Simon and Harvey Starr). The third part assesses the adequacy of the different models, using empirical data analysis (Zeev Maoz) and computer simulation (Dina A. Zinnes and Robert G. Muncaster). The concluding chapter (Nehemia Geva, Steven B. Redd, and Alex Mintz) introduces three new challenges to the student of foreign policy decisionmaking. Collectively, the authors present the most current thinking about "cognitive" and "rational" decisionmaking on war and peace.

NOTE

1. According to one leading scholar of the foreign policy process (Brecher 1995), the cognitive-rational debate represents "a fundamental, all-encompassing divide in the study of world politics." Brecher, however, sees these approaches as complementary rather than contradictory strategies.

Part 1

Rational and Cognitive Approaches to International Conflict

2

A Rational Choice Approach to International Conflict

James D. Morrow

Rational choice approaches to international conflict have generated a set of important and empirically supported propositions since the early 1980s. Utility and game theory, both originally applied in economics, are the key tools for the statement and explication of theories of choice in international conflict. Utility theory accounts for the choices of individuals deciding in isolation, game theory for individuals' choices when all their choices can affect the outcome.

Although utility theory was used first to explain international conflict (e.g., Bueno de Mesquita 1981), game theory is a natural tool for understanding conflict (e.g., Bueno de Mesquita and Lalman 1992). Conflict is strategic interaction; the actions of both sides determine whether war occurs, and actors in international crises choose their actions in part for the anticipated effect of those actions on others. Game theory provides a rigorous tool for explaining choices in strategic interaction. In particular, noncooperative game theory provides a powerful tool for explicating theories addressing critical elements of international crises—credibility, dynamics, and perception. But the role of these rational choice theories is often misunderstood. This chapter addresses three questions: First, what is rational choice and its role in explanations of conflict? Second, what restrictions do the central assumptions of game theory place on how we think about conflict? And third, what are the broad implications of a rational choice approach for the study of international conflict?

Before I begin with the substance of this chapter, let me state my commitment to the scientific study of international conflict and what my commitment entails. At a minimum, science demands and creates consensual knowledge among a scientific community based on the empirical testing of logical theories. The creation of consensual knowledge requires explicit theory and explicit testing. The former assists scientists in determining what the logic of a theory is and whether that logic is correct; the latter assists scientists in determining both the outcome of a particular test and whether that evidence tests the conclusions of a theory. Obviously, the process of science involves more than just explicit arguments and tests. But at a minimum, explicit logic and tests are central to scientific understanding. The details matter.

Because the details matter, it is imperative that we spell them out. I claim that many objections to rational choice theory arise because of the details of such theory. I am not saying that we should ignore such objections because they address the details. Rather, many of the details of rational choice theory that appear objectionable in the abstract are substantially innocuous. Assumptions that appear highly restrictive in the abstract prove to be quite flexible in practice. Those details place little or no restriction on possible theories of international conflict.

This last point is important. *The* rational choice theory of conflict does not exist. Rather, rational choice methods are a way to elaborate competing theories of international conflict. They provide the basic tools for explicating general theoretical statements. Of course, other sets of basic tools exist; psychological approaches could provide a different set of tools for explicating theory. The task of judging the value of such tools is difficult. Because we test theories—not the tools used to elaborate them—we cannot judge the value of these tools directly by evidence. Instead, we ask whether the tools lead to productive lines of research. Rational choice methods have led to novel hypotheses supported by evidence across a large number of cases (e.g., Bueno de Mesquita and Lalman 1992; Fearon 1994; Kim and Morrow 1992; Morrow 1989b). They have also produced a body of models that challenge the accepted wisdom in the field and lead to substantially different ways of thinking about central issues in international conflict (e.g., Fearon 1995; Powell 1990). Now I turn to what those methods require us to accept.

WHAT IS RATIONAL CHOICE?

Rational choice is a simple idea: Actors do what they believe is in their best interest at the time they must choose. Stated this way, the idea is so simple as to be innocuous. The purchase of rational choice methods is created by specifying what this simple statement means.

How do we specify what actors believe is in their best interest? First, we define outcomes, the final results of the combination of choices and influences beyond the actors' control. Outcomes are mutually exclusive and exhaustive; that is, one and only one outcome will result. Second, we define actions, the choices available to each actor. In parallel to outcomes, an actor chooses one and only one action in a choice. Finally, we specify the mechanism that leads from chosen actions to outcomes. Each actor has a preference ordering over the outcomes; that is, it can rank the outcomes from best to worst, allowing for the possibility of ties in the order. Preference orders are complete—for each pair of outcomes, one is at least as good as the other—and transitive—if one outcome is at least as good as a second and the second is at least as good as the third, then the first is at least as good as the third.

An actor chooses an action to produce preferred outcomes. Which action is chosen depends on both an actor's preferences over outcomes and its knowledge about how actions produce outcomes. If each and every action produced one outcome with certainty, chosen actions would follow directly from preferences over outcomes: An actor would just choose the action that produced the outcome ranked highest among the set of outcomes that could result. But we usually believe that actors are not certain about the consequences of their actions. Such lack of certainty is represented by a probability distribution for each action that gives the probability of each outcome's occurring if that action is chosen.

Uncertainty makes a theory of choice more difficult to specify.[1] Preferences over outcomes are not sufficient to lead to complete preferences over actions when actors are not certain about what outcomes each action produces. We need more than just preferences over outcomes to account for a choice between an action that produces the best and worst outcomes with equal probability and one that always produces a middling outcome. Rational choice approaches commonly, but not always, assume that actors are expected utility maximizers. We assume that actors also have complete preferences over the set of all possible gambles over the outcomes. Gambles are probability distributions over a set of outcomes or other gambles and provide a way to formalize actions. The expected utility theorem states that if preferences over gambles observe four conditions, then there exists an index, called utility, over the outcomes such that the preferences over gambles are given by their expected utilities. The expected utility of a gamble is the utility of each possible outcome multiplied by the probability of that outcome's occurring in the gamble. One gamble is preferred to another only if its expected utility is greater.

The four conditions of the expected utility theorem are that preferences over gambles are (1) complete, (2) transitive, (3) continuous in mixtures, and (4) independent from equal substitutions. The first two conditions have been defined earlier and ensure a preference order over gambles. The third condition, also known as the Archimedean axiom, asserts that for any three gambles ranked in order, there exists a gamble over the best and worst gambles such that the actor is indifferent between it and the middle gamble for certain. If such a gamble could not be found, then either the best gamble is so good that the decider in question will take any nonzero chance of gaining it no matter the cost of the worst gamble, or the worst gamble is so bad that the decider will accept any chance of avoiding it no matter the attractiveness of the best gamble. Such behavior is bizarre in its extremes. We then are assuming that none of the outcomes is so attractive or so unattractive as to produce such extreme behavior.

The fourth condition, called the independence axiom, asserts that preferences between gambles are not altered by a partial substitution of another gamble in both. Begin with two gambles, G and H, G preferred to H. Consider two compound gambles, G' and H', with a parallel structure— each gives an identical chance of a given gamble F and the complementary probability to G and H, respectively. The independence axiom asserts that G' must be preferred to H' because G is preferred to H. The choice between G' and H' is independent of the chance of F because F is equally likely in both G' and H'. Decisions should not be changed in the face of equal substitutions. None of the four conditions seems objectionable. Given all four, preferences over gambles can be represented by a utility function that is linear in probabilities.

At this point I must make two points about the role of the expected utility hypothesis in rational choice approaches. First, one can have rational choice theories without assuming expected utility. When actors can predict the consequences of their actions, preferences over outcomes are sufficient; utilities are not needed to determine preferred actions. Niou and Ordeshook's models of balance-of-power theory (Niou, Ordeshook, and Rose 1989; Niou and Ordeshook 1990) are an example of a rational choice theory that does not require the expected utility hypothesis. Their models require only preference orderings over the set of outcomes, which are distributions of resources.

Second, the expected utility hypothesis leads to a flexible model of individual choice for the construction of models of international politics. The expected utility hypothesis does not restrict the set of possible outcomes, actors' preferences over those outcomes, the set of available actions, or what actors believe about how actions lead to outcomes. We must address those questions to develop models of international conflict, and expected utility approaches attune us to the variety of individual responses that are possible within a decisional setting.

In one sense, prospect theory and the poliheuristic theory are rational choice approaches. Both assert that actors are trying to achieve preferred ends through their choices. Prospect theory claims that choices are inconsistent with utility functions that are linear in probabilities. Psychological experiments produce behavioral deviations from this condition of utility theory. The poliheuristic theory claims that we must study the cognitive heuristics that actors use in evaluating alternatives. Different actors use different heuristics. But the core view of purposive actors is the same in all three approaches. The argument here is about whether an expected utility framework can represent choices. The best demonstration that it cannot is a logical proof that sets of observed choices are not consistent with any possible utility function.

Experiments are often offered as evidence that choices are inconsistent with utility theory. For example, Mintz and Geva (Chapter 5) describe experiments on information processing relevant to the poliheuristic theory. The information available in the experiments combines states of the world and different facets of outcomes into summary measures. For example, experimental subjects can examine information on the political, military, economic, and diplomatic consequences of the courses of action available. But these different facets are not distinct outcomes; rather, they are partial descriptions of likely outcomes. They are not mutually exclusive and exhaustive; we expect political, military, economic, *and* diplomatic consequences for any action. Neither the underlying set of outcomes nor a probability distribution over them is given to the subjects. The descriptions of consequences include the effects of uncertainty. Utility theory says nothing about how actors will combine the information available in these experiments because the experimental design has already combined the outcomes and probabilities in the available information. Further, utility theory, as used in economics and political science, is an external recreation of choices; it is *not* a representation of cognitive process. Psychologists may interpret utility theory as requiring that all facets of an outcome and all available information must be used in a decision, but this interpretation is a non sequitur. *Nothing in the assumptions of utility theory supports this interpretation.* These experiments do not contradict utility theory or its use in international politics.

Even with the flexibility of the expected utility hypothesis, there is a large body of evidence from experimental psychology and economics that people sometimes deviate from expected utility maximization. These deviations typically violate the independence condition of the expected utility theorem. However, there are good reasons to believe that such deviations do not pose a mortal threat for the application of the expected utility hypothesis to international conflict. First, there are versions of utility theory that do not use the independence condition (Machina 1987, 1989). Economic models using such generalized utility theory do not generate results substantially different from those using expected utility theory.

Second, alternatives to utility theory that do not assume the independence condition, like prospect theory, are based on the close empirical study of the decisions of individuals. But international conflict is the study of the actions of states rather than those of individuals. It is a significant leap of faith to believe that a theory of choice developed empirically to account for the decisions of individuals can also account for the actions of a state. The application of utility theory to international conflict does not suffer from this problem of using a theory of individual choice to represent collective choice. The expected utility theorem states that if the preferences of an actor, whether state or individual, satisfy the conditions of the theorem, then that actor's choices can be represented by a utility function. There is no assumption that the actors are individuals. There may be good reasons to believe that the actions of states are not consistent and so cannot be represented by a utility function (Bueno de Mesquita 1981, pp. 12–18; but see also Morrow 1988). But given the assumption that state action is consistent, the expected utility theorem shows that such actions can be represented by a utility function.

Prospect theory has no such logical basis. It does not have a central theorem that states the conditions that decisions must satisfy in order to be represented by its constructs. The use of prospect theory to represent the decisions of states requires the leap of faith that a theory of individual choice can represent the choices of collectives. Applications of prospect theory to international relations recognize this point and typically focus on the choices of important individuals in government (e.g., Farnham 1992). Such studies usually assert, rather than demonstrate, that observed choices are inconsistent with utility theory. Such assertions may say more about the authors' failure to understand utility theory than about the ability of utility theory to account for actions.

So far I have said little about what the actors know about the links between their actions and the final outcome. We expect that actors cannot perfectly anticipate the consequences of their actions and so choose under uncertainty. But how much do actors know about their situation, and how well can they process the information available to them? Rational choice models typically limit the uncertainties in a situation and delineate them precisely. Each actor has a set of beliefs over the uncertain elements of the situation and updates those beliefs using Bayes's law when it acquires new information. Information may be costly, and actors may choose not to collect information because of such costs. However, actors always have a good understanding of the nature of the uncertainties facing them because those uncertainties must be spelled out. They know what states of the world are possible, and they hold some beliefs about the relative probabilities of the different states.

Bounded rationality, the undoubtedly correct observation that people have limited abilities for calculation and deduction, is commonly held to be an alternative to rational choice. But bounded rationality is rarely defined precisely. What limits exist on human abilities, and how do individuals process information? When bounded rationality has been spelled out explicitly, it produces the same behavior as some rational choice models. Satisficing, the idea that people select the first acceptable alternative that they find, is a rational choice procedure when actors face search costs. Hierarchies and organizational procedures provide an efficient solution to the coordination of the activities of many individuals on one task. The idea of bounded rationality is attractive in the abstract, as is the idea of rationality. Most of the objections to rational choice theory arise from the specific content of what rational choice means, not to the general idea that people pursue their self-interest as they understand it. But because the details matter, progress in understanding international conflict requires specific models of bounded rationality. Will those specific models prove to be as attractive as the general concept? We can know only by developing such models.

The issue of bounded rationality is important in game theory.[2] A main source of uncertainty in games is the actions of the other players. Bounded rationality could have a profound impact on the inferences the players can make about each other's moves and so what moves they choose to make. I return to the issue of bounded rationality in the following section, on the assumptions of game theory.

WHAT DOES GAME THEORY ASSUME?

International conflict involves the actions of two or more parties trying to influence each other. Game theory is the appropriate tool from choice theory for building models of international conflict. In utility theory the choice of one actor and impersonal forces beyond that actor's control produce the outcome. The impersonal forces are modeled by a random process. In game theory the choices of multiple actors and impersonal forces beyond their control produce the outcome. Again, the impersonal forces are modeled by a random process. But the choices of the actors cannot be: Actors must consider what moves the others will make when choosing their own moves. I call a player's anticipations of other players' moves its conjecture about how the game will be played. Conjectures can be modeled by probability distributions, just like beliefs about the state of the world. Players choose their actions to produce preferred outcomes using their conjectures to determine which outcomes are likely given each action. Unlike beliefs in utility theory that are unconstrained, conjectures in game theory recognize that the other players are choosing their actions to achieve the outcomes they prefer.

Before elaborating on the development of this idea in the concept of equilibrium in game theory, I first specify what is meant by a game.[3] The extensive form of a game delineates what choices each player has, the order of those choices, what outcomes are possible, how the players' choices produce outcomes, what each player knows when it must choose, and the utility each player has for each outcome. The game tree gives all possible choice points in a game, called choice nodes; the actions available to the moving player at each choice node, called branches; and the points where the game ends, called terminal nodes. One and only one player is assigned to each choice node, and one and only one outcome to each terminal node. Chance events can be included by treating chance as a player who moves with fixed and known probabilities. Each player's choice nodes are partitioned into information sets; when a player moves, it knows at which information set it is but not at which node within that information set. Information sets describe what the player knows about prior moves when it faces a choice. Each player has a utility function over the set of possible outcomes; payoffs are the utility each player receives from each outcome. Finally, we assume that the extensive form of the game is common knowledge among the players—that is, all players know it, they know that all other players know it, and so on through all possible levels of knowledge about one another's knowledge. A game is played under perfect information if all information sets contain only one node. Under perfect information, every player knows all prior moves when it must choose. A game is played under complete information if all the players' utility functions for outcomes are common knowledge.

A strategy for a player is a complete plan to play the game; it must specify a move for each information set of the player. Strategies simplify strategic analysis. We ask what strategy a player should play in response to the other player's strategies. (I talk in terms of two-person games here, but most of the concepts generalize directly to n-person games.) A best reply for a player against a given strategy of the other player is the strategy that gives the first player at least as high a payoff against the given strategy as any other strategy of the first player. If a strategy gives a player a higher payoff than any other against a fixed strategy of the other player, we say it is a strict best reply. Rational players should play best replies against what strategy they think the other player is playing. A strategy is dominant if it is a strict best reply against all strategies of the other player. Obviously, rational players should play a dominant strategy if they have one; they always do worse with any other strategy regardless of which strategy the other player plays. But very few games have dominant strategies. Typically, a player's best reply depends upon the strategy of the other player.

What should rational players do when they do not have dominant strategies? Can we place any restriction on what strategy each expects the other to play? One strategy strictly dominates another for a player if the first strategy always produces a higher payoff than the second. Rational players should never play a strictly dominated strategy. This observation leads to a first restriction on what conjectures players can hold about one another's strategies: rationalizability. Rationalizable strategies are found through a process of iterated elimination of strictly dominated strategies. Begin by eliminating all strictly dominated strategies for all players. Evaluate the remaining strategies to see if any are now strictly dominated on the smaller set of remaining strategies for the other player. Eliminate the now-dominated strategies and continue the process until no strategies can be eliminated. Any strategy that remains is rationalizable.

Rationalizability is a minimal condition on conjectures for rational actors. It assumes that all players are rational and that their rationality is common knowledge. Each player does not want to play a strictly dominated strategy and can anticipate that the other player will not play a strictly dominated strategy. Its conjecture about the other player's strategy arises from the common knowledge of the players' rationality and the game. Irrational moves are not expected to occur. By "rational" here, I mean only that a player's payoffs capture its preferences over lotteries among the possible outcomes. Unfortunately, players have multiple rationalizable strategies in most games. Any rationalizable strategy is a best reply for some conjecture that the other player is playing one of its rationalizable strategies (otherwise, the first player's strategy would be strictly dominated). Rationalizability, then, places a mild restriction on conjectures.

Under rationalizability, players can hold incorrect conjectures. They can believe that the other player will play a strategy other than the strategy it plays. Because best replies depend upon a conjecture about the other player's strategy, a player holding an incorrect conjecture would want to change its strategy. Equilibrium, in contrast, assumes that the players' conjectures are correct. To use game theoretic lingo, the players hold a common conjecture about how the game will be played (Brandenburger 1992). Equilibria are sets of strategies where each player's strategy is a best reply against the other player's strategy. Neither player wishes to change its strategy because it correctly anticipates the other player's strategy and plays a best reply against that strategy.

Why might the players hold such a common conjecture? There are three standard answers to this question. First, they may share common experience playing the game that leads them to share a common conjecture about how they will play. Second, some strategy pair may be distinguished from all others, making it a focal point. Each player then expects the other to play its focal strategy. Third, preplay communication could allow them to develop a common conjecture. All three are plausible explanations of why common conjectures might exist, but none of them is sufficient to guarantee that a common conjecture will exist. For example, communication can help the actors coordinate behavior, but it does not guarantee that they will.

It may seem that the assumption of a common conjecture is implausible in international conflict. Why should we believe that actors correctly anticipate each other's future moves in a crisis? The three reasons given for why a common conjecture might arise do not appear to hold in conflicts. Although the parties may have a common history of crises, repeated crises between the same two nations often have different outcomes. The parties do communicate, but communication through threats is part of what we would like to explain about conflict. Finally, there does not appear to be a clear focal point. Bargaining games typically have many equilibria, of which equal division is a possible focal point. But equal division does not appear to be a common outcome of crises.

The assumption of correct conjectures in equilibrium does not imply that both players can anticipate completely one another's future actions in a dispute. They would if they were playing pure strategies, where each player makes one and only one move from each information set. But many games have mixed strategy equilibria. A mixed strategy for a player specifies a probability distribution for each of its information sets. A player playing a mixed strategy must be indifferent among the pure strategies that are part of the mix. Otherwise, some pure strategy would be a best reply to the other player's strategy.

Players do not choose randomly among moves in a mixed strategy; rather, the probabilities represent the uncertainty of the other player about what the moving player will do. This interpretation of mixed strategies, due to Harsanyi (1973), assumes that a player's knowledge of the other player's payoffs is not complete. Small variations in payoffs unknown to the other player determine which move in the mixed strategy is the moving player's best reply. Mixed strategies, then, represent situations where the players are uncertain about one another's future actions. Each actor knows what actions it will take at each information set, but neither can anticipate the other's actions completely. The assumption of equilibrium does not deny the possibility that the actors' conjectures are uncertain about one another's future actions. It does require that their actions be best replies in response to their conjectures.

Uncertainty about one another's actions is the common conjecture in a mixed strategy equilibrium. Mixed strategy equilibria, I argue, should be preferred to pure strategy equilibria in models of international conflict. We generally believe that actors are uncertain about each other's future actions in a crisis. The common conjecture of uncertainty in a mixed strategy equilibrium captures this belief formally. In a pure strategy equilibrium, the actors can anticipate each other's moves completely, and those anticipations prove to be correct in equilibrium. International cooperation may exhibit the common conjecture needed to form such expectations, and pure strategy equilibria may be appropriate in models of cooperation. But conflict thrives on uncertainty, and we should select those equilibria where the players are uncertain about each other's future actions over those where they can anticipate such future choices.

Mixed strategies pose a particular problem if the players' preferences do not satisfy the independence condition. The probabilities of each pure strategy in a mixed strategy are calculated to make the other player indifferent among the pure strategies in its mixed strategy. Such probabilities may not exist when players' preferences do not satisfy independence. Equilibrium in beliefs (Crawford 1990) generalizes the concept of equilibrium to cases where the players' preferences do not satisfy independence. In an equilibrium in beliefs, each player holds a probabilistic conjecture or belief about the other player's strategy. Each player plays a best reply given its conjecture. Further, every strategy in a player's conjecture must also be a best reply against the other player's conjecture. Equilibrium in beliefs generalizes equilibrium, particularly mixed strategy equilibrium, to actors with preferences without independence. Each player plays a definite strategy but is uncertain about the other player's strategy.

So far I have discussed best replies at the level of strategies, that is, complete plans to play the game. But extensive-form games specify a sequence to the moves in a game. Further, our common understanding of international crises suggests that the interaction is sequential rather than simultaneous. Each side responds to the threats and offers of the other in turn. Sequence has an important effect on the judgment of best replies. Best replies should be judged at the level of individual moves instead of complete strategies. Players cannot commit themselves to particular moves in the future, but choosing a strategy at the start of the game does so.

Best replies must also be judged for moves that are possible in a game but do not occur in a particular equilibrium. The strategies in a given equilibrium produce moves that are made; those moves are said to be on the equilibrium path. Other decision nodes are not reached when that given equilibrium is played; they are said to be off the equilibrium path. The trick is that moves off the equilibrium path affect behavior on the equilibrium path. In a possible deterrence game, the challenger will be deterred if the defender carries out its threat. But if the challenger is always deterred, the threat does not need to be carried out. The challenger's decision to back down, which is on the equilibrium path, depends on the defender's decision to carry out the threat, which is off the equilibrium path in this example.

Backward induction provides the simplest way to check whether moves off the equilibrium path are best replies. You begin by checking moves at the end of the game, that is, those that lead only to terminal nodes. Choose the move that produces the best outcome for the moving player, then work backward through the tree to solve preceding moves by assuming that players making later moves will make the moves solved earlier. Continue the process to the initial move of the game. Backward induction gives a unique solution (up to indifference between outcomes).[4] However, backward induction can be applied only to games of complete and perfect information, when all players know all prior moves from each of their decision nodes.

Backward induction cannot be performed when a player faces some uncertainty when it must decide, that is, has an information set with multiple nodes. This problem is solved by defining a player's beliefs for each of its information sets with multiple nodes. Beliefs, given by a probability distribution over the nodes of an information set, give the likelihood that the moving player is at each node in the information set should that information set be reached. Beliefs, then, capture hypotheses about what moves have occurred before a player moves that it cannot verify within the game.

Because conjectures are correct in equilibrium, beliefs in equilibrium must be based on the other player's strategy. A perfect Bayesian equilibrium is formed from beliefs and strategies together. The strategies are best replies given the other player's strategy and the player's beliefs, and the beliefs are consistent with both players' strategies on the equilibrium path.

Perfect Bayesian equilibrium is the central solution concept for games of incomplete information. Incomplete information means that the players do not know one another's payoffs.[5] Such games are modeled by assuming that each player is one of several possible types, where each type has a different set of payoffs. The other player knows the set of possible types but not which particular type the other player is. Beliefs in games of incomplete information give the probability of each different type of other player and are thus closely connected to conjectures. If a player knew the other player's type, it could predict the other player's future moves. A player may be able to infer the other player's type from its earlier moves and so have a better idea about the other player's future moves.

Perfect Bayesian equilibrium unifies perception and action. Beliefs depend on strategies and strategies on beliefs. Beliefs in games of incomplete information can act like perceptions. Beliefs change with the other side's actions as the game unfolds, so that beliefs depend on actions. But beliefs also help determine actions because a player's best reply from any given move depends on its conjecture about the other player's future moves. Updated beliefs depend on both initial beliefs and how well the types of other players separate—distinguish themselves by making different moves. Conjectures also change as beliefs are updated. If different types will make different moves in a game, learning the other player's type improves the ability to predict its moves. In this way, perfect Bayesian equilibrium models learning, changes in perceptions, and how perceptions affect actions.

Psychological approaches to international conflict consider all these concepts empirically. Conjectures and beliefs are treated as exogenous variables where the relationship between the two is open and poorly specified. Sometimes the choice of strategy appears to be dictated by a simple cause-and-effect relationship, but strategic interaction is more complex. Preferences over outcomes, which we should expect to vary across actors, also affect choice of strategy. An empirical approach to conjectures and beliefs faces the problem that those concepts may not be amenable to ex ante analysis. Conjectures and beliefs reside in the heads of actors, leaving only scant direct historical record. Such concepts are easier to study ex post than ex ante. Before a crisis, actors understandably try to conceal evidence of their conjectures and beliefs from outside observers. After a crisis, observers can comb papers for indications of actors' thought processes, but the actors may have incentives to misrepresent them in their memoirs.

To date neither prospect theory nor the poliheuristic theory has addressed strategic interaction. Because we believe that strategic interaction is central to international conflict, rational choice methods are superior to those models. Of course, either model of decision could be adapted to strategic settings. But they will have to face the same questions that game theory has already faced. What restrictions do we place on the conjectures that players hold about each other's actions, for example? The assumption of rationality helps us begin to answer these questions in ways that may be difficult for these other approaches to match. Rationalizability allows us to eliminate strictly dominated strategies because rational actors would never use strategies that always made them worse off. Both prospect theory and the poliheuristic theory claim that actors deviate from the tenets of expected utility theory. Actors might then use strictly dominated strategies under these models, particularly if the dominating strategy were mixed rather than pure. Quite simply, we do not know how these perspectives treat strategic interaction. Models of strategic interaction could probably be built on either approach, but that work has not been done yet. Rational choice theorists have struggled with the difficult problem of strategic interaction since the 1940s.

Game theory, however, does not yet present a complete theory of strategic interaction. Perfect Bayesian equilibrium is the commonly accepted form of equilibrium at this time. It fails to address some important questions. For example, as I have mentioned, beliefs off the equilibrium path can influence behavior on the equilibrium path. One side in a conflict may be willing to carry out an incredible threat because of inferences it draws about the other side's type. The first side's willingness to carry out such a threat may be sufficient to deter the other side. Then the move where the threat would be carried out will not occur in equilibrium, that is, off the equilibrium path (Nalebuff 1991). Perfect Bayesian equilibrium places only weak restrictions on beliefs off the equilibrium path. Restrictions on beliefs try to deal with this issue (Cho and Kreps 1987; Banks and Sobel 1987), but they are not generally accepted. The concept of equilibrium has not yet reached a final stage of development. We should not be surprised if there are further developments in what equilibrium means in a game.

Some suggestions for advancing equilibrium try to address the problem of multiple equilibria (e.g., Harsanyi and Selten 1988). Many games have multiple equilibria, and equilibrium theory does not give a unique solution to these games. The possibility of multiple equilibria does not imply that game theory cannot provide testable hypotheses. When a game has multiple equilibria, not all strategy pairs are equilibria. Observing behavior that matched a nonequilibrium pair of strategies would falsify a hypothesis based on such a game. The existence of multiple equilibria also shows us how conjectures could affect behavior. Different equilibria require different common conjectures about the game. If we can find clear ex ante evidence about what conjecture the actors share, then we can predict a specific strategy pair. Although this possibility allows for some independent role for conjectures, that role is more limited than complete exogeneity of conjectures as in psychological approaches.

As noted earlier, equilibrium does not provide an explicit argument about why the actors share a common conjecture; it assumes they hold one. Binmore (1990) describes two possible approaches to the question of how common conjectures arise, the eductive and the evolutive. The former contends that the actors arrive at equilibrium strategies through reasoning out the positions of both players. The latter argues that equilibrium strategies arise through trial and error. An eductive approach assumes that fully rational actors can reach closure and agree on what strategy pairs they will play. It would claim that equilibrium theory to date is incomplete and that a complete equilibrium theory would give a unique strategy pair as a solution to a game. An evolutive approach assumes that evolution rather than rationality is the proper model for equilibrium theory. Players observe the results of their strategies to eliminate strategies that are failing. They improve failing strategies by random mutation. Over time, both players should converge on an equilibrium pair of strategies. Reality lies somewhere between the two views; actors evaluate their possible strategies both prospectively and retrospectively.

This point brings me back to bounded rationality. Bounded rationality could pose significant problems for game theory. Equilibrium theory assumes that the rationality of both players is common knowledge. If the players have different levels of cognitive capabilities, a player's best reply depends in part on how much it knows about the other player's cognitive abilities. If the other player is limited in its ability, the first player may be able to exploit its limitations. Such considerations expand the set of strategies that are part of some equilibrium and raise the question of what the players know about one another's cognitive abilities.

Game theorists have adopted two approaches to bounded rationality in the recent literature. Finite automata theory represents players as simple computing machines composed of states (e.g., Banks and Sundaram 1990). Each state dictates one move for the player, and the machine shifts from state to state based on the actions of the other player. Evolutionary game theory uses evolution as the model of bounded rationality (e.g., Young 1993). Strategies are chosen because they succeed in competition with other strategies. Both approaches focus on repeated games, which limits their applicability to international conflict. Both approaches generally find that solutions converge on Nash equilibria of the stage game—the game played in each iteration of the repeated game. Then bounded rationality may bring us back to the same results as a fully rational game theory.

Bounded rationality also leads us to wonder about the large role of common knowledge in game theory. Game theory assumes that many things are common knowledge: the players' rationality, their payoff functions, the game itself, and their common conjecture. Common knowledge is a strong condition, but it avoids the messy problem between players of inferring what the other knows. The formal analysis of information below the level of common knowledge (do we call this uncommon knowledge?) is quite involved (Geanakoplos 1992). In practice, informational asymmetries can be modeled within a game that formally meets the common-knowledge requirements. Games of incomplete information make payoffs private information, while the range of possible payoffs is common knowledge. Arguments that players are "irrational" often mean nothing more than that those players take actions that are different from those of most players in their situation. Such "irrationality" can be represented by a type with different payoffs that make the "irrational" actions preferred (e.g., Kreps and Wilson 1982).

Game theory does make strong assumptions about the conditions of strategic interaction. Without those assumptions, the analysis of strategic interaction is an indeterminate morass. Other approaches, such as prospect theory and the poliheuristic theory, do not deal with these assumptions explicitly. We do not know what range of conjectures is acceptable or how conjectures arise initially and how they are revised as the parties interact. We do not know what information is common knowledge or the status of information that is not common knowledge. We do not know if and how the players differ in their cognitive capabilities and what they know about one another's abilities. Game theory cuts the Gordian knot of strategic interaction with simple, powerful assumptions. Such assumptions may be unwarranted, but it is up to others to show how to untie the knot of strategic interaction before they dismiss game theory.

WHAT DOES RATIONAL CHOICE THEORY TELL US ABOUT CONFLICT?

This final section states three general lessons the rational choice approach offers us for understanding international conflict. Rational choice methods can be used to formalize different theories of international conflict. A rational choice approach entails a commitment to writing down explicit models of international conflict. The exact conclusions of those models depend on their exact assumptions. Rather than review specific hypotheses of particular rational choice models, this section presents the general lessons of a rational choice approach. Game theory has important implications for how we study conflict in general. These implications appear to be generic across many specific models, although I illustrate my points with some specific examples.

The Interaction of Strategic Choices

Strategic interaction is central to game theory; actions are chosen both for their immediate effect and for the effect they have on the other player's choice. In decision theory, actions are selected to produce preferred outcomes. In game theory, all the players' choices, even those choices not carried out in equilibrium, influence the outcome. Then an actor in a game must think about the other player's motivations and possible choices when it decides. Choices cannot be considered in isolation. Studies that examine one side's decision separate from others are likely to produce misleading results.

I illustrate the effects of strategic interaction on choices with the literature on the balance between offense and defense (e.g., Quester 1977; Jervis 1978). When the offense is advantaged over the defense, there are benefits to attacking first if war occurs: Surprise is achieved, and enemy forces can be attacked before they are prepared for battle. Snyder (1984, p. 214) summarizes the conclusion of this literature: "War is more likely, the stronger the offense relative to the defense." The argument goes further to include an element of strategic interaction (due to Schelling 1965). Both sides have to worry that the other will strike first. If an actor believes that the other side will strike, then it would reasonably try to gain the first-strike advantage for itself.

But multiple responses are possible to the threat of a first strike (Powell 1989, 1990 discusses this point as it applies in a nuclear crisis). War is averted if the parties can find a mutually agreeable settlement to their dispute. Both sides prefer a settlement closer to their own interests. In bargaining over a possible settlement, a side must weigh the effects of offering an additional concession. If its offer is accepted, it loses the value of the additional concession. The additional concession also increases the chance that the other side will accept its offer, preventing war. War occurs when one side decides that it is better off fighting than continuing to negotiate. A first-strike advantage increases the value of war to the side holding it. If an actor knows that the other side holds a first-strike advantage, it is willing to make more attractive offers to the other side. The gain in reducing the chance of war outweighs the loss of the additional concession if the offer is accepted. Such offers are more attractive to the side with the advantage, and so a peaceful settlement may be more likely.

My point here is not that first-strike advantages lead to peace but rather that first-strike advantages influence both actors' decisions in different ways. A side holding a first-strike advantage is more willing to fight, and so its opponent is more willing to make concessions to avoid war. The effect of first-strike advantages on the probability of war is indeterminate in general. In some situations it may raise the probability of war and in others lower it. Knowing what circumstances produce increased chances of war requires specific models.

Selection on Unobservables

The events that occur are selected from the set of all possible events, and unobservable factors drive that selection. Consequently, we cannot correct for this selection bias.[6] Any event we observe is the consequence of some actor's choice. Actors choose to engage in conflict because they see some benefit in doing so. They resist threats because they believe they are better off resisting than giving the threatening power what it wants. Otherwise, a crisis does not occur because one of the two sides is unwilling to engage in conflict. Thus we as analysts cannot treat the historical record as a simple random sample. Events occur precisely because they are different from the typical case; history is a selection from the set of all possible events.

Further, actors decide on the basis of factors that cannot be observed apart from their choices. For instance, it is commonly believed that resolve—a nation's determination to prevail in a conflict—plays a large role in nations' willingness to fight in a crisis.[7] There may be prior indicators of a nation's resolve, such as prior commitments or strong trading relations, but one nation cannot ascertain another nation's resolve before a crisis. A nation's resolve is known only to itself in advance of a crisis; it is a nation's private information.

Actors make their judgments on the basis of both their own private information and publicly available information. Their own resolve plays a large role in their choices. When they judge the other side's motivation, they can rely only on the publicly available information. An actor facing an unfavorable situation according to the accessible information will choose to pursue conflict only when it has a substantial advantage in its private information. Similarly, such an actor will resist threats only if it holds an advantage in its private information. *Then actors select the cases that occur on the basis of variables we cannot observe—the actor's private information.* Nations with greater resolve are more likely to initiate, resist, and escalate in a crisis. We cannot correct for such selection effects because we cannot measure the variables that drive the selection process.

Selection effects on unobservable variables have an important implication for empirical tests. Success in crises depends on both the public and private dimensions of power. Ex post measures of resolve should predict the outcomes of crises better than ex ante measures. Resolve to fight depends on military capability, which is easily observable, and willingness to fight, which is not observable before combat. Measures of resolve based on observed actions should predict better than measurable capabilities, and they do (Maoz 1983).

Because ex post measures should always fit better than ex ante measures, historical studies of crises may be inherently biased. Careful historical methods try to separate out ex post judgments and rely on ex ante information alone. But the selection of cases is often driven by the outcome of the crises, not by the ex ante circumstances. Researchers cannot separate themselves from their knowledge of the events later and so may contaminate their analyses.

We can compare the relative frequency of different types of cases for evidence of selection effects. For example, there are a number of disputes between major and minor powers. Within that set, the major power is much more likely to initiate the dispute than is the minor power by a ratio of roughly three to one (Morrow 1989a). If both sides have equal opportunity to initiate a dispute, we have evidence that major powers are more likely to choose to begin a dispute than minor powers within major-minor dyads. A major power's advantage in military capabilities increases the chance that it will win a war, increasing its bargaining power in a crisis.

The selection effects argument shows that direct analysis of cases can lead to foolish conclusions. Kugler (1984) argues that nuclear weapons have no deterrent effect because there have been a number of crises since 1945 where a nonnuclear power has challenged a nuclear power and won, either in a crisis or war. But Fearon (1994) shows that these cases are dramatically different from the cases where a nuclear power challenges a nonnuclear power during the same period.[8] Whenever a nonnuclear power challenges a nuclear power, it does so in an area that is recognized as a peripheral interest of the nuclear power, as Vietnam was for the United States. Nuclear powers often challenge a recognized interest of a nonnuclear power, as unification of Vietnam was for the North Vietnamese. Nonnuclear powers challenge nuclear powers only when the nuclear power has little interest in the outcome, and in many such cases they prevail over the nuclear power. The conclusion that such evidence casts doubt on nuclear deterrence theory is a faulty inference.

Strategic Uncertainty and the
Problems of Ex Post Case Studies

The strategic uncertainty of a crisis suggests that comparisons across many cases test hypotheses more effectively than detailed study of a single case. I argued earlier that mixed strategy equilibria should have precedence over pure strategy equilibria in the study of international conflict. We generally believe that the parties are uncertain about one another's actions in a crisis, and mutual uncertainty is the common conjecture in a mixed strategy equilibrium. Actors choose precise actions on the basis of factors that are not common knowledge before and during the play of the game. Otherwise, each side could determine the other's strategy from those common-knowledge factors. Then we should not be able to predict precisely actions taken in a particular crisis. Individual case studies are poor tests of rational choice models. Ex post reconstructions of historical events use information that the actors could not have at the time, subtly influencing us away from the strategic problems they faced. Instead, the predominance of mixed strategy equilibria prescribes that we look for patterns in behavior across a number of crises to test our theories of international conflict.

Rational choice methods have been applied to study individual cases (e.g., Zagare 1977). After the fact, a game can be designed that fits a set of facts about a specific event. Unfortunately, such ex post reconstruction cannot explain the case precisely because the game cannot fail to fit the specified facts of the case. Consequently, rational choice theorists (including Zagare himself) have moved away from trying to explain individual cases. This observation is directly relevant to one of Stein and Welch's criticisms of rational choice methods (see Chapter 4). They claim that psychological approaches provide better "descriptive accuracy" than rational choice methods in accounting for individual cases. However, ex post reconstruction is not a test of a theory precisely because it cannot fail to explain the facts that the analyst defines as relevant.[9] Further, psychological approaches, by definition, must perform at least as well as rational choice methods because the former accept all of the variables that the latter recognize as important to explaining a case. Psychological approaches add new variables and invoke more complex combinations of the variables they share in common with rational choice methods into their candidate explanations. By their very nature, psychological approaches must provide greater descriptive accuracy simply because they use all the variables of rational choice methods and then add more variables. Greater descriptive accuracy of individual cases is not a test of the superiority of one method over another.

Theories of international conflict must necessarily be simplifications of reality. The presence of mixed strategy equilibria makes comparisons across many cases the appropriate way to test competing theories of international conflict. Rational choice methods have led to novel hypotheses that are supported by evidence across a large number of cases (e.g., Bueno de Mesquita and Lalman 1992; Fearon 1994; Kim and Morrow 1992; Morrow 1989b). Stein and Welch (Chapter 4) claim that the lack of structure in international crises renders rational choice methods impotent. If so, how can such methods find empirically supported results?

CONCLUSION

This chapter has provided a brief introduction to rational choice methods and their implications for the study of international conflict. Such methods offer a way to formalize conflictual situations. Many objections to rational choice methods in the abstract prove to be less pressing in practice. The methods are more flexible than is commonly thought, allowing us to build models of competing theories of international conflict that help us better understand both the conclusions of those theories and how to test them.

Utility theory, the starting point for rational choice methods, provides a simple and flexible model of choice. The structure of states, choices, and outcomes forces us to define fully situations in international conflict before analyzing them. At the same time, utility theory does not restrict the range of preference over outcomes or beliefs about states that actors can hold. Its axiomatic base allows us to apply it to collectivities as well as individuals, if their choices are consistent.

Game theory is the primary rational choice tool for analyzing international conflict. It is the best-developed model of strategic interactions available. Like utility theory, game theory forces us to define precisely situations before we assess them. Game theory demonstrates that strategic interaction is not just an immediate extension of a model of individual choice. Preferences over outcomes and beliefs about underlying states alone do not always determine strategic choices; common conjectures matter as well. Strategic logic limits the conjectures that players can hold about other players' actions. Game theory alerts us to the importance of strategic interaction and of selection on unobservable variables when we study international conflict.

Prospect theory and the poliheuristic theory are other models of choice under uncertainty. Neither offers the axiomatic bases of utility theory nor a theory of strategic interaction parallel to game theory. Both may eventually prove superior to existing rational choice methods. To date, the proponents of these methods have not shown that their models explain actions in international conflict that are logically impossible under rational choice methods and that their methods can be used as a foundation to explicate theories of international conflict as can rational choice methods. Such approaches hold promise, but their proponents have much work to do before we can compare these methods to rational choice.

NOTES

This chapter has benefited from the remarks of the participants at the conference "Decision Making on War and Peace" and a seminar presentation at the Center for International Security and Arms Control at Stanford University. I would like to thank Bruce Bueno de Mesquita and Scott Sagan for their comments. I retain all responsibility for the views presented here.

1. For convenience, I do not make the classical distinction between risk and uncertainty here. Risk is a situation where the probability of each outcome given each action is definable and known to all actors. Uncertainty occurs when the probability of an outcome given an action is unknown or not meaningful. Under uncertainty, probability distributions reflect an actor's degree of belief about the likelihood of outcomes given an action. Both risk and uncertainty require more than ordinal preferences over outcomes.

2. The best discussions of game theory and bounded rationality are Binmore 1990, pp. 151–231, and Kreps 1990, pp. 150–177. Sargent 1993 discusses explicit models of bounded rationality in macroeconomic theory.

3. Morrow 1994 is an accessible introduction to noncooperative game theory for political scientists.

4. If there are no chance moves, backward induction requires only preferences over outcomes, not complete utility functions.

5. Players could have limited information about some aspect of the game other than each other's payoffs. For ease of exposition, I limit myself to uncertainties over payoffs.

6. Morrow 1989a is the first treatment of selection effects in the context of a formal model of international conflict. Fearon 1994 is the clearest statement of this point.

7. It is not clear what resolve corresponds to in a formal model of crises. The definition of resolve in the literature confounds several factors. Different elements of many formal models of crises, such as risk attitudes and the relative utility of the status quo compared to the outcomes of winning and losing, produce effects that parallel those often attached to resolve.

8. Bueno de Mesquita and Riker (1982) present evidence on the level of escalation of crises as a function of whether each side possesses nuclear weapons.

9. An ex post reconstruction could fail to explain facts of the case that are excluded from its construction.

3

Prospect Theory and the Cognitive-Rational Debate

Jack S. Levy

Prospect theory—which posits that people evaluate choices with respect to a reference point, overweight losses relative to comparable gains, engage in risk-averse behavior in choices among gains but risk-acceptant behavior in choices among losses, and respond to probabilities in a nonlinear manner—is now a leading alternative to expected utility as a theory of choice under conditions of risk (Kahneman and Tversky 1979). It has served as the basis for major research programs in social psychology, organizational behavior, management science, investment and insurance analysis, and consumer economics, and it has recently begun to attract attention in political science and international relations.[1] Prospect theory's growing influence in political science derives from the rich and intriguing set of hypotheses that it generates and also from the fact that it is often perceived as a "psychological" alternative to rational economic models of behavior.

My argument is that prospect theory does not fit neatly into the cognitive-rational debate. Some aspects of prospect theory, including loss aversion and domain-sensitive risk orientations, are quite compatible with rational choice theories and their underlying microeconomic foundations. Other aspects of the theory (especially the editing of choice problems and in particular the selection of the reference point around which individuals frame and evaluate choices), though theoretically underdeveloped, will undoubtedly have more in common with process-oriented cognitive theories than with rational economic theories.

My aim in this chapter is to assess the "debate" between prospect theory and rational choice. I begin with a brief description of prospect theory and some of its hypotheses about international behavior. I then consider some of the theoretical and methodological problems that plague efforts to apply these hypotheses to international relations and to test them against the evidence and against alternative rational choice explanations. I give particular emphasis to problems of external validity, the ability to generalize from laboratory findings to the complex world of international relations. I consider the limitations of a theory of individual decisionmaking for a theory of state foreign policy and for a theory of strategic interaction between states, and end with a discussion of fruitful avenues for future research on prospect theory and international relations.

A BRIEF REVIEW OF PROSPECT THEORY
AND THE EXPERIMENTAL EVIDENCE[2]

In expected utility theory, actors aim to maximize their expected utility by weighting the utility of each possible outcome of a given course of action by the probability of its occurrence, summing over all possible outcomes for each strategy and selecting that strategy with the highest expected utility. The theory assumes that an actor's utility for a particular good depends on net asset levels of that good and that preferences do not depend upon current assets. Current assets affect marginal utilities and therefore choices given a particular allocation of assets, not preferences over outcomes or terminal states.

I should note a few other sources of confusion concerning expected utility theory. First, most applications of expected utility theory in the social sciences add the auxiliary assumption (Simon 1986) that individuals have diminishing marginal utility for most goods, and this is reflected by a concave utility function. This assumption is descriptively accurate and theoretically useful for many types of behavior, but it is not an essential component of the theory, and violations of diminishing marginal utility are not necessarily violations of expected utility theory.

In addition, violations of expected utility are not necessarily violations of rational choice. Expected utility theory is based on a set of axioms that allows us to construct a Von Neumann–Morgenstern (1944) utility function from ordinal preferences (Morrow 1994, pp. 29–32). Rational choice is defined more broadly to require a consistent and transitive preference order and the selection of the preferred alternative (Young 1975, pp. 364–365), but it makes no further axiomatic assumptions. The prospect theory assumption of a nonlinear combination of probabilities and utilities, for example, violates expected utility theory but may be consistent with broader versions of rational choice.

Evidence from the experimental laboratory demonstrates that people deviate from the predictions of expected utility theory in a number of ways. To begin with, people tend to be more sensitive to changes in assets than to net asset levels, to *gains* and *losses* from a *reference point* rather than to levels of wealth and welfare (Kahneman and Tversky 1979, p. 277). This *reference dependence* (Tversky and Kahneman 1991, p. 1039) is the central analytic assumption of prospect theory. It violates the expected utility postulate of an individual utility function that is defined over levels of assets.[3] Reference dependence is reflected by the fact that an individual may prefer x to y when x is currently a part of her endowment but prefer y to x when y is part of her endowment.[4]

The importance of reference dependence derives from the fact that people treat gains and losses differently: They overvalue losses relative to comparable gains. The evidence for this phenomenon of *loss aversion* is quite robust and persuasive (Kahneman and Tversky 1979; Tversky and Kahneman 1986, 1991; Kahneman, Knetsch, and Thaler 1991). People tend to value what they have more than comparable things that they do not have, and the disutility of relinquishing a good is greater than the utility of acquiring it. Loss aversion is reflected by the greater steepness of the value function on the loss side than on the gain side.

One consequence of loss aversion is that people often refuse to sell an item in their possession at a price they would not even have considered paying for it in the first place, so that selling prices tend to exceed buying prices. This overvaluation of current possessions is the *endowment effect* (Thaler 1980, pp. 43–47), and it has been repeatedly substantiated in a variety of laboratory tests. The magnitude of the endowment effect is considerable. The typical ratio of selling prices to buying prices is about two to one, though sometimes it is as high as three or four to one (Knetsch and Sinden 1984, 1987; Knetsch 1989; Kahneman, Knetsch, and Thaler 1990, p. 1336, 1991; Hartman, Doane, and Woo 1991, p. 142; Tversky and Kahneman 1991).[5]

Another consequence of loss aversion and the endowment effect is a tendency toward status quo choices. People treat the costs of moving away from the status quo as losses and the benefits of moving away from the status quo as gains and then overweight the former relative to the latter; consequently, people stay at the status quo more frequently than expected utility theory would predict. This *status quo bias* is demonstrated in a number of experimental and field studies of consumer and investment behavior (Samuelson and Zeckhauser 1988; Knetsch and Sinden 1984; Knetsch 1989; Hartman, Doane, and Woo 1991).

Loss aversion is one dimension of the asymmetry of losses and gains. Another is an asymmetry in observed *risk orientation* in the domains of losses and gains. People tend to be risk-averse with respect to gains and risk-acceptant with respect to losses. This means that individual value functions are usually concave in the domain of gains and convex in the domain of losses, with a *reflection effect* around the reference point (Kahneman and

Tversky 1979, p. 268). This pattern has been found repeatedly for a variety of individuals and situations, but it may break down for very small probabilities or for catastrophic losses (Kahneman and Tversky 1979; Fishburn and Kochenberger 1979; Slovic and Lichtenstein 1983; Tversky and Kahneman 1986; Quattrone and Tversky 1988; Slovic et al. 1977).

Note that loss aversion and the asymmetry in risk orientation are analytically distinct. Loss aversion is reflected by the greater steepness of the value function for losses than for gains, whereas risk orientation is reflected in the S-shaped curvature of the value function. It is possible to have loss aversion in choices among certain outcomes that involve no lotteries and therefore no risk. In fact, the preceding discussions of loss aversion, the endowment effect, and the status quo bias all referred to choice behavior under conditions of certainty, where there are no risky gambles, and Tversky and Kahneman (1991) have developed a model of loss aversion in riskless choice.

Because of the asymmetrical treatment of gains and losses and the importance of the reference point in defining these distinct domains, the identification of the reference point, or *framing*, can have a critical effect on choice. Under some conditions a change in frame can result in a change in preferences even if the values and probabilities associated with outcomes remain the same. This has been demonstrated repeatedly in laboratory experiments (Kahneman and Tversky 1979; Tversky and Kahneman 1986; Grether and Plott 1979; Slovic and Lichtenstein 1983; Tversky, Slovic, and Kahneman 1990).

In many simple choice problems, the reference point is largely predetermined by the situation. In a static situation that involves a well-defined status quo, for example, the status quo is likely to serve as the reference point. Thus Tversky and Kahneman (1991, pp. 1046–1047) argue that "the reference state usually corresponds to the decision maker's current position," but they concede that this is not always the case and that expectations, aspirations, social norms, and social comparisons as well can influence the framing of the reference point.

Variations in the way people select reference points are particularly likely to arise in dynamic situations, where there is no well-defined and salient status quo that might serve as an obvious focal point for framing. In a situation that involves a sequence of successive choices rather than a single choice, for example, it is not clear whether an actor will define her reference point in terms of her asset position at the beginning of the series of choices (the cumulative frame) or with respect to her asset position after a series of actions have already been taken (the current frame).

The key hypothesis associated with prospect theory is that people *accommodate* to gains more rapidly than to losses. Moreover, they accommodate rather quickly. This *instant endowment effect* (Kahneman, Knetsch, and Thaler 1990, p. 1342) is important because it suggests that after a series of gains an individual will treat the possibility of a subsequent setback as a loss rather than as a forgone gain, overweight it, and engage in risk-seeking behavior to maintain her cumulative gains against that loss. After a series of losses, however, an individual will not accommodate, or "renormalize" (Jervis 1992), as quickly but instead adopt the cumulative frame and engage in risk-seeking behavior in an attempt to eliminate those losses.

This asymmetry in the way people renormalize to gains and to losses has serious implications for conflict, cooperation, and bargaining in international relations and elsewhere. If A seizes territory from B, for example, prospect theory suggests that B will take excessive risks to recover its losses while A will take excessive risks to maintain its gains (Levy 1992b, pp. 284–292). This phenomenon raises some interesting questions regarding how different people accommodate to change, in what direction, how quickly, and under what conditions. The literature provides few answers to this question—other than to say that framing is highly subjective, poorly understood, and basically unexplored.

Because people sometimes frame around expectation or aspiration levels rather than the status quo, and because the status quo may be difficult to define in many dynamic situations, the concept of the status quo bias is misspecified. The bias is really a *reference point bias,* a greater tendency to move toward the reference point than expected utility theory predicts. Theoretically, the hypothesized status quo bias is generally stabilizing in the sense that it reinforces the status quo, but the hypothesized reference point bias may be destabilizing whenever the reference point deviates from the status quo.

Reference dependence and framing effects are critical with respect to debates regarding rational choice. If people always framed around the status quo, it would be possible to subsume loss aversion and the reflection effect within expected utility theory by positing an S-shaped utility function with a steeper slope on the loss side. But preference reversals induced by changes in frames rather than subjective utilities or probabilities are much more difficult to reconcile with the axioms of expected utility theory, the logic of which requires that identical choice problems should yield identical results. Evidence that behavior varies depending on whether the glass is seen as half empty or half full does not easily lend itself to a rational choice explanation.

Another respect in which individual choice behavior appears to deviate from the predictions of expected utility theory is in the response to probabilities. Whereas expected utility theory posits a linear combination of utilities and probabilities, experimental studies reveal a tendency toward a *nonlinear response to probabilities.* Studies beginning with Allais (1953) have shown that individuals overweight outcomes that are certain relative to outcomes that are merely probable. Because of this *certainty effect* (Kahneman and Tversky 1979, p. 265), people attach greater value to the complete elimination of risk than to the reduction of risk by a comparable amount. This is graphically illustrated in an experiment involving a hypothetical game of Russian roulette, where people are willing to pay far more to reduce the number of bullets in a revolver from one to zero than from four to three, even though the changes in expected utility are equivalent (Quattrone and Tversky 1988, p. 730).

People are also likely to overweight small probabilities and to underweight moderate and high probabilities, in contrast to the equal weight of utilities and probabilities in expected utility theory. Consequently, except for choices involving small probabilities, people tend to give more weight to the utility of a possible outcome than to its probability of occurrence. But there is one qualification: Although small probabilities are overweighted, extremely small probabilities generate unpredictable behavior.[6] Sometimes people ignore extremely unlikely events and essentially assume that they have a zero chance of occurring, but at other times they exaggerate the probability of highly unlikely events (Kahneman and Tversky 1979, pp. 282–283). This unpredictability of behavior with respect to extremely small probabilities is illustrated by the wide range of individual responses to the dangers of AIDS or natural disasters.

Kahneman and Tversky (1979) developed prospect theory to integrate these observed patterns into an alternative theory of risky choice. They distinguish two phases in the choice process. In the *editing phase,* the actor identifies the reference point, available options, possible outcomes, and value and probability of each of these outcomes. In the *evaluation phase,* the actor combines the values of possible outcomes (as reflected in an S-shaped *value function*) with their weighted probabilities (as reflected in the *probability weighting function*) and then maximizes over the product (the "prospective utility").

It is important to note that choice behavior with respect to risk is determined by the combination of the value function and the probability weighting function and not by the value function alone. Although this combination usually generates risk aversion with respect to gains and risk acceptance with respect to losses, the overweighting of small probabilities can trigger a reversal of risk propensities under certain conditions, depending on the precise shapes of the two functions (Kahneman and Tversky 1979; Levy 1992a, pp. 183–184).

The reason for such reversal is fairly intuitive. In a choice between a certain outcome and a lottery involving midrange probabilities, the certainty effect leads to the overweighting of certain gains and therefore to greater caution, whereas the overweighting of certain losses encourages the risky choice to avoid the certain loss. This helps to explain the tendency to sell winners too early (to lock in a certain gain) and to hold losers too long (and thus risk a larger loss in the hope of avoiding a certain loss) (Shefrin and Statman 1985). If probabilities are small, however, the over-weighting of the small probability of a gain increases the attractiveness of the lottery and induces more risk-seeking behavior. Similarly, the over-weighting of a low-probability loss decreases the attractiveness of the lottery and makes a risk-averse choice more likely.

Note that these conditions of small probabilities are precisely the conditions under which people engage in gambling and buy insurance (the insurance premium being a certain loss). Prospect theory provides a straightforward explanation of both of these phenomena, whereas expected utility theory cannot easily explain both gambling and the purchase of insurance by the same person.

Thus the existence of small probabilities is a necessary but not sufficient condition for risk aversion in the domain of losses and risk acceptance in the domain of gains. This possibility is frequently ignored in recent discussions of prospect theory in political science. This is particularly serious in international relations, where choices involving small probabilities but large consequences are quite important.

Prospect theory generates an intriguing set of hypotheses about foreign policy choices and international interactions—hypotheses about risk-seeking behavior to avoid losses or to maintain recently acquired gains, the influence of sunk costs, the greater difficulty of compellence as opposed to deterrence, the difficulty of cooperating with others to distribute losses or of coercing the adversary to accept losses,[7] and a variety of other patterns of behavior.

These hypotheses appear to explain patterns of behavior that do not fit easily into standard rational choice models, but we must overcome some serious conceptual and methodological problems before we can utilize prospect theory as a reliable framework for explanation in international politics. Although there are ongoing debates regarding the internal validity of the experimental findings upon which prospect theory is based,[8] the more serious issues concern the external validity of the laboratory findings (or the extent to which they can be generalized beyond the laboratory to the complex world of international relations) and the theoretical relevance of a theory of individual decisionmaking to strategic interaction among collective state actors. To these I now turn.

THE GENERALIZABILITY OF LABORATORY FINDINGS[9]

The descriptive generalizations upon which prospect theory is based emerge from experimental research in highly structured laboratory settings that are unlikely to be replicated in the ill-structured world of international relations. In the laboratory, subjects are given a choice between a certain outcome and a lottery that involves two or more possible outcomes with known values and probabilities. The framing of the reference point is basically determined by the way in which the analyst sets up the choice problem. The analysis is facilitated by the use of monetary outcomes or in some cases mortality rates or inflation and unemployment rates, which are measurable on an interval scale and which can be roughly scaled into utilities. The experiments control for the possible effects of extraneous variables or randomize them over a large number of subjects. Each subject is given a onetime choice and receives a payoff that depends on her choice alone and not on the choices of adversaries. Analysts construct their research designs in such a way that expected utility theory and prospect theory predict different choices, so that it is relatively straightforward to interpret the results of most of these experiments.

The choice problems that foreign policy leaders typically face rarely satisfy these conditions. The framing of the reference point is subjective, hard to predict, and hard to measure. The same is true for the probabilities and utilities that political leaders attach to outcomes—and in fact the identification of possible options and their consequences.[10] There are usually two risky options rather than one, for doing nothing or selecting the status quo or a negotiated agreement also involves risks. These risks are compounded by two factors: Each option has future consequences that require a balancing of present and future risks, and these consequences are a function of others' choices as well as one's own. Thus which of the options is more risky is often difficult to define conceptually or measure empirically.

While laboratory studies focus on the evaluation of prospects under static conditions of current risk, then, foreign policy decisionmaking involves the critical tasks of defining the situation, editing the choice problem, and then evaluating options under dynamic and interactive conditions of present and future uncertainties. Consequently, it is extremely difficult for the analyst to determine whether an actor selects a particular option because of framing, loss aversion, risk orientation, and the overweighting of the probability of certain outcomes or simply because it is more highly valued in terms of a standard cost-benefit calculus based on expected value. Thus it is difficult to distinguish empirically between a prospect theory explanation and an expected utility explanation.

The problem of determining empirically how an actor defines her reference point is particularly troubling. If we cannot establish the reference point, and do so independently of the behavior we are trying to explain, then prospect theory and its key hypotheses of loss aversion, the endowment effect, and the reflection effect cannot be tested and have no explanatory power. Did Khrushchev withdraw Soviet missiles from Cuba because he defined his reference point as the situation that existed before the missiles were installed, framed the issue of withdrawal as one of forgoing gains rather than suffering losses, and consequently preferred the certainty of returning to the precrisis status quo to the gamble of a showdown with the United States, which might turn out much better or very much worse for the Soviet Union?[11] Or had Khrushchev accommodated to the gains of having nearly operational missiles in Cuba, framed his reference point around the new status quo, defined any withdrawal as a loss, calculated that his losses could be minimized by a public U.S. pledge not to invade Cuba and by assurances that the United States would withdraw its missiles from Turkey, and concluded that the risk of crisis escalation that would follow from his failure to withdraw the missiles would be intolerable for the Soviet Union? In the absence of independent evidence regarding how Khrushchev defined his reference point, it is difficult to differentiate empirically between these two explanations.

Given the methodological problems involved in empirically differentiating a prospect theory explanation from a rational choice explanation based on expected value maximization, how should we evaluate the theoretical and empirical utility of these two theoretical frameworks? I have argued elsewhere (Levy 1992b, pp. 296–297) that rational choice/expected utility theory is more parsimonious than prospect theory because it is axiomatically based and because it requires fewer parameters for full specification. In addition, rational choice is normatively appealing, whereas prospect theory makes no explicit normative claims (Tversky and Kahneman 1986, p. S272).

On these grounds I argued that in case study applications of prospect theory the burden of proof should be on the proponent of prospect theory to test her theory or explanation against a rival rational choice explanation and to show not only that the evidence is consistent with a prospect theory explanation but also that the theory provides a better explanation of that behavior than does a rational choice explanation based on a straightforward expected value calculation (Levy 1992b, pp. 296–297).

THEORETICAL LIMITATIONS OF PROSPECT THEORY

What Does Prospect Theory Attempt to Explain?

We need to be clear about what prospect theory does and does not purport to explain. Prospect theory is a theory of choice under conditions of risk. It is not a complete theory of decisionmaking, however, because it focuses only on explaining choices given the basic parameters of the decision problem—the available options, the possible outcomes of each option and the values and probabilities associated with each, and the framing of the reference point. These basic parameters themselves are taken as given and treated exogenously. In its current form, therefore, prospect theory is a theory of the evaluation of prospects but not a theory of the editing of choices (Levy 1992a, p. 190).

This is an important limitation of the theory, particularly for the purposes of explaining the complex world of international politics, as one can plausibly argue that much of the explanatory power in international politics lies in the specification of the problem, the options, the values and probabilities of possible outcomes, and the framing of the reference point. Although this is ultimately an empirical question, prospect theory currently has little to say about the editing process.[12]

Nearly all of these same concerns (except for the framing of the reference point) apply as well to expected utility and other decision theories. How people define and structure a choice problem and how they specify the number and variety of options, the possible outcomes associated with each along with their utilities and probabilities, and the shape of the utility function are all exogenous to the model. The analyst provides this information and in doing so introduces auxiliary assumptions that are a necessary component of any theory of choice and that may have considerable explanatory power. It is clear that these auxiliary assumptions and the question of their empirical validity require as much attention as does the formal decision model itself.

These auxiliary assumptions concern both the basic parameters of the choice problem and the processes through which the actors generate those parameters. Although expected utility theory has been criticized for excessive reliance on the "as-if" assumption (Friedman 1953)—for its focus on behavioral outcomes and exclusion of the question of how those outcomes are arrived at—the same criticism can be made of prospect theory, or at least of the evaluation phase of prospect theory. Both expected utility and the evaluation phase of prospect theory are *structural* theories rather than *process* theories. Given certain parameters of the choice problem, they attempt to explain choices or outcomes, not the processes through which those choices come about (Abelson and Levi 1985, p. 235).[13]

In Simon's (1976) terms, both expected utility theory and prospect theory are concerned with "substantive rationality" rather than "procedural rationality." Behavior is substantively rational when it involves the optimization of given goals under given conditions and constraints. Substantive rationality is a function of goals and situational constraints but not intervening reasoning processes. Procedural rationality, in contrast, depends on the appropriateness of the intervening reasoning processes (Simon 1976, pp. 130–131). Thus the question whether or not people actually engage in the hypothesized intervening calculations is essential for the validity of hypotheses on procedural rationality but not for hypotheses on substantive rationality. Whereas neoclassical economics and formal decision theory are concerned primarily with substantive rationality, most theories of judgment and choice in social psychology are primarily process-oriented.

It is in this sense that prospect theory does not fit neatly into the cognitive-rational debate. The evaluation phase of prospect theory—which includes a well-developed and formalized theory that incorporates loss-aversion, an S-shaped value function, and a probability weighting function and which has captured most of the attention in applications of prospect theory to international relations—has more in common with rational economic theories than it does with process-oriented cognitive theories. But once it is more fully developed, the editing phase of prospect theory—which includes the framing of the reference point and the specification of options, outcomes, utilities, and probabilities—will undoubtedly have more in common with theories centered on cognitive processes.

That prospect theory in its current form explains just the evaluation phase of choice suggests only that the theory is incomplete, not invalid; in the same way, that many of the key parameters in expected utility theory are exogenous is a reflection of the scope of the theory, not its validity. It is clear that a theory that explains both the editing and evaluation phases of the choice problem (including the framing of the reference point and the specification of the problem in terms of options, outcomes, values, probabilities, and perhaps also the intervening processes through which these parameters are arrived at) would be superior to prospect theory as it now stands, in that it would explain everything that prospect theory currently explains and more and thus constitute a progressive problem shift (Lakatos 1970). Which choices people make given the basic parameters of the choice problem is hardly a trivial question, however, and in the absence of a more complete theory of choice, prospect theory should be evaluated in terms of how well it explains the half of the choice problem it purports to explain, not its failure to explain the other half. There are other, more serious theoretical limitations of prospect theory as a framework for understanding international relations and foreign policy.

From Individual Choice to Collective Choice

Prospect theory is a theory of individual choice. What we want to explain in international politics, however, is the foreign policy behavior of states as collective decisionmaking groups. The concepts of individual framing, loss aversion, and risk orientations were developed for theories of individual decisionmaking and tested on individuals, not on groups, and it is not clear that these concepts apply equally well at the collective level.

True, in a number of cases, particularly in authoritarian regimes, a single individual plays such a dominant role in decisionmaking that the application of the unitary actor assumption is a reasonable first approximation. The unitary actor model may also be applied to more pluralist regimes on crisis issues in which the threats to state interests are sufficiently clear that either there is little disagreement as to the nature of the threats or what to do about them or there is a shift in decisional power to a single leading actor.

Although prospect theory and its concepts of framing, risk orientation, and the reflection effect can be usefully applied to individual cases in situations where the validity of the unitary actor assumption is empirically demonstrated, this does not help us much when it comes to a theory of foreign policy decisionmaking that is generalizable across many different types of situations. We need a theoretical solution to the aggregation problem.

Rational choice theory has a similar aggregation problem, of course, but in important respects rational choice theory has made more progress toward solving this problem. Prospect theory lacks anything comparable to rational theories of bureaucratic politics to explain how individual preferences, political power, and private information get translated through the political process into choices for the state or organization (Allison 1971; Bendor and Hammond 1992). It also lacks anything comparable to rational theories of coalition formation to explain how preferences get aggregated. There is nothing in principle that excludes prospect theory from doing something like this, although the roles of framing and the nonlinear probability weighting function introduce additional layers of conceptual and mathematical complexity.

One problem in aggregating individual preferences is that the behavior of groups with respect to risky choices is not necessarily congruent to the aggregation of the risk orientations of individual members, as demonstrated by the substantial body of literature on "choice shifts." Early work in group dynamics emphasized the "risky shift" phenomenon, the tendency for groups to favor riskier choices than do the individual members of the group (Pruitt 1971). Janis (1982), for example, argues that "groupthink," or a tendency toward excessive concurrence seeking in small groups, is likely to generate illusions of omnipotence, omniscience, and invulnerability of the group, and these illusions lead members to downplay uncertainties about outcomes and adopt riskier courses of action. More recent work tends to support a more balanced "group polarization" hypothesis, in which groups tend to move either toward riskier or more cautious policy orientations, depending on the circumstances (Myers and Lamm 1976; Minix 1982; Hart 1991, pp. 264–266).

Loss aversion and risk orientation both depend on framing, of course, and this presents another difficult set of analytical issues for group decisionmaking. In individual cases where the application of a unitary actor assumption is reasonable, we can focus on the frame and decision calculus of the dominant decisionmaker. For the purposes of a general theory of foreign policy, however, the concept of a collective frame around which a collective value function and collective probability weighting function are constructed to generate a collective risk orientation involves an unacceptable reification of individual-level concepts. It is more useful to focus on the individual level and talk about how individual frames influence individual evaluations of outcomes and orientations toward risk to generate (along with probability weighting) individual policy preferences. If a particular outcome is especially costly because it is seen as a loss relative to a reference point, there is no reason why that cannot be incorporated into an actor's utility function.

The framing of choice problems in collective settings involves an important strategic component. At the same time that individuals are framing and reframing the decisions they face, they may be trying to manipulate how other decisionmakers frame their choice problems. In fact, part of the political bargaining may take place not directly over policy preferences or even over cost-benefit calculations, but over the reference point that others select to frame their problems (Maoz 1990a). This applies to domestic politics as well as to bureaucratic politics, and part of leaders' efforts to gain the support of domestic publics lies in attempting to shape the way these publics frame the issue. The aim is to influence the other to frame a particular outcome as a forgone gain rather than as a loss in order to minimize the costs to others of accepting that outcome (Levy 1996b).

All of this suggests that one critically important task for future research involves the theoretical development and empirical validation of linkages between loss aversion, the reflection effect, and framing effects at the individual level and decisionmaking at the collective level. The development of a formal theory of collective choice based on the microfoundations of prospect theory would be particularly useful. This is an ambitious theoretical task, but other work can be done short of this that would add to the utility of prospect theory for international relations.

Hypotheses of framing, loss aversion, the reflection effect, and the certainty effect can also be used to supplement bureaucratic politics or other theories of foreign policy by helping to explain the policy preferences of key actors in the political process. Heads of organizations may be more concerned about maintaining their organizational power and budgets than increasing them and may treat temporary budgetary increases as a permanent part of the organization's endowment. These considerations should be reflected in their evaluations of outcomes and in their policy preferences. Similarly, domestic publics may be influenced more by policies that hurt their standard of living than those that improve it, more by policies that harm the national interest than those that enhance it, and they may be more likely to punish political leaders for failures than to reward them for successes. In this "two-level game" (see Chapter 7) involving loss-averse domestic publics, even political leaders who were not themselves influenced by loss aversion or framing would find it in their interest to behave as if they were.

We see that prospect theory does not need to be developed into a full-blown theory of collective choice in order to enhance our understanding of foreign policy. Hypotheses of framing, loss aversion, and the reflection effect can be useful in supplementing other established theories of foreign policy by helping to specify some of the parameters that are exogenous in those models, including in particular the preferences of authoritative decisionmakers or of key bureaucratic and domestic political actors. These hypotheses can also help to explain negotiation and bargaining among domestic actors. Certainly an important task for future research is to develop these ideas and to specify how prospect theory hypotheses can be integrated into broader models of the foreign policy process (including rational choice models). Something like this is necessary, because a theory of individual choice cannot be useful as a theory of foreign policy unless it is integrated into a theory of the policymaking process.

From State Foreign Policy to Strategic Interaction

Just as it is necessary to move from a theory of individual choice to a theory of collective choice in order to provide a complete explanation of foreign policy, it is also necessary to move from a theory of decision to a theory of strategic interaction to provide a logically complete explanation of international behavior. Here in particular, prospect theory lags far behind rational choice theory, which has supplemented expected utility as a theory of choice with game theoretic and spatial models of strategic interaction (Bueno de Mesquita and Lalman 1992; Morrow 1994; Morgan 1994).

It is clear that a major theoretical task for prospect theory is to incorporate the assumptions of reference dependence, loss aversion, the reflection effect, and nonlinear response to probabilities into a theory of strategic interaction. Such a "behavioral game theory" (Camerer 1990) has yet to be developed. It is a technically difficult project that most international relations theorists will prefer to leave to economists or economic psychologists, but there are other ways to make prospect theory more useful for understanding strategic interactions between states.

One task, as I suggested in my earlier discussion of collective decision theory, is to use the hypotheses of framing, loss aversion, and the reflection effect to help specify the values actors attach to various outcomes and thus to their preferences over outcomes. If a particular outcome is especially costly because it is seen as a loss relative to a reference point, the analyst can easily incorporate such effects of loss aversion into the payoff structure.

There is also work to be done related to the bargaining process itself. The expanding literature on negotiation and bargaining theory from a behavioral perspective provides a number of ideas to build on and apply to international politics or to domestic politics (Rubin and Brown 1975; Pruitt 1981; Neale and Northcraft 1991). The impact of framing on bargaining (Bazerman 1983; Neale and Bazerman 1985; Neale, Huber, and Northcraft 1987) is particularly significant and needs to be explored further in the context of international politics. One important hypothesis that could be more fully developed relates to the concept of "concession aversion": If bargainers treat their concessions to the adversary as losses and what they get in return as gains, they will overvalue the former relative to the latter and be less inclined to make concessions or reach negotiated settlements than rational choice theories of bargaining would predict (Levy 1996b).

It would also be useful to explore the role of framing in the bargaining process. One question is the extent to which an actor attempts to influence the adversary's frame or the adversary's perception of the actor's own frame, and particularly whether political leaders attempt to make it easier for adversaries to make concessions by encouraging them to view those concessions as forgone gains rather than losses. Moreover, do leaders try to reinforce their own bargaining positions by trying to convince adversaries that they define their own possible concessions as losses, thus increasing the sense of loss and presumably leaving the actors less inclined to make further concessions and in fact more deserving of additional compensation?

CONCLUSION

I have argued that prospect theory has an ambiguous status with respect to rational choice theory. In important respects the theories are very different. Taken as a whole, prospect theory clearly differs from expected utility theory in that the nonlinear probability weighting function deviates from the expected utility principle and thus violates one of the axioms upon which expected utility theory is based. Moreover, the central analytic assumption of reference dependence in prospect theory and the implication that preferences over outcomes may be dependent upon the reference point against which those outcomes are defined and evaluated do not fit easily with the more general rational choice assumption of a transitive preference order over outcomes. Finally, although a theory of the editing phase of the choice problem, and particularly a theory of the framing of the reference point, has yet to be developed, it seems pretty clear that such a theory will have more in common with process-oriented cognitive theories than with rational economic theories.

Still, many other specific components of prospect theory are quite compatible with rational choice theory in general and with expected utility theory in particular. Expected utility, for example, can easily accommodate an S-shaped utility function that is steeper below the inflection point to incorporate loss aversion. Both are theories of value maximization. Expected utility theory and prospect theory, or at least the evaluation phase of prospect theory that has been the primary focus of research in the literature, are also similar in that they share many of the same limitations. Each exogenizes the basic parameters of the choice problem (the available options, their possible outcomes, the probabilities and utilities associated with each, and—for prospect theory—the framing of the reference point) and provides a theory of choices or decisional outputs given those decisional inputs. Thus each focuses on choices or outcomes and not the processes through which they are generated. In this sense neither prospect theory nor expected utility theory provides a complete theory of decision-making, though the development of a theory of framing would add to prospect theory one component of a theory of preferences.

Another similarity between expected utility theory and prospect theory is that each is a theory of individual choice and for this reason cannot by itself explain either the foreign policy behavior of collective state actors or the patterns of interaction among states in the international system. The former requires a theory of how individual preferences get aggregated into state decisions, and the latter requires a theory of strategic interaction. In this sense, rational choice theories are more fully developed than is prospect theory. Through bureaucratic politics and theories of coalition formation, rational choice theory has made important steps toward developing a theory of collective decisionmaking based on expected utility, and through game theory it provides an interactive theory of strategic choice. Prospect theory lags behind rational choice theory in both of these respects. Thus the extension of prospect theory into a theory of collective choice and a theory of strategic interaction, along with the development of a theory of framing, are its most urgent theoretical tasks.

It would be a mistake, however, to see prospect theory and rational choice or expected utility theory exclusively in competitive terms. It is possible that components from each of these theories can be integrated to develop more powerful explanations of political behavior with a minimal loss of parsimony. One important task for future research would be to explore how loss aversion and the reflection effect might be incorporated into rational choice theories of foreign policy and international politics. Can we build better theories of bureaucratic politics or domestic sources of foreign policy by using loss aversion and risk-seeking behavior to avoid losses to help specify the preferences of individual actors, and thus give greater empirical content to the shape of the utility function? Can we incorporate loss aversion and the reflection effect into theories of bargaining in a way that enhances the descriptive accuracy of those theories without undermining their theoretical coherence? Can theories of bargaining and influence be expanded to incorporate the role of interactive framing, in which each actor attempts to influence the other's reference point and the other's perception of his own reference point?

In these and other ways, we need to make greater efforts to combine the elegance and analytic power of rational economic explanations of international behavior with more descriptively accurate assumptions about individual behavior.

NOTES

I would like to thank Jeffrey Berejikian, William Boettcher, William Clark, Patrick James, Cliff Morgan, and Michael Sinatra for helpful comments on earlier versions of this chapter.

1. For empirical applications of prospect theory in international relations, see Farnham 1992, McDermott 1992, McInerney 1992, Richardson 1992, Taliaferro 1994, Berejikian 1995, Weyland 1996, and Mintz and Geva 1997b. For experimental studies, see Geva and Mintz 1994; Mintz and Geva, Chapter 5; and Kowert and Hermann 1994.

2. This section builds on Levy 1992a, 1996b.

3. Although standard utility-based game theory does not allow for reference dependence, Brams's theory of moves (1994; see also Chapter 6 in this volume) generates equilibria that are sensitive to the position from which one begins and thus incorporates a form of reference dependence.

4. This is a statement about preferences over outcomes, not changes on the margin.

5. There is an important qualification here. The evidence suggests that the endowment effect does not apply to normal commercial transactions. Money expended on an item is not treated as a loss, and goods purchased for eventual sale or barter—as opposed to use—generally do not generate an endowment effect (Kahneman, Knetsch, and Thaler 1991, p. 200). This finding has important implications for the role of bargaining chips in negotiations.

6. Although there is no conclusive evidence as to the specific point at which overweighting shifts to underweighting or whether this point varies significantly across individuals or conditions, preliminary evidence suggests that it falls in the .10–.15 range (Hershey and Schoemaker 1980).

7. The theory suggests that it is easier to cooperate with others to distribute gains or to deter the adversary from making gains.

8. Let me summarize briefly. Economists argue that observed anomalies in expected utility theory are the artifacts of experimental procedure and can be explained by standard economic theory. Subjects are faced with hypothetical rather than real choices and consequently have few incentives to expend the mental effort to make optimum decisions in complex choice problems. They are confronted with

unfamiliar problems in one-shot experiments and have no opportunity to learn through the discipline and incentives of market institutions. Finally, subjects in bargaining experiments have an incentive (or at least a habitual tendency) to misrepresent buying and selling prices. With real choices that involve ample financial incentives and opportunities for learning, economists argue, the anomalous behavior should disappear.

These are plausible hypotheses, and experimental economists as well as social psychologists have redesigned experiments in an attempt to control more fully for the effects of these other variables. (For an influential early study, see Grether and Plott 1979. For useful reviews of this experimental literature, see Cox and Issac 1986, Roth 1995, Camerer 1992, 1995, and Levy 1997.) The consensus is that although alternative experimental designs with better controls reduce somewhat the magnitude of the systematic anomalies in expected utility theory, those anomalies do not disappear. This conclusion draws further support from empirical studies of consumer, insurance, and financial market behavior in natural settings. I conclude that loss aversion, the reflection effect, and framing effects persist in individual choice behavior and cannot be fully explained by rational economic theory.

9. See also Jervis 1992, Levy 1992b, 1997, Shafir 1992, and Stein 1992b.

10. On some of the problems with probabilities, see Boettcher 1995.

11. Technically, this scenario undoubtedly involved a mixed outcome (both gains and losses relative to the reference point).

12. Some applications of prospect theory to international relations have explored the possible impact on framing of affect (Farnham 1992) and of historical learning or analogical reasoning (McDermott 1992; Taliaferro 1994; Levy 1994).

13. Another similarity between expected utility theory and prospect theory is that both are compensatory theories of decisionmaking (Abelson and Levi 1985, pp. 259–261). The difference is that while expected utility theory posits a linear combination of the value and probability for each possible outcome, prospect theory posits that values are weighted by a nonlinear function of probabilities. For an application of a noncompensatory model to international relations, see Chapter 5.

4

Rational and Psychological Approaches to the Study of International Conflict: Comparative Strengths and Weaknesses

Janice Gross Stein & David A. Welch

What information would be useful to explain or predict interstate conflict? Proponents of rational choice theory and those of psychological approaches provide different answers to this question. The differences between those answers have profound implications for building, testing, and making practical use of theory.

With few exceptions, those who study world affairs through the rational choice lens and those who do so through the psychological lens rarely enter into meaningful dialogue. In addition to employing fundamentally different concepts, by and large they seek the answers to rather different questions. Thus it is difficult to compare the relative success of their "normal science" (Kuhn 1970). Certainly, economists and psychologists have engaged in a lively debate on the question of whether human beings are "rational," and if not, whether rational actor assumptions are nevertheless useful. But students of international conflict have had relatively little to add to this debate because the associated issues have nothing to do with international politics in particular.

Nevertheless, proponents of rational choice and psychological approaches to the study of international conflict each claim, in effect, analytical superiority over the other. Our chief purpose in this chapter is to judge the relative usefulness of the two approaches with reference to their own aspirations. As a prelude to that discussion, we offer a brief overview of cognitive and motivational psychology's challenge to rational choice. We then examine what rational and cognitive approaches to the study of international conflict try to do and assess the difficulty of attaining those goals. We conclude that psychological approaches to international conflict have quite different (and much more limited) aspirations than do rational choice approaches but that they are significantly more tractable, owing to the nature of the domain and ambiguities in the concept of rationality (Green and Shapiro 1994, pp. 13–32).

THE RATIONALITY ASSUMPTION
AND DECISION COMPLEXITY

Rational choice theory proceeds from a simple and intuitive idea: If we know what people want, we can explain and predict what they do. It assumes merely that people are cognitively competent to match means to ends and to rank options accordingly. In standard formulations, a rational analysis simply needs information about what people want, what alternatives are open to them, and what they know (or can reasonably be expected to figure out) about the likely costs and benefits of the alternatives (cf. Elster 1986, p. 16; Monroe 1995, p. 2).[1] In many cases this information may be readily discoverable or determined by the structure of the choice problem itself. Thus the promise of rational choice theory is to permit reliable explanations and predictions of behavior in a variety of contexts on the basis of relatively little information about the actors themselves, and certainly without having to know their life histories or reconstructing the phenomenology of choice.

But behind the superficial simplicity of the concept of rationality lies a great deal of ambiguity. Must someone have the *best* reasons possible, including the information necessary to make a true expected utility calculation, to make a "rational" choice, or is it sufficient that she merely have clear goals and reasons for believing that her actions will lead her to attain them (Simon 1995b)? Does it matter what goals she pursues (e.g., can suicides, masochists, altruists, and martyrs be rational)? How we resolve these ambiguities has important implications for how we conceive, employ, and evaluate rational choice theory. In general, the weaker the set of requirements, the larger the number of choice situations that meet the scope conditions for rational choice theory; but the more difficult the problem of modeling, the less precise the prediction and the greater the danger of tautology.[2]

Decisions that leaders face in foreign policy making—including decisions about war and peace—typically involve many uncertainties about the available options, their likely costs and benefits, and the value trade-offs they entail. On a weak understanding of rationality, we may nonetheless describe almost all leaders of states as "rational," because they virtually always have some notion of their goals and some reasons (though not necessarily the best reasons) for believing that their choices will promote those goals. But on a strong understanding of rationality, these choices are almost never rational. Well documented cases of foreign policy decisionmaking consistently show that leaders typically have inadequate information about their options; that they make significant errors in judging costs, benefits, and likelihoods; and that they do not attempt to make expected utility calculations. The decisions they face implicate so many values in unforeseeable ways that leaders are unable to sort out the trade-offs.[3]

It is precisely in complex decisionmaking situations such as these that a theory of choice is most needed and would be most useful. But it is precisely here that rational choice theory helps us least. If we are working with a strong understanding of rationality, we cannot estimate the parameters necessary to conduct a rational analysis; if we are working with a weak one, the analysis yields no determinate prediction.[4] But human beings normally do not permit the complexity of decision problems to stand in the way of action. They still make choices. Psychology helps us to see how people cope with complexity and uncertainty.

PSYCHOLOGICAL APPROACHES TO CHOICE

While actual processes of human choice remain somewhat mysterious, it is increasingly clear that people do not make "rational" choices in more than the weakest sense of the term, except in trivial cases. Human beings are not expected utility maximizers.[5] Many rational choice theorists would insist that this is not a telling criticism of rational choice theory, whose purpose is not descriptive accuracy but predictive power. Whether or not the unrealism of rational choice assumptions is an impediment to rational choice theory is an issue we take up later. For the moment, however, we simply survey some of the more important insights of psychology into how people do make decisions.

Cognitive Models

Cognitive psychology explains deviations from rational actor assumptions about judgment, estimation, and choice by looking at the simple rules people use to make timely responses to complex and ill structured problems. There is no single cognitive theory of choice, and cognitive psychologists have identified no dominant decision rule. Indeed, this has not been their goal. Instead, they have concentrated on identifying and categorizing the filters through which people process information and the simplifying mechanisms they employ to help them make sense of the world. As our

discussion indicates, the impact of these filters and simplifying mechanisms varies from context to context and from individual to individual.
Many lead to conflicting expectations about judgment and behavior. Thus
cognitive psychology is far from being a true competitor to rational choice
in the quest for a general, transposable theory of choice. Nevertheless,
cognitive psychology has enhanced our understanding of the reasons why
people deviate from the rational ideal.

Schemata, heuristics, biases, and information processing. One of the core
insights of cognitive psychology is that people's prior beliefs strongly affect (and often distort) information processing. Attribution theory emphasizes the importance of "schemata" in determining how people interpret
new information in the light of preexisting beliefs (Fiske 1986; Iyengar
1991; Iyengar and McGuire 1993; Kelley 1972; Lau and Sears 1986;
Reder and Anderson 1980; Schank and Abelson 1977; Thorndyke and
Hayes-Roth 1979; Walker 1988).[6] Attribution theories do not assume that
an individual's collection of schemata forms a coherent whole. They do assert that schemata, once formed, are resistant to change (Lau and Sears
1986; Lebow and Stein 1993; Ross, Lepper, and Hubbard 1975; Vertzberger 1990).[7]

Heuristics can also impair processes of rational revision and judgment
(Kahneman, Slovic and Tversky 1982; Nisbett and Ross 1980; Von Winterfeldt and Edwards 1986). Heuristics are rules people use to test the
propositions embedded in their schemata and may be thought of as conve-
nient shortcuts or rules of thumb for processing information. Three of the
best documented heuristics are *availability, representativeness*, and *anchoring*. The availability heuristic refers to people's tendency to interpret
ambiguous information in terms of what is most easily available in their
cognitive repertoire (Pryor and Kriss 1977; Ross and Sicoly 1979; Taylor
1982; Tversky and Kahneman 1973). The heuristic of representativeness
refers to people's proclivity to exaggerate similarities between one event
and a prior class of events, typically leading to significant errors in probability judgments or estimates of frequency (Kahneman and Tversky 1972,
1973; Tversky and Kahneman 1982). The heuristic of anchoring refers to
people's tendency to estimate the magnitude or degree of something by
comparing it with an "available" initial value (often an inaccurate one) as
a reference point (Fiske and Taylor 1991, pp. 250–256, 268–275).

Cognitive biases also result in errors in attribution. The egocentric
bias leads people to exaggerate their own roles as determinants of the actions of others. The proportionality bias leads people to make inappropri-
ate inferences about the intentions of others based on the apparent costs
and consequences of their actions. The fundamental attribution error leads
people to exaggerate the importance of dispositional over situational factors

in explaining the behavior of others and to attribute greater coherence and meaning to others' behavior than the evidence warrants (Fiske and Taylor 1991; Kahneman, Slovic, and Tversky 1982; Nisbett and Ross 1980, pp. 72–99).

While each of these heuristics and biases has been amply documented in the laboratory, they often generate contradictory predictions about inference and estimation in real-world situations (Lebow and Stein 1993). These inconsistencies make it difficult to integrate these processes into general theories of decisionmaking and severely constrain their predictive value. As explanations, they are overdetermined: Any pattern of inference and judgment can be accounted for ex post facto by one among the several heuristics and biases that have been identified above. In drawing on cognitive models to explain a pattern of attribution by foreign policy leaders, analysts currently get little theoretical guidance on which bias is relevant under what sets of cognitive and situational conditions. It remains for cognitive psychologists to specify the conditions that make one process of causal attribution more likely than another.[8]

Revision of inference and estimates. Conservatism does not hold unconditionally. Schemata *do* change, although they tend to change gradually over time, rather than undergo quick and far-reaching conversions. Schema theory has not yet developed an integrated set of propositions about why schemata change.[9] The centrality of schemata, their refutability, the diagnosticity of discrepant information, the pattern of attribution, and cognitive complexity have all been identified as predictors of the likelihood of revision and, by extension, of change in judgment. Change is in part a function of the rate at which discrepant information occurs and its diagnosticity. Contradictory evidence dispersed across many instances should have a greater impact on schemata than a few isolated examples (Crocker, Hannah, and Weber 1983). As people consider information inconsistent with previous beliefs, they incorporate into their schemata the conditions under which the schemata do not hold, permitting gradual change and adjustment (Higgins and Bargh 1987, p. 386). Important schemata are challenged only when there is no other way to account for contradictory data that people consider diagnostic. Even the strongest schema cannot withstand the challenge of strongly incongruent information or a competing schema that fits the data better (Markus and Zajonc 1985). Cognitive psychologists have not, however, established thresholds for "strongly" incongruent and diagnostic information.

Significant change in schemata about another also occurs when subjects are exposed to incongruent information and are persuaded that the behavior is not arbitrary but reflects the nature of the target. Change occurs when inconsistent information is attributed to dispositional rather than situational factors (Crocker, Hannah, and Weber 1983, p. 65). The general tendency to prefer situational to dispositional attributions to account for incongruent behavior explains why change occurs so infrequently (Jones and Nisbett 1971; Kelley 1967; Ross 1977; Ross and Anderson 1982). Again, cognitive psychologists have not identified the conditions under which people make uncharacteristic attributions to dispositional factors.[10]

Change is also a function of cognitive complexity, or the intricacy of the cognitive rules used to process information about objects and situations. Cognitive complexity refers to the structure or the organization of cognition rather than to the content of thought. Complexity has somewhat contradictory effects on schema change. The more complex the cognitive system, the more capable is the decisionmaker of making new or subtle distinctions when confronted with new information (Suedfeld and Rank 1976; Suedfeld and Tetlock 1977; Tetlock 1985). Experts with highly complex cognitive schemata are more sensitive to new information than novices with low cognitive complexity, whose schemata are likely to be fixed and rigid (Conover and Feldman 1984).[11] But because experts have more relevant information, they can more easily incorporate inconsistent information as exceptions and special cases. Incongruent data therefore have less impact on their schemata than they would have on those of novices (Higgins and Bargh 1987).

Processes of cognitive change are poorly specified. Theories of social cognition have yet to identify when various schemata are invoked to guide the processing of new information, when people assimilate inconsistent information into a schema, when they adjust the schema to the evidence, and when they reject one schema in favor of an alternative (Jervis 1986; Tetlock and Levi 1982, p. 73). Moreover, cognitive theories do not model explicitly the processes that link environmental stimuli to schemata and explain how and when schemata change accordingly (but cf. Erber and Fiske 1984; Tetlock and Boettger 1989). Until they do, social cognition will remain incomplete as a theoretical tool in the analysis of foreign policy decisions. Critics rightly contend that the neglect of context is disturbing; the *social* in social cognition research is largely absent (Kuklinski, Luskin, and Bolland 1991, p. 1346).

More helpful are several strands of theory and research about the solution of "ill structured" problems and learning from failure. A problem is well structured when there is a well-established goal, known constraints, and identified possible solutions. Sometimes even the solution to the problem is established. Generally, problems in foreign policy are ill structured. Goals are often multiple and vaguely defined, one or more constraints are open, information is ambiguous and incomplete, and little may be known about the solution to the problem. Learning is the construction of new representations of the problem, the development of causal relations among the factors, the identification of constraints, and the organization of relevant knowledge.[12] Initially ill structured problems become well structured during the representation process, which largely determines the solution (Voss and Post 1988, pp. 281–282). From this perspective, choice can be modeled as a function of problem representation.

Drawing on models of bounded rationality and satisficing within organizational contexts, a second strand of research examines the liabilities of success and the benefits of failure in improving organizational decisionmaking (Sitkin 1992). Failure that challenges the status quo can draw attention to problems and stimulate the search for solutions. Only certain kinds of failures promote revision: Highly predictable failures provide no new information, but unanticipated failures that challenge old ways of representing problems are more likely to stimulate new formulations. Responding to failure, leaders can "learn through experimentation" (Campbell 1969; Hedberg 1981). Revision in response to failure can provoke a series of sequential experiments that generate quick feedback and allow for a new round of trial-and-error experimentation.[13] This kind of model captures the dynamics of social cognition far more effectively than the statics of schema theory, where the perceiver is a "passive onlooker, who . . . doesn't *do* anything—doesn't mix it up with the folks he's watching, never tests his judgments in action or interaction" (Neisser 1980, pp. 603–604, cited in Kuklinski, Luskin, and Bolland 1991, p. 1346). The trial-and-error model does not represent information processing as a neat linear process with clear causal antecedents but as a messy, dynamic, interactive process.

Motivational Models

Motivational psychology is based on a very different set of premises than is cognitive psychology. Growing out of the Freudian tradition, it takes as its starting point human needs—among them the needs to avoid fear, shame, and guilt and the needs for self-esteem, social approval, achievement, and effective control. Motivational psychologists argue that these needs bias information processing and result in more or less the same kinds of cognitive impairments described by cognitive psychologists. Unlike cognitive biases, which are ubiquitous because they stem from inherent limitations in the human capacity for information processing, motivated biases are either individual-specific ("push" models) or situation-specific ("pull" models).[14]

"Push" models of behavior explain observable biases in information processing in terms of individual personality structures and the diverse ways in which they mediate deep-seated, universal human needs, particularly the need for efficacy and control. Research suggests that when people have alternative sources of information available, their selection of relevant data is often shaped by the relative desirability of the conclusions that the alternative sources provide (Kruglanski 1980, 1986; Kuhl 1986; Raynor and McFarlin 1986; Tesser 1986; Trope and Ginossar 1986; Zukier 1986). Motivational factors may predispose people to make situational or dispositional attributions. Undesirable actions by disliked targets are far more likely to be interpreted by dispositional attributions than are undesirable actions by liked targets (Regan, Straus, and Fazio 1974).

"Pull" models emphasize situations and the needs, fears, and anxieties they arouse in individuals. A "pull" model of motivation directly related to foreign policy decisionmaking emphasizes affect and the ways in which stress—generated by time pressure, fear of loss, and reluctance to assume responsibility for decisions—is responsible for inadequate search, biased estimates of probability, superficial decisionmaking, premature commitment, and insensitivity to information that a decision may have been poor (Janis 1982, 1989; Janis and Mann 1977). This kind of motivational model is more sensitive to situational variables than are cognitive models and relates political situations to coping strategies and associated motivational biases.

Psychology and the "Theory" of Choice

Theories must be judged by the usefulness of their assumptions, how well they specify their scope conditions, and their logical coherence. All three are essential if a theory is to have explanatory and predictive power. The fundamental assumptions of psychological theories are realistic in the sense that they accord with empirical evidence, although some questions arise with respect to how well psychological theories travel from the laboratory to the real world. More problematic, psychological theories generally do not specify their scope conditions. In addition, they are often logically inconsistent with one another (Lebow and Stein 1989; Simon 1985; cf. Jervis 1986, pp. 327–328; Tetlock and Levi 1982, p. 73). At its present level of development, therefore, the psychological approach to the study of choice does not hold out the prospect of general, transposable theories of decisionmaking.

Owing to space constraints, we confine much of our discussion in this section to cognitive theories, although many of the same points apply to motivational theories mutatis mutandis.

The importance of context. Cognitive psychology developed in the laboratory. Biases and heuristics were discovered in the course of experiments in which college students were asked to perform judgmental tasks in strictly controlled environments. The laboratory differs from the real world in a number of important ways (Ebbeson and Koncini 1980; Funder 1987), raising questions about the transposability and operationalizability of cognitive psychological concepts in naturalistic settings.

Attribution studies typically ask subjects explicitly to determine why an event occurred, whereas most events occur in the absence of specific causal questions. The elicitation procedure itself may systematically bias the results of the studies.[15] Moreover, the tasks subjects are asked to perform in experiments are generally trivial and highly structured. They are also unrelated to other tasks and judgments the subjects are likely to perform outside the laboratory. Judgments made by political leaders on foreign policy issues, by contrast, are often interrelated and range from the trivial to the significant.

People's recognition of the importance of a decision may influence their thoroughness in collecting and evaluating information and their choice of decisionmaking rules (Jervis 1986). They may be less likely to use cognitive shortcuts and may rely on different heuristics and biases when they confront judgmental tasks of great importance to them.[16] The availability, representativeness, and anchoring biases—the three most-studied biases in the laboratory—may be less relevant when people make important decisions on subjects they know something about. Some clinical evidence indicates covariance between biases and other situational factors, including decisional complexity, time pressure, and the substantive knowledge, experience, and personality of the decisionmaker (Johnson 1988; Linville 1982b). Biases may matter less in foreign policy decisionmaking than they do in the laboratory because the continuous environment of foreign policy decisionmakers gives them feedback that often permits them to approach decisions incrementally, repeatedly correcting for past mistakes (Gettys, Kelley, and Peterson 1973; Jungermann 1983; Lindblom 1959; Winkler and Murphy 1973). Theories of social cognition do not take all of these differences into account. Attribution and judgment are not generic processes: They are governed by principles that are highly context-dependent.

Competing predictions. Cognitive psychologists have yet to develop an integrated set of propositions to explain distorted attribution, estimation, and judgment. As it is presently formulated, cognitive psychology consists of a collection of discrete insights into phenomena whose relationships to one another remain largely unspecified. For instance, cognitive psychology does not systematically identify the conditions or domain of different heuristics and biases. Some research suggests that heuristics and biases are mutually supportive and appear together in clusters. Yet the behavioral predictions of some of the most important biases are contradictory. Future research must identify the linkages among heuristics and biases and determine which will prevail in situations in which two or more predict different responses.

Cognitive models, as they are currently formulated, do not satisfactorily identify the critical variables that differentiate the likelihood of competing outcomes. Cognitive psychologists must attempt to build a theory or theories that establish a hierarchy among biases and heuristics and specify why, how, and when one dominates another.

The need to link schemata to information processing and choice. Cognitive psychology has yet to develop phased models of information processing that systematically link kinds of prior schemata to processes of attribution, which in turn result in inference and judgment. Cognitive models do not link central schemata systematically to heuristics and biases and to substantive and situational factors, nor do they specify the relationship among the different stages in information processing. Models that systematically link kinds of schemata to processes of attribution and subsequent changes in schemata need to be tested not only against behavior in the laboratory but also against evidence of foreign policy decisionmaking.

The interaction of cognition and motivation. Analysts must consider the interactive impact of cognitive and motivational factors in explaining bias (Simon 1995a). Since the mid-1970s, cognitive and motivational approaches have generally been treated dichotomously. Cognitive psychologists assumed that people are motivated only to be accurate in their attributions and judgments (Higgins and Bargh 1987). This was in part a function, first, of the dominance of behaviorism and then of the rapid growth of research in cognitive psychology, which gave little attention to motivational factors and treated human beings as "naive scientists" or "cognitive misers." Indeed, while some psychologists treat cognition and affect as separate systems that operate largely independently of one another, others see motivation as an alternative explanation of cognitive process,[17] and still others deny the relevance of motivational factors at all (Zajonc 1980; Zajonc, Pietromanco, and Bargh 1982).[18] Nisbett and Ross (1980, pp. 12–13), who are typical of this last approach, dismiss motivated biases as analytically unimportant. "With so many errors on the cognitive side," they argue, "it is often redundant and unparsimonious to look also for motivational errors."[19] Earlier motivational psychologists similarly ignored generic cognitive processes.

More recently, however, psychologists have begun to consider the interactive effects of cognition and affect on processes of attribution and judgment, and to treat personal and motivational factors not as adjuncts to cognition but rather as constitutive parts (Zukier 1986). Some experimental studies treat cognition as the antecedent variable and examine how cognitive complexity, cognitive organization, and the fitting of new information to affect-laden schemata shape affective reactions to new stimuli (Fiske 1981, 1982; Linville 1982a, 1982b; Mandler 1975; Strongman 1978;

Tesser 1978). Psychologists have also examined how feelings shape the way people think. Studies suggest that deeply felt needs and intense emotions affect information processing and interrupt both attention and memory (Arkin, Appleman, and Burger 1980; Bradley 1978; Miller 1976; Miller, Norman, and Wright 1978; Nielson and Sarason 1981; Sicoly and Ross 1977; Tetlock 1980). As we have noted, affect toward the target, as well as the desirability of the consequences, also influences the use of situational and dispositional information in processes of attribution. Arousal can also influence attribution; it has been shown to intensify positive and negative responses (Clark 1982; Gollwitzer, Earle, and Stephan 1982).[20] In related research, moderate stress has been shown to enhance effective information processing, whereas extreme stress degrades performance (De Rivera 1968; Janis and Mann 1977; Lanzetta 1955; Maoz 1995, pp. 391–432; Holsti and George 1975; Lebow 1981, pp. 115–147, 268–273; George 1986).

To the extent that people are motivated not only or even largely by accuracy but by other important needs as well, we must question the proposition that inaccurate or biased inference is due solely to cognitive limitations. A review of the experimental literature on social cognition suggests that people are better conceived as "creatures of compromise," where people's judgments and inferences are understood in terms of the competing motivations they are trying to satisfy. The criterion is not how much of the relevant information people can consider but rather how much of their motivational set they can satisfy. The motivation to be accurate is only one factor in the larger motivational set (Higgins and Bargh 1987, p. 415; see also Kruglanski and Ajzen 1983).

PSYCHOLOGICAL APPROACHES TO
THE STUDY OF INTERNATIONAL CONFLICT

Identifying the psychological processes involved in decisionmaking is difficult enough in the laboratory; it is a daunting task in a naturalistic setting. It requires a great deal of information to determine, for instance, whether President Kennedy's interpretation of the Soviet deployment of strategic missiles to Cuba in 1962 as a deliberate, opportunistic challenge—rather than a fear-driven, defensive gamble—is best explained in terms of his Soviet foreign policy schema, the egocentric bias, his affective response to deception, or some combination of these (and/or other) factors. Indeed, in this specific case, although we can determine with high confidence *that* Kennedy made incorrect inferences about Soviet motives (Allyn, Blight, and Welch 1989/1990; Blight, Allyn, and Welch 1993; Lebow and Stein 1994), the available record does not permit us to determine exactly *why* he did so. The most we can do in this case is to offer plausible psychological explanations for his error.

The high information demands for psychological explanations of international conflict, coupled with the various difficulties we surveyed in the previous section, mean that psychological explanations of international conflict are few in number compared to rational choice analyses and consist almost exclusively of pretheoretical discussions or in-depth case studies with limited theoretical goals (e.g., Dawes 1992; De Rivera 1968; Hermann 1974, 1980; Holsti 1989; Holsti and George 1975; Janis 1982; Jervis 1976; Jervis, Lebow, and Stein 1985; Lebow 1981; Lebow and Stein 1994; Mandel 1986; Stein 1992a, 1994; Welch 1993). The earliest case studies were psychobiographical (e.g., Allport 1958; George and George 1956; Hermann 1974, 1980; Lane 1959; Lasswell 1948; Maslow 1970; Volkan and Itzkowitz 1984).[21] Later efforts attempted to employ psychological approaches to explain the dynamics of specific events or classes of events, usually acute international crises.[22]

Psychologically informed case studies provide powerful explanations of specific events, but what general inferences about international conflict do they permit? Are they predictive? The most significant theoretical accomplishments to date of psychological approaches to the study of international conflict have been critical rather than constructive: for example, challenging the postulates of rational deterrence theory (Jervis, Lebow, and Stein 1985; Lebow 1993; Lebow and Stein 1994) and its associated view, "proliferation optimism" (Blight and Welch 1994). Such studies clearly demonstrate that leaders who face decisions about war and peace are not in fact expected utility maximizers, and they catalogue a number of typical deviations from rational norms. To the extent that these studies follow the logic of critical-case testing, and also in proportion to their representativeness, they advance our understanding of the dynamics of international conflict by reducing the set of competing explanations of state behavior. Additionally, they provide important cues for further lines of inquiry. However, neither individually nor collectively do they lead to lawlike generalizations, even highly contingent ones. Thus, while they enable us to identify patterns, tendencies, and various typical errors, they have not led to the specification of models that would enable analysts to predict exactly what kinds of patterns, tendencies, and errors are likely under what conditions.

PROSPECT THEORY

Prospect theory is a behavioral alternative to rational choice theory derived from empirical observations of subjects' choices rather than from a normative ideal. It does not specifically employ or presuppose cognitive or motivational concepts, although the choice behavior it describes is consistent with the expectations of some psychological theories. We digress to examine it here briefly because it represents in some sense a middle ground between rational and psychological approaches to the study of international conflict. Readers will find a more detailed discussion of prospect theory in Chapter 3.

Behavioral decision theorists have demonstrated experimentally that subjects routinely violate the assumptions of rational choice under certain circumstances and in systematic ways (Kahneman, Slovic, and Tversky 1982; Kahneman and Tversky 1979; Quattrone and Tversky 1988; Tversky and Kahneman 1981, 1986, 1992). Among the crucial insights of prospect theory are that people assess alternatives not on the basis of their prospective net assets (i.e., their expected utilities) but in relation to a reference point defining an acceptable outcome; that a crucial desideratum in choice is the prospective loss or gain relative to this reference point; that people consider losses more painful than gains pleasurable; and that people will accept poor gambles in order to avoid certain losses but will shun uncertain prospects of large gains in favor of smaller sure gains, even though the risky choice might have a higher expected utility.[23]

According to prospect theory, the selection of a reference point is central to the assessment of options and the choices people make. But there is at present no theory for predicting which reference points people will choose. Psychologists and economists have identified a number of processes that systematically bias people in favor of the status quo as a reference point. One of these is known as the endowment effect: People demand more to give up an object than they would be willing to pay to acquire it in the first place. Forgone gains are less painful than perceived losses, and therefore, over the long run, people's expectations tend to converge on the status quo (Kahneman, Knetsch, and Thaler 1991; Knetsch 1989; Sinden and Sinden 1984; Thaler 1980). In addition, prospect theory suggests that people will normalize (i.e., adjust their reference points) more quickly for gains than for losses, reinforcing the status quo bias. Yet the status quo does not always serve as a decisionmaker's reference point. People who are dissatisfied with a status quo will often take great risks to reach what they consider an acceptable state of affairs. In many cases this may follow a loss from a previous reference point for which they have not normalized; they will therefore strive to restore an earlier (acceptable) status quo. In other cases people's aspirations, expectations, or conceptions of entitlement may provide the appropriate frame of reference for understanding their risk-taking behavior (Stein 1992b, pp. 215–216; Welch 1993, pp. 23–25). Thus any attempt to apply prospect theory to the study of foreign policy choice at present requires treating reference points as exogenous.

There are two key reasons why prospect theory is not yet in a position to mount a full challenge to rational choice in the quest for general, transposable theory. First, just as with psychological theories, there are some reasons to wonder how well prospect theory travels from well-defined experimental choice situations to complex, unstructured, real-world choices. Second, the value function prospect theory postulates is not well defined, and appears not to be well behaved at the extremes. Accordingly, it has not yet yielded to formal mathematical representation (but cf. Tversky and Wakker 1995).

Thus prospect theory has not yet reached the level of development at which it could serve as a robust tool for predicting choice.[24] Nevertheless, in the few studies directly comparing post hoc explanations of foreign policy choices, prospect theory appears to provide a better fit with the evidence than does rational choice (see, e.g., Farnham 1994; Stein and Pauly 1993), suggesting that its central insights are relevant to and useful for foreign policy analysis.[25]

RATIONAL CHOICE APPROACHES TO
THE STUDY OF INTERNATIONAL CONFLICT

The comparative advantage of psychological approaches is descriptive accuracy and post hoc explanatory power; the comparative advantage of rational choice is theoretical elegance. In contrast to psychological approaches, rational choice analyses of international conflict abound and typically have more ambitious theoretical goals. Rational choice aspires to provide a transposable deductive apparatus for the formal analysis of interstate interactions. Relatively few rational choice theorists aspire to descriptive accuracy in specific cases; instead, they insist that treating states *as if* they were unitary rational actors yields dividends in explanatory and predictive power (e.g., Bueno de Mesquita 1984, 1989; Bueno de Mesquita and Lalman 1986; Bueno de Mesquita, Newman, and Rabushka 1985). Yet in our view rational choice has not led to cumulation of useful knowledge about international conflict. As this is a controversial claim, it requires careful explication.

The first difficulty stems from the ambiguities of the rationality assumption itself, to which we referred in the first section: The weaker the content of the assumption, the larger the number of choice situations that meet the scope conditions; but the more difficult the problem of modeling, the less precise the prediction and the greater the danger of tautology. Suppose that we adopt a weak conception of the rationality assumption—namely, that leaders have clear goals and reasons (good or bad) for believing that their actions will attain their goals. Empirically, this assumption will accurately describe most leaders facing a choice about war or peace. However, this weak variant of the rationality assumption places virtually no constraints upon the operationalization of the concept of reasons. Further, it provides no logical criteria for predicting one choice rather than another when leaders have reasons for both waging war and not waging war (for this we would need auxiliary assumptions sufficiently powerful that the resulting model could no longer be described as a rational choice model at all, since the rationality assumption would not be pulling any weight), and it would make it trivially easy to "explain" any particular decision in retrospect.

A stronger rationality assumption would avoid many of these pitfalls. Let us specify that a "rational" choice is the expected-utility-maximizing choice, and let us further specify that only certain preference orderings are allowed (namely, leaders will always prefer a marginal increase in the coercive capacity of their state to any increment of any other good, such that no leader will be willing to sacrifice any degree of security to promote, say, a humanitarian or other moral objective). Such an assumption provides a logical criterion for predicting one choice rather than another when leaders have "reasons" for both waging war and not waging war (the leader will pick the alternative with the higher expected utility), and the logical criterion can easily be modeled mathematically. However, we know that leaders do not—indeed, cannot—make expected utility calculations except in trivially simple choice situations where we do not need the elaborate edifice of rational choice "theory" to predict behavior, because the simple logical meaning of the word "preference" suffices. Thus the scope conditions for a general theory of choice based upon a strong conception of rationality exclude all of the interesting cases of international conflict.

Proponents of rational choice nevertheless insist that this does not stand in the way of useful applications of rational choice theory. Two arguments in particular are commonly deployed in defense of this view: that treating leaders *as if* they were rational actors predicts choices about international conflict, notwithstanding the unrealism of the assumption; and that by means of simplified representations of strategic interactions, rational choice theory can yield explanatory and predictive knowledge about choices otherwise obscured by empirical detail.

The "As-If" Defense of Rational Approaches to the Study of International Conflict

Those who concede that people are not normally expected utility maximizers often maintain that it is nonetheless defensible (and useful) to treat them *as if* they were. According to this view, propounded most effectively by Milton Friedman (1953), the superior performance of theories premised on empirically inaccurate assumptions is a fully sufficient justification for employing the assumptions. The claim that people may be assumed to be "rational" for purposes of theory building in social science has been criticized as a violation of the covering-law principle of scientific progress because it relies upon an idealization without an empirical referent (Moe 1979). However, we leave aside the larger philosophy of science question to consider the simpler (and unobjectionable) claim that an increase in predictive accuracy justifies such a move.

It is easy to see the attraction of an "as-if" rationality assumption in the economic realm. Suppose that our objective is to predict the quantity of widgets produced in a highly competitive market. One way to facilitate such a prediction is to make two simplifying (though inaccurate) assumptions: (1) that the widget market is *perfectly* competitive and (2) that firms are fully informed, rational profit maximizers. In a perfectly competitive market, firms are price-takers, and they maximize profit by producing widgets until the marginal cost of production equals marginal revenue. We need only estimate the demand function for widgets and the factor costs of production to arrive at a reasonably good estimate of total production volume, even though firms are not, in fact, rational profit maximizers (they have neither the information nor the organizational competence to make the necessary calculations). This approach works because *if the market is competitive enough*, then firms that are relatively efficient and just so happen to hit upon or come close to ideal production volumes will do well in the marketplace and will survive, whereas inefficient firms and firms that over- or underproduce will fail. The outcome we wish to predict—production volume—will be roughly the same whether or not firms are rational profit maximizers, because poor performers will be selected out of the market. Assuming that firms are rational profit maximizers is therefore useful, as it draws our attention to the parameters we need to estimate in order to make a reasonably accurate prediction of production volumes, and the unrealism of the assumption does not materially affect the analysis.

As the foregoing illustration makes clear, however, the utility of the rational actor assumption depends upon the context in which it is employed. A highly competitive market in homogeneous goods structurally constrains agents according to a small number of fixed and knowable parameters. The large number of producers, the essential similarity and interchangeability of their products, and the formal identity and large number of transactions in the marketplace are environmental constants with which neither firms nor economists need bother themselves further. The stakes for producers are clear, as are their organizational imperatives. In short, specifying production volumes in the highly competitive widget market represents an extremely well structured decision problem for widget producers and a tractable analytical problem for economic analysts armed with a spare set of as-if assumptions.

In contrast, decision problems in international politics are generally ill structured and are less tractable analytically. In cases of actual or potential international conflict, leaders are often uncertain about the stakes; their organizational imperatives are clear only when stated at an extremely high level of abstraction ("state survival" or "security"; "power"; "the national interest"; etc.) and must be interpreted and reformulated as precise objectives in the light of specific contingent circumstances (a difficult and controversial task in the best of times); they face—and must choose among—a wide variety of options, typically with no way of meaningfully estimating payoffs and probabilities; and the actions of any one player can have a powerful effect on the structure of the decision problem itself.[26] In short, international conflict, in contrast to microeconomics, is not fertile soil for as-if theorizing because crucial parameters are neither fixed nor objectively knowable. As-if rationality assumptions in such a domain yield no determinate predictions.

As we have seen, psychological approaches fare no better in the quest for general theories of choice and provide no superior set of behavioral assumptions for formal, deductive analyses of international conflict. Yet they are much better suited to explanation in particular cases, because they draw the analyst's attention to leaders' *subjective* judgments and estimates of stakes, options, costs, benefits, and probabilities and help render those judgments and estimates intelligible by providing a set of theories, concepts, and categories with which to interpret them.

Simplified Representation

Much rational choice scholarship on international conflict deals with the apparent complexity and indeterminacy of the subject matter through a strategy of simplified representation. Prisoners' Dilemma, for example, is a common metaphor for many real-world strategic interactions and is used to estimate crisis stability or arms race stability in particular strategic contexts, sometimes solely on the basis of players' preferences over outcomes in a single-play simultaneous game. Such simplified representations are often analytically tractable in the sense that equilibrium solutions to games (when they exist) yield determinate predictions of behavior (Brandenburger 1992; Snidal 1986).

Implied in any strategy of simplified representation is the claim that the abstraction captures the essence of a decision problem for national leaders, notwithstanding their own confusion and uncertainty about stakes, options, costs, benefits, likelihoods, and the interests, goals, and intentions of the adversary. The claim is prima facie plausible when reality and representation are isomorphic, and it becomes prima facie less plausible as the isomorphisms break down. It is immediately apparent that the very considerations that led us to call into question the use of as-if rationality assumptions in the study of international conflict (although not necessarily in micro-economics) lead us to suspect that while simplified representation might be a useful analytical strategy in well structured decision problems, it is unlikely to help in the study of international conflict. International conflicts do not arise out of the blue and cannot reasonably be treated as single-play simultaneous games. The more we abstract from leaders' subjective judgments and estimates, the less the formal representation describes the choice situation leaders actually face. In seriously ill structured decision problems, the very choice of game to use as a representation of a strategic interaction (and the specification of players' preference orderings) represents an arbitrary stipulation that undermines the analytical utility of the representation itself.[27]

While simplified representations therefore tell us a great deal about what *analysts* believe about the essential nature of decision problems, they do not lead to reliable explanations and predictions when the underlying decision problems are ill structured. There are several ways, of course, to improve the degree of isomorphism between representation and reality—for example, by studying iterated rather than single-play games, by formulating more nuanced payoff matrices, by modeling games with imperfect information, and so forth (Kreps and Wilson 1982; Morrow 1989a). But truly ill structured decision problems have resisted rational analysis thus far, and it is difficult to see how the behavior of nonrational agents in ill structured decision problems can be predicted by even the most sophisticated rational models.

The Performance Defense of Rational Models

An obvious rejoinder is that rational models have in fact demonstrated their explanatory and predictive value empirically and that, as a class, they outperform all contenders. Indeed, Bruce Bueno de Mesquita (1984, pp. 344–349) has reported favorable systematic comparisons of the performance of his particular expected utility model (Bueno de Mesquita 1981) with other rational models in the domain of international conflict, and he claims a successful point-prediction rate of over 90 percent across a variety of political decisionmaking domains for a related model based upon Black's median voter theorem (Black 1958; Bueno de Mesquita, Newman, and Rabushka 1985).[28] Such a success rate would seem to require no further justification. Moreover, Bueno de Mesquita and his colleagues have progressively applied their approach to a broader and broader set of phenomena, in accordance with covering-law principles of scientific knowledge and progress, making a strong prima facie case for its superiority to competing approaches on Lakatosian grounds.[29]

As a group, rational choice approaches to the study of international conflict have no competitors. There are no theories of comparable generality with comparable goals founded explicitly upon nonrational assumptions. For reasons we discussed above, cognitive and motivational psychology at their current level of development are in no position to mount such a challenge. Strictly speaking, therefore, Lakatosian criteria do not apply to the so-called rational-cognitive debate, because neither represents a true competitor to—and therefore neither can falsify—the other. Lakatosian criteria apply only *within* each genre. Nevertheless, the strong claims made on behalf of the performance of rational choice approaches to the study of international conflict warrant consideration. Bueno de Mesquita's research program is clearly the most impressive example of its type. It is therefore worth assessing its contribution to the study of international conflict qua rational choice theory.[30]

Bueno de Mesquita's model assumes that states may be treated *as if* they were unitary expected utility maximizers choosing between a fixed menu of alternatives, depending upon the specific behavior under study (e.g., attack/do not attack; resist/yield; escalate/do not escalate; support initiator/remain neutral/support initiator's opponent; etc.). For each option, it is necessary that the analyst (though not the actual leaders of states) be able to estimate the appropriate probability and utility of each alternative course of action, in order to perform the necessary expected utility calculation. In the original formulation, Bueno de Mesquita estimated utility by comparing states' alliance portfolios,[31] and he estimated probability of gaining or losing by comparing national capabilities as reflected in military, industrial, and demographic measures, adjusted for distance (Bueno de Mesquita 1981, pp. 101–109).[32]

The crucial question we must ask is whether (and, if so, in what sense) this is an "expected utility" model. Certainly the formal mathematical presentation of the model is consistent with such an interpretation, both in notation and in functional form. But the application, ancillary assumptions, operationalization of concepts, and abstraction of the model suggest that it is not.

Bueno de Mesquita notes that "being rational simply implies that the decision maker uses a maximizing strategy in calculating how best to achieve his goals. The rationality assumption tells us nothing about how actors form their preferences but rather shows how actors behave, given their preferences" (Bueno de Mesquita 1981, p. 31). But preferences are endogenous to the model, and option menus are arbitrarily constrained across the entire set of interstate interactions to which the model applies. The model does not make—and does not permit—an attempt to determine empirically the option sets leaders *actually* construct or their subjective preferences. It would therefore seem to entail a particularly strong rationality assumption. Yet the parametric constraints of the choice situations to which the model is meant to apply are insufficiently strong to vindicate the "as-if" justification of such a strong rationality assumption. Unlike producers of widgets in a perfectly competitive market, who would disappear from the observed sample of producers if they did not truly behave as if they were profit maximizers—and where we can know precisely what behavior would maximize profit—states do not disappear from the observed sample of states if they make suboptimal decisions. Unlike widget producers in a perfectly competitive market, states have nothing they must maximize in order to survive. There are various things they must provide at some minimal level in order to survive, but these are not deducible from the choice situation, and even if they were, the minimal levels would not themselves be predictable from the model. In other words, the nature of the choice situation to which Bueno de Mesquita's model is meant to apply is one that does not permit us to know that a true expected utility maximizer *would* make the choices predicted by the model, as opposed to others not predicted by the model. A weakly rational decisionmaker might make those choices, but the model does not rest upon a weak assumption of rationality (indeed, for the reasons we have already discussed, it could not do so, given its theoretical aspirations). In sum, we cannot justify the conclusion that the model employs an "as-if" expected utility maximization assumption, and it is doubtful whether it is even meaningful to describe it as a "rational choice" model.[33]

The point becomes clearer when we consider the model's data validity (King, Keohane, and Verba 1994, p. 25). In well-understood cases where it is possible to make reliable judgments about the sign and/or rough magnitude of decisionmakers' true expected utility estimates, Bueno de Mesquita's often widely miss the mark. For example, in the Crimean War, where Bueno de Mesquita estimates the expected utility of war with Russia for Turkey at $-.756$, the historical record clearly shows that Turkey strongly preferred waging war against Russia to the status quo (Kinglake 1863; Temperley 1964; Welch 1993). In addition, in the case of the Cuban missile crisis, Bueno de Mesquita estimates the United States' expected utility from a conflict with the Soviet Union to be positive (.314), whereas—had he thought in those terms—President Kennedy clearly would have assigned a strongly negative expected utility for war with the Soviet Union (Blight, Allyn, and Welch 1993; Garthoff 1989; Lebow and Stein 1994).[34] Bueno de Mesquita's indicators of probability and utility do not appear to be valid.[35]

All models, of course, involve simplifications and abstractions from reality, and it is not unusual to operationalize concepts in terms of indirect or surrogate indicators. Bueno de Mesquita certainly has a model with which to predict a variety of behaviors in international politics. Calling into question the interpretation of the model as an expected utility model does not ipso facto call into question its predictive value (merely its interpretation and therefore its *explanatory* value). In this respect, Bueno de Mesquita's model might be thought of as analogous to the theory of quantum mechanics, a theory with predictive value but with an uncertain interpretation (Lahti and Mittelstaedt 1987; Laurikainen and Montonen 1993).[36]

A similar point applies to the model derived from Black's median voter theorem employed by Bueno de Mesquita and his colleagues to make point predictions of political events (e.g., Wu and Bueno de Mesquita 1994). The model predicts choice as a function of a contest between interested parties on the basis of three variables: the capabilities of each, the preferred outcome of each, and the salience of the issue to each. This model exogenizes not only these three variables but also the identification of relevant parties.[37] Most simply, one might conceive of policy choice in this model as the vector sum of the weighted preferences of the parties. This is a representation with great intuitive appeal. However, the model neither operationalizes—nor even requires—the concept of expected utility maximization. The analyst employing it is wholly indifferent to the sources or nature of the parties' preferences, their individual processes of decision, or their computational skills. Since the rationality assumption does no work in the model, it cannot meaningfully be described as an "expected utility" or a "rational choice" model. Again, this is not necessarily an indictment of its value as a predictive tool: With good-quality, exogenously derived inputs, such a model might well have a high rate of predictive success.

While the as-if justification does not appear to be available to so-called expected utility or rational choice models in the study of international conflict, and as there are grounds for doubting whether it is even appropriate to describe such models as "expected utility" or "rational choice" models, there is no reason in principle why scholars could not attempt to formulate, operationalize, and employ models whose independent variables were true measures of probability, utility, and uncertainty. It would be instructive to evaluate such models and compare their performance in Lakatosian terms to existing rivals that claim to be—but are not—"rational" models. If such true expected utility models employed measures of *purely subjective* judgments, it would be odd if they did not predict choice perfectly, within the constraints of observational error: People do not make choices believing that better ones are available. If they were to employ measures of *objectively knowable* probabilities, utilities, and uncertainties, it is likely that their performance would be less than perfect, for reasons identified by cognitive psychologists, motivational psychologists, and behavioral decision theorists. But in any case such objectively knowable probabilities and utilities are generally not available in this field.

CONCLUSION

The foregoing suggests that cognitive and motivational psychology have different (and much more limited) theoretical goals than do rational choice approaches to the study of international conflict but that those goals are more readily achieved. On balance, the psychological study of international conflict is likely to be the more fruitful avenue of inquiry.

There are three crucial reasons why psychology is more congenial to the study of international conflict than is rational choice analysis. First, international conflict is a relatively rare phenomenon (crises and wars represent a minute proportion of total interstate interactions), and international conflicts generally have important unique features. It is therefore difficult for analysts and decisionmakers alike to identify among historical antecedents a significant number of "like" cases on crucial dimensions from which to tease out probability distributions, or on the basis of which to derive behavioral proclivities from circumstantial constraints. Accordingly, leaders of states must confront conflicts without a repertoire of generally accepted and empirically defensible principles of conflict management. Cognitive psychology sheds light on how leaders cope with this uncertainty: They commonly interpret ambiguous situations in the light of personally salient historical experiences or employ behavioral rules of thumb that reflect idiosyncratic "lessons of history" (Khong 1992; Lebow 1981; Neustadt and May 1986; Richardson 1993). Since these are idiosyncratic variables that nonetheless strongly influence problem representation, judgment, and estimation, they greatly complicate rational choice analysis. This is not a significant barrier to rational choice analysis in other domains (for example, in the study of micro- or macroeconomic phenomena) where decision problems typically concern well-understood, large-*n* classes of formally identical events (purchases, sales, investments, and so forth) with which decisionmakers are extremely familiar.

Second, because leaders tend to seek guidance in "lessons of history," their behavior changes over time in response to prior historical events. International conflict as a subject of study is therefore a moving target, constantly evolving self-referentially (Jervis 1991/1992). While this greatly complicates formal deductive rational choice analysis, it does not represent a serious obstacle to psychological analysis, with its more modest theoretical goals.

Third, international conflicts virtually always represent ill-structured decision problems. Few (perhaps none) of the crucial pieces of information

necessary to conduct a rational choice theoretic analysis—stakes, preferences, options, costs, benefits, likelihoods—are given by the structure of
the interaction but are instead constructed by decisionmakers through
processes of introspection, attribution, and estimation. It is consequently
difficult to justify formal abstractions from real-world decision problems
of the kind rational choice theorists seek. Problem representation is a significant variable in any international conflict, and the concepts and methods of psychology are comparatively well suited to understanding problem
representation. In such a domain of study, "as-if" assumptions of rationality yield no determinate predictions, and simplified representations that
are analytically tractable are insufficiently isomorphic with reality to permit valid inferences from the representations themselves to the behavior of
actors in the real world. Rational approaches fail to deliver, therefore, that
which they promise: the master key to unlock the myriad secrets of international conflict.

> *Such knowledge is too wonderful for me;*
> *it is high, I cannot attain unto it.*
>
> —Psalm 139:6

NOTES

The authors would like to acknowledge the invaluable assistance of Steven Bernstein, Peter Feaver, Joy Fitzgibbon, and Gillian Manning, as well as the financial
support of the Social Sciences and Humanities Research Council of Canada.
  1. For the purposes of this essay, we assume that readers are familiar with the
formal requirements of rational choice theory concerning actors' preference orderings.
  2. The dangers of tautological applications of rational choice are evident in
Riker 1995.
  3. On complex decisions, see, for example, Steinbruner 1974, pp. 15–18. For
critical assessments of the application of economic assumptions to the study of politics, see Monroe 1991; Rosenberg 1995.
  4. In some cases it may be possible to compensate for the inherent complexity
of decisionmaking situations by representing them in simplified or abstract forms
that *are* analytically tractable (e.g., by representing the nuclear arms race between
the United States and the Soviet Union as a single-play Prisoners' Dilemma).
Whether or not this strategy pays dividends depends upon the degree of isomorphism between reality and representation. We take up this issue later in the chapter.
  5. For a treatment of psychological and behavioral theories of choice, see
Sniderman, Brody, and Tetlock 1991.
  6. A schema is a working hypothesis about some aspect of the environment and
may be a concept of the self (self schema), other individuals (person schema),
groups (role schema), or sequences of events in the environment (scripts) (Fiske and
Taylor 1991, p. 140; Fiske 1986). In addition to using them to organize their interpretations of their environments, people use schemata to develop scripts for action.

7. The postulate that schemata are resistant to change can be interpreted as consistent with statistical logic if people assign a low variance estimate to their expectations. Psychological research contradicts this interpretation through repeated observations that exposure to discrepant information strengthens rather than undermines existing schemata (Anderson 1983; Anderson, Lepper, and Ross 1980; Hirt and Sherman 1985). The strengthening of schemata after exposure to contradictory information results from the processes of reasoning people use to explain away the apparent inconsistency (Crocker 1981; Kulik 1983; O'Sullivan and Durson 1984; Srull 1981; Wyer and Gordon 1982).

8. Some research proposes that the fundamental attribution error is most likely to occur when the observed behavior is consistent with prior beliefs about the actor (Kulik 1983). Consistent behavior is especially likely to be attributed to dispositional factors even when there are compelling situational explanations. Dispositional attributions are likely to be highly accessible for consistent behavior, and the readily available belief that the actor is "just the kind of person" who would engage in such behavior may make people insensitive to situational factors that might have evoked the inconsistency. The representative bias may therefore help to explain the occurrence of fundamental attribution errors when observed behavior is consistent with prior beliefs. But when behavior disconfirms prior beliefs, subjects are, contrary to the expectations of the fundamental attribution error, sensitive to situational factors.

It may not be that situational or distributional attributions depend upon the information itself, but instead upon its availability and accessibility (Higgins and Bargh 1987). Attributions may also depend critically upon the relationships among the various stages of information processing.

9. In large part because schema theories focus on whole schemata, they are relatively static. For a critical review of the static quality of schema theory, see Kuklinski, Luskin, and Bolland 1991.

10. In parallel research, psychologists who work with the affective concept of attitude rather than the concept of schema have noted that turning-point decisions, or decisions that deviate significantly from the pattern of prior decisions, depend on resolving the contradiction between the attitude toward object and the attitude toward situation in favor of the latter (Auerbach 1986).

11. Those who possess multiple judgment dimensions are also likely to possess rules of abstraction that facilitate the integration and comparison of information. They tend to produce alternative interpretations of new information but by using their capacity for abstraction and integration are able to resolve these ambiguities (Bennett 1975, pp. 33–35; Vertzberger 1990, pp. 134–137).

12. For theoretical discussion, see Newell and Simon 1972; Reitman 1965; Simon 1973; Voss et al. 1983; Voss and Post 1988; Voss et al. 1991; cf. Levy 1994. For applications to international politics, see Mendelson 1993; Nye 1987; Stein 1994.

13. For a discussion of the importance of "theory in action," see Argyris and Schon 1978. For an analysis of "action bias," see Peters and Waterman 1982.

14. See Hoyenga and Hoyenga 1984, pp. 21–63, for discussion of "push" and "pull" models. Attribution theory is similarly premised on the fundamental need to understand, predict, and control. In related research Seligman (1975) examines the impact of attributional processes on emotional states and cognitive biases. He suggests that the intensity of anxiety and fear stimulated by an aversive situation is a function both of the unpredictability of the feared outcome and inability of the individual to control the situation. When individuals attribute lack of control to

their stupidity or inability, they experience a particularly acute form of "personal helplessness" that results in depression and learning deficits. See also Miller, Norman, and Wright 1978.

15. Pyszczynski and Greenberg (1981) and Enzle and Shopflocher (1978) similarly demonstrate that direct attributional questions may instigate attributional processes that do not occur in the absence of such questions. Both of these studies focus on the onset of attribution rather than on the impact of attributional processes on prior beliefs.

16. Nisbett and Ross (1980, pp. 220–222) dispute the hypothesis that important judgments will encourage the adoption of more explicit and articulated cognitive processes. They also argue (pp. 250–254) that laboratory procedures often result in an *underestimation* of the magnitude of inferential failings.

17. For example, cognitive psychology identifies the general tendency for people to make dispositional rather than situational attributions when they explain consistent behavior but to prefer situational rather than dispositional attributions when they explain inconsistent behavior. Motivational psychology helps to explain this puzzle through the proposition that undesirable actions by disliked targets are far more likely to be interpreted through dispositional attributions than are undesirable actions by liked targets.

18. Trope (1975) also argues that differences in behavior as a function of achievement-related motives are primarily due to differences in cognitive information seeking, not affective arousal.

19. For discussion, see Fiske and Taylor 1991, pp. 326–337.

20. A careful review of the most important evidence, however, suggests that these data are also open to cognitive explanations, in part because of the elasticity of cognitive models. As Tetlock and Levi note (1982, p. 83), because the cognitive paradigm has so many theoretical degrees of freedom, it can explain almost anything.

21. For methodological discussion, see Alexander 1988, 1990; Carlson 1988; Kren and Rappoport 1976; Runyan 1984, 1988; and Gronn 1993.

22. For example, several scholars have used the Janis and Mann model, or components of it, to explain faulty strategic and political decisions and the insensitivity of the leaders who made them to information suggesting that their choices would have disastrous consequences. These cases include the pre-1914 Russian, Austrian, German, and French military plans; German policymaking in the July 1914 crisis; postwar U.S. grand strategy; the Cuban missile crisis; the Middle East wars of 1967, 1969, and 1973; and the Falklands/Malvinas War of 1982 (Blight 1990; Larson 1985; Lebow 1981; Snyder 1984; Stein 1985a, 1985b; Lebow 1985).

23. For example, in a choice involving prospects of monetary gains, Kahneman and Tversky's subjects preferred a sure gain of $3,000 to an 80 percent chance of winning $4,000 (and a 20 percent chance of winning nothing) by a four-to-one margin. The expected utility of the preferred alternative was 3,000 x 1.0 = 3,000; the expected utility of the second alternative was 4,000 x .8 = 3,200. The same problem framed in terms of losses illustrated dramatically different preferences. By a margin of more than eleven to one, respondents preferred an 80 percent chance to lose $4,000 (and a 20 percent chance to lose nothing) to a sure loss of $3,000. They therefore chose the alternative with the lower expected utility (–3,200 vs. –3,000) (Kahneman and Tversky 1979, p. 26). This nicely illustrates the claim that people are risk-acceptant with respect to losses and risk-averse with respect to gains.

24. Even if it had, prospect theory and expected utility theory would predict different choices only in narrowly defined circumstances. For many—and perhaps

most—choices people face, the expected-utility-maximizing choice would also be preferred by someone who is risk-averse in the domain of gains and risk-acceptant in the domain of losses.

25. For critical discussion, see Shafir 1992.

26. The Cuban missile crisis provides an instructive illustration. Neither U.S. nor Soviet decisionmaking bodies reached consensus on the stakes in the confrontation, the set of options that should be on the table, the possible costs and benefits of the options, or the likelihood of realizing gains or suffering costs. Neither side understood the motives or intentions of the other. Both sides were completely unable to forecast with any meaningful accuracy the likely reactions of the other to any particular moves of their own. As a result, individuals on both sides of the confrontation had wildly differing estimates of the merits and dangers of taking hard and soft lines (Blight, Allyn, and Welch 1993; Blight and Welch 1990, 1994; Lebow and Stein 1994).

27. Snyder and Diesing, for example (1977, pp. 114–115), cannot decide whether the Cuban missile crisis is better modeled by Prisoners' Dilemma or Called Bluff.

28. For revisions and extensions of the model, see Bueno de Mesquita 1983, 1985; Bueno de Mesquita and Lalman 1986, 1988, 1990; Wu and Bueno de Mesquita 1994.

29. "A scientific theory T is falsified if and only if another theory T' has been proposed with the following characteristics: (1) T' has excess empirical content over T: that is, it predicts novel facts, that is, facts improbable in the light of, or even forbidden by, T; (2) T' explains the previous success of T, that is, all the unrefuted content of T is included (within the limits of observational error) in the content of T'; and (3) some of the excess content of T' is corroborated" (Lakatos 1978, p. 32).

30. In what follows, we presume readers are familiar with Bueno de Mesquita's model. Space will not permit a more extensive examination here. For a typical critique that addresses a broader range of issues, see Majeski and Sylvan 1984.

31. Bueno de Mesquita uses four categories—defense pacts, nonaggression or neutrality pacts, ententes, and no alliance—as ordinal indicators of the utility of states' policies for each other, on the assumption that states will be willing to sacrifice policy autonomy to others only in proportion to the similarity of their preferences (Bueno de Mesquita 1981, pp. 114–115).

32. For this, Bueno de Mesquita used the composite national capabilities scores developed by the Correlates of War project. The model also built in terms for uncertainty (specifically, uncertainty about the utility for third parties of a state's policy) and risk-taking (a function of vulnerability to attack as indicated by the capabilities of nonaligned states; see Bueno de Mesquita 1981, pp. 118–125). We set aside these indicators and subsequent revisions to the original model, as discussion of them adds nothing to our analysis of the relevant points.

33. A model that required direct estimation of the subjective utilities and subjective probabilities of a subjectively constructed value set *could*, of course, be described as an expected utility model (see, e.g., Stein and Tanter 1980).

34. Indeed, it is difficult to find examples of cases where leaders made decisions believing that alternatives were, on balance, preferable. Thus a weak conception of rationality courts tautology when invoked as an explanation of behavior.

35. Endogeneity may be part of the reason why Bueno de Mesquita's use of alliance portfolios to estimate utility is invalid (King, Keohane, and Verba 1994,

pp. 185–196): It is plausible that alliance portfolios may be a function—and therefore not a valid predictor—of propensities to wage war. A three-month lag does not seem to be an adequate check against this problem (Bueno de Mesquita 1981, p. 114).

36. Here we do not take up the issue of the model's predictive value, which would depend upon a more thoroughgoing examination both of the model's design and of the quality and replicability of the data employed to test it.

37. The high success rate claimed for this model raises interesting questions about the explanatory and predictive value of the model originally formulated in Bueno de Mesquita 1981, since it would appear to vindicate the view that foreign policy choices are a function of the interactions of domestic players, not a function of the unitary rational choices of a leader taking his or her cues from systemic indicators.

Part 2

Alternatives to Rational Choice and Prospect Theory

5

The Poliheuristic Theory of Foreign Policy Decisionmaking

Alex Mintz & Nehemia Geva

How a decisionmaker chooses a certain policy from a portfolio of alternatives has been a central concern of political analysis for many years. Most studies of foreign policy behavior have attempted to answer the question of *what* accounts for the behavior of nations, typically using linear models connecting the policy choice (the dependent variable) to a set of explanatory (independent) variables. Considerably less attention has been given to the question of *how* policymakers actually make decisions. Consequently, research in foreign policy decisionmaking has often sacrificed process validity in the quest for outcome validity.

There are presently two leading foreign policy decisionmaking paradigms. The first is based on the classical or rational acftor model originally posited by Von Neumann and Morgenstern in the 1940s to explain microeconomic decisions (see also Brams, Chapter 6; Morrow, Chapter 2). The second is based on the cybernetic perspective, whose groundwork was laid by Herbert Simon (1957, 1959) in his research on bounded rationality and later refined by John Steinbruner (1974). In this chapter we introduce a third perspective—the poliheuristic theory of decisionmaking—as an alternative to the rational actor and the bounded rational/cybernetic paradigms in international relations. This theory is drawn in large part from research on heuristics done in experimental cognitive psychology (see also Stein and Welch, Chapter 4).[1] In the following pages, we describe the core tenets of this theory and test experimentally its validity using a new research platform: the foreign policy "decision board" simulator.

The poliheuristic decisionmaking theory highlights the cognitive mechanisms that mediate foreign policy choices and behavior. The theory incorporates the conditions surrounding foreign policy decisions as well as the cognitive processes themselves (i.e., the why and how of decision-making), thus addressing both the contents and the processes of decisions. Knowing which decision *process* is actually being adopted, that is, the extent of sensitivity (or lack of it) of the decisionmaker to the order of alternatives, the order of dimensions, and the valence of the information, may help shed light on *why* a certain alternative was chosen. Moreover, knowledge of the process may give us insight into political manipulative and framing effects that may have led to a particular decision.

The "poli" part of the name we chose for the theory implies two key premises of our formulation. First, at the core of this theory is the assumption that political leaders, as cognitive managers, employ "poly" (many) heuristics in a two-stage decision process consisting of: (a) an initial screening of available alternatives, and (b) an analytic or lexicographic rule of choice to select the best alternative from the subset of remaining alternatives in an attempt to minimize risks and maximize rewards. Second, political leaders measure success and failure, costs and benefits, gains and losses, and risks and rewards using *poli-tical* units (see Mintz and Geva 1997a for a fuller description of the theory).

THE POLIHEURISTIC THEORY OF DECISION

A Two-Stage Poliheuristic Process

Extensive experimental research led Abelson and Levi (1985) to conclude that people use different decision rules while making decisions. Stress, task complexity, and familiarity with alternatives are all variables that trigger the use of particular decision rules (Beach and Mitchell 1978). Suedfeld and Tetlock (1992, p. 55) also point out that human beings as cognitive managers "react to specific challenges and opportunities and adjust their styles of decision making to situational factors" (see also Fiske and Neuberg 1990; Tetlock 1986). Elsewhere (Mintz and Geva 1997a) we note that policymakers use a mixture of decision strategies. We distinguish between decision rules that are based on the *rejection* of alternatives (e.g., on the basis of political calculations) and heuristics that are based on the *acceptance* of alternatives. We also point out that the domain in which a decisionmaker operates (gain or loss) has an impact not only on the risk propensity of the decisionmaker (as implied by prospect theory) but also on the selection of a particular decision rule. We show further that foreign policy decisionmaking often entails a two-stage process in which the first step involves the elimination of certain alternatives from the choice set, and the second consists of an analytic process of choosing an alternative that minimizes risks and guarantees rewards. The first phase in the decision process typically involves a nonholistic (nonexhaustive) search, to select a subset of alternatives using simplifying heuristics (see Mintz 1993; Mintz and Geva 1997a). Often foreign policy decisions are based on the adoption of alternatives (employing a lexicographic heuristic) or the rejection of alternatives (using Elimination by Aspect rule) on the basis of one or at most a few critical dimensions. The second phase typically involves a maximizing or lexicographic decision rule for selecting an alternative from the subset of surviving alternatives. Thus we posit that not only do decisionmakers change strategies in coping with different decisions, but that they also use a mixture of decision strategies en route to a single choice. Mintz and colleagues (1995) provide strong evidence for the two-stage process of decisionmaking in a study of high-ranking national security decisionmakers. We therefore focus in this chapter on other aspects of the poliheuristic theory.

The Political Ingredient of the Poliheuristic Theory

Self-interest has commonly been used in explaining individual behavior in markets. Mueller (1993, p. 78) notes that political actors are to be endowed with the same motivations as agents in their market roles. Both are similar in their pursuit of self-interest; they differ only with respect to the environments in which they operate.

Politicians value gains and losses in political terms. Domestic politics is the essence of decision. Politicians are concerned about their level of support, challenge to their leadership, and prospects of political survival. The relevant "currency" of political leaders while making political decisions is public support and approval. Their popularity serves as an indicator of their political power (and chances of survival in power). Translated into economic terms, popularity signifies political "worth."[2] Politicians are thus concerned with losing political "capital." Leaders' perceptions of the political consequences of their actions play a decisive role in how they choose to deal with foreign policy crises (DeRouen 1993). Because loss aversion overrules all other considerations, leaders are driven more by avoiding failure than by achieving success (Anderson 1983).

It is well documented that a theory of the causes of international conflict requires an understanding of the role domestic politics plays in foreign policy decisions. Works on the diversionary theory of war (Levy 1989; Russett 1990a, 1990b), the political incentive explanation of the use of force (Geva, DeRouen, and Mintz 1993; Mintz and Geva 1993), regime type and interstate conflict (Chan 1984; Dixon 1993, 1994; Gochman 1993; Hermann and Kegley 1995; Maoz and Russett 1993; Russett 1993, 1995; Small and Singer 1976), domestic opposition to the use of force (Bueno de Mesquita and Lalman 1990), and more generally the literature on "linkage politics" (Rosenau 1969; Wilkenfeld 1972) and two-level games (e.g., Putnam 1988; Simon and Starr, Chapter 7) have all addressed this phenomenon. But while these studies capture the salience of domestic politics to foreign policy decisions, they fall short of recognizing the *noncompensatory* nature of the decision process. In fact, no study views "satisficing" the domestic politics criterion as a prerequisite for the use of force in a noncompensatory decisionmaking environment. Domestic politics becomes the sine qua non, and subsequently multiple outcomes need not be assessed alongside a multitude of trade-offs (see Axelrod 1976; DeRouen 1993). Consistent with prospect theory, where losses loom greater than gains (Levy, Chapter 3; Tversky and Kahneman 1986), the political dimension is important in foreign policy decisions not so much because politicians are driven by public support but because they are averse to loss and would therefore reject alternatives that may hurt them politically: Because a low score in the political dimension cannot be compensated for by a high score in some other dimensions, politicians are not likely to adopt unpopular policies.

Processing Characteristics of the Poliheuristic Model

The poliheuristic theory holds that main processing characteristics of decisionmaking are: (1) nonholistic, (2) dimension-based, (3) noncompensatory, (4) satisficing, and (5) order-sensitive.

Nonholistic/nonexhaustive search. The poliheuristic model of foreign policy decisionmaking assumes that actual decisionmaking behavior is not even boundedly rational. Instead, it employs simple heuristics. Heuristics compensate for incomplete information as they provide cognitive shortcuts to intricate foreign policy matters by organizing the information so as to facilitate the decision process (Sniderman, Brody, and Tetlock 1991, p. 19). According to the poliheuristic model, comparisons of policy options are made within a (very) restrictive alternative set and attribute set. Nonholistic models employ a simplified process whereby the decisionmaker sequentially eliminates or adopts alternatives "by comparing them to each other, or against a standard, either across dimensions or across alternatives" (Sage 1990, p. 233). Holistic decisionmaking is cognitively demanding, while nonholistic, heuristic-based models are typically streamlined by rules that offer cognitive shortcuts. The selection of an alternative is not based upon the detailed, conscious consideration of all aspects of the alternatives. Rather than choosing an alternative that maximizes utility on the basis of an exhaustive comparison process or selecting an alternative that satisfices a certain criterion, the theory suggests that foreign policy decisions are often grounded in the rejection or adoption of alternatives on the basis of one or at most a few dimensions. According to Mintz (1993,

p. 599), rather than relying on "holistic decision rules . . . that require the evaluation and comparison of all alternatives across different dimensions, the decision maker adopts heuristic decision rules that do not require detailed and complicated comparisons of relevant alternatives, and adopts or rejects undesirable alternatives on the basis of one or a few criteria." For example, Freedman and Karsh (1991) report that during the Gulf crisis of 1990–1991, Iraqi president Saddam Hussein rejected the option of withdrawal from Kuwait because of the supreme importance he placed on the factor of "survival at any cost."

The poliheuristic model differs from the other process models of foreign policy decisionmaking as it is typically associated with a nonexhaustive, dimension-based search. Thus a decision is being made prior to the completion of the consideration of all alternatives along all dimensions (Mintz 1993; Mintz and Geva 1997a). The poliheuristic model employs less cognitively demanding decision procedures than expected utility theory, subjective expected utility theory, or other multiattribute utility models.

Dimension-based model. The poliheuristic model implies an attribute, or dimension-based, process rather than an alternative-based search. The decision consists of a selective processing pattern in which the decision-maker devotes differing amounts of time and uses nonconstant amounts of information across alternatives. In the poliheuristic model, an alternative that does not meet a certain threshold of the most important dimension will be discarded (Mintz 1993). In this model the expected gain in a critical dimension should be higher than a certain threshold level. If the expected gain along a critical dimension is below the threshold value, then the alternative is eliminated. A dimension can be conceived as an organizing theme (OT) for related information and variables (Ostrom et al. 1980). Thus if the decisionmaker is concerned with the political implications of a decision, then public opinion polls, the leader's popularity, the state of the economy, domestic opposition, and other variables related to this general organizing theme may be used to evaluate the consequence of a chosen alternative. The number of criteria and variables to be considered for a particular OT may vary across alternatives. One alternative may be rejected on the basis of only one criterion (e.g., how it scores in public opinion polls), while another alternative may be rejected/accepted on the basis of polls, editorials, and more. The sequence of the variables that enter the process is usually determined by the availability of information, its structure, and its relevance to the theme. The decisionmaker uses such a process for the first OT, then moves to the second OT (dimension) while operating along the same principles.

Noncompensatory decisionmaking. The poliheuristic model of foreign policy decisionmaking suggests that foreign policy decisions are typically based on a noncompensatory strategy: If a certain alternative is unacceptable in a given dimension (e.g., it is unacceptable politically), then a high score in another dimension (e.g., the military balance of forces) *cannot* compensate for or counteract it, and hence the alternative is eliminated. In this sense, the model is nonadditive: Alternatives are eliminated if a score on a critical dimension(s) is below a cutoff.[3] The model enables the decisionmaker to reject or accept an alternative on the basis of one (or a few) dimensions rather than to evaluate an alternative along all other dimensions. According to Mintz (1993), political leaders almost by definition take into account (explicitly or implicitly) political factors and consequences while making policy decisions. The noncompensatory principle of the poliheuristic model suggests, then, that leaders will "eliminate options that are below the 'cutoff' level on the political dimension. Thus one set of calculations that enters into the political leader's decision-making calculus is political, [the other is] substantive (e.g., economic, strategic, diplomatic, legal, social, psychological, and so on). The context of the [substantive] dimension(s) that enters into the calculus of decision making varies as a function of the substance of the decision" (i.e., it can be economic, military, etc.) (Mintz 1993, pp. 601–602). The noncompensatory principle suggests, however, that regardless of the score on the substantive dimension, the debate concerning use of force is moot if this alternative is likely to politically damage the leader.[4] Remaining options are then evaluated (sequentially) based on how they score on other dimensions.

The noncompensatory process does not always continue until only one alternative is left. There are situations where several remaining alternatives all pass a threshold value and are then considered in a more analytic/rational process (or by selecting a lexicographic decision rule). "Even when one alternative is left (by default), a final refinement of the default choice is typically performed by trying to minimize costs and maximize benefits" (Mintz 1993, p. 600). Such noncompensatory models are more likely to be used in complicated decision environments because they are cognitively easier.

"Satisficing" decision principle.   The poliheuristic model represents a decisionmaking process in which alternatives are not rejected or adopted on the basis of a maximizing rule. Since the theory employs some form of elimination by dimensions, it can be classified as "satisficing" and not optimizing (Mintz and Geva 1997a). The model is concerned with finding "acceptable" rather than maximizing alternatives because it allows the possibility that not all dimensions will be considered before a decision is made. The idea behind the poliheuristic model, then, is to quickly eliminate (or adopt) alternatives based on one or a few noncompensatory dimensions, simplifying the information search and the evaluation phases of the decision process (Mintz and Geva 1997a; Payne, Bettman, and Johnson

1988, p. 534). The strategy consists of comparing alternatives to predetermined values along a selected set of dimensions instead of evaluating each alternative on each dimension and comparing the sum expected utilities of all alternatives. According to Suedfeld and Tetlock (1992, p. 67), in the actual world "values, alternatives, probabilities, and outcomes are not as clear as is required for ideal decision making. The need to make many choices in a short period of time, the complexity of the interactions that determine outcomes, and the uncertainty surrounding probabilities, all compel human beings to make their choices by bounded rationality: a simplified model of the decision environment."

Order-sensitive search. Most foreign policy decisionmaking models on the use of force in international relations accept implicitly or explicitly the invariance assumption that is a central premise of analytic/rational and compensatory models. The invariance assumption requires "that preference order among prospects should not depend on how their outcomes and probabilities are described and thus that two alternative formulations of the same problem should yield the same choice" (Quattrone and Tversky 1988, p. 727; see also Kahneman and Tversky 1984). According to the poliheuristic model, the invariance assumption is violated not only when the situation or the alternatives are described differently (see Mintz and Geva 1997a, ch. 8) but also when variations are introduced in the order in which alternatives and dimensions are presented to decisionmakers. The dimension-based process of the poliheuristic decisionmaking model implies that the choice of a particular alternative may depend on the order in which particular dimensions (diplomatic, economic, military, political) are invoked.

In sum, the poliheuristic model captures the heuristic nature of the foreign policy decisionmaking process. While we propose that political leaders may employ more than one decision strategy en route to a foreign policy choice, their initial search process can be described as nonholistic, dimension-based, noncompensatory, satisficing, and order-sensitive.

The decision process as outlined by the poliheuristic model is more simplified than the expected utility or cybernetic models of decision. Furthermore, whereas expected utility models are concerned primarily with predicting the outcome of decisions rather than with accounting for the underlying *cognitive processes* that govern decisionmaking, the poliheuristic theory attempts to account for both process and outcome validity. The model is an alternative to the expected utility model (see Bueno de Mesquita and Lalman 1990, 1992; Morrow, Chapter 2), the cybernetic theory (see Ostrom and Job 1986), and the prospect theory (see Levy, Chapter 3) approaches to the use of force and foreign policy decisionmaking in international relations (see Zinnes and Muncaster, Chapter 9).

Placing the Poliheuristic Theory in Context

The poliheuristic theory is compatible with a host of contingency theories of decision and judgment that attribute to decisionmakers the ability to adapt the decision process to changing environmental demands and to their own personal cognitive makeups (Abelson and Levi 1985; Beach and Mitchell 1978; Payne, Bettman, and Johnson 1988, 1993; Tetlock 1992). The choice of a decision heuristic is contingent on the costs of the process and the potential benefits of the outcome (see Beach and Mitchell 1978). The changes in the decision process may reflect situational changes (see Maoz, Chapter 8) as well as ripening of the decision process itself. In this sense, the poliheuristic model extends previous research that only identified decision heuristics (Tversky and Kahneman 1974) with an analysis of the conditions that influence the selection of one heuristic over another (see details in Mintz and Geva 1997a). We concur with Suedfeld and Tetlock (1992) that decisionmakers react to specific challenges and opportunities in the environment. Political leaders' utilization of more than one decision strategy in a two-stage process is thus a functional/pragmatic adaptation to the complex environment in which choices are made.[5]

In this chapter we apply the poliheuristic theory to decisions on the use of force, but the model can also explain decisions *not* to use force in a crisis. In such instances the decisionmaker anticipates that the alternative to use force will have a low utility in the political dimension that cannot be compensated for in the substantive dimension. Examples include President Eisenhower's 1954 decision not to use force in Dien Bien Phu (see De-Rouen 1993) and the Israeli government's 1973 decision not to use a preemptive strike on the eve of the Yom Kippur War, as the expected positive military consequences of these actions could not have compensated for the negative utility in the political dimension (both in the domestic and international arenas).

In the remainder of this chapter, we introduce a new research technology we use to test some of the key propositions of the poliheuristic theory of decision and report preliminary results.

EXPERIMENTAL DEMONSTRATION

The application of the experimental method in political science is not new (see Geva, DeRouen, and Mintz 1993 for a brief overview). The experimental design we utilized in our study allows for careful manipulation of the theoretical propositions outlined above. The principal drawback of the experimental approach is the problem of external validity—generalizing from subject behavior in a highly constrained laboratory setting to a more intricate natural environment. However, Morgan and Wilson (1990, pp. 1–2) argue that

> careful experimental controls ensure that strong statements can be made concerning the congruence between theory and experiment. Such an approach can address important questions when seeking to test abstract, theoretical concepts. If subjects in a carefully controlled laboratory setting do not behave in accordance with the prediction of a model it is highly unlikely that actors in complex natural settings will do so.

According to these authors, "at a very basic level experimental evidence can provide some indication as to whether a theory 'makes sense' and points to where additional theoretical and empirical work will be most fruitful." The study utilizes a new technology—the foreign policy decision board simulator—to focus on the processing characteristics of the poliheuristic model (i.e., the holistic-nonholistic and the alternative-based vs. dimension-based heuristics).[6] The decision board enables both process tracing and structural analysis (Ford et al. 1989) of key propositions derived from the poliheuristic model of decisionmaking.[7]

The Decision Board

The core structure of the decision board platform is a matrix of decision alternatives and decision dimensions. The intersection of the decision alternative and dimension, the information bin (IB), contains information that indicates an evaluation (or consequence) V_{ij} of an alternative i along a dimension j.

Information boards have typically been used to study the processes of information acquisition en route to a decision (see Billings and Marcus 1983; Billings and Scherer 1988; Payne, Bettman, and Johnson 1988). Common dependent variables in those studies were the amount of information subjects consumed and mainly the order in which this information was collected. In most cases researchers paid less attention to the resulting choice of the decisionmaker. In this chapter, as we are interested also in the input-output relationships within the decision process, we include in the decision board features from the structural analyses of decisionmaking research.

The experiments are structured as a decision task that consists of a choice of one of A_i action alternatives evaluated along D_j different dimensions, that is, as a 4 x 4 matrix. The values (V_{ij}) inside the matrix represent the evaluation of a given alternative (A_i) on a given dimension (D_j).

Processing implications of the decision board. Before dressing our decision board with foreign policy scenarios, we outline the processing implications of the poliheuristic strategy within the structure of the decision board. In other words, we specify how the theory will behave within this skeleton matrix of A_i x D_j alternatives and dimensions.

As we pointed out above, the common heuristics associated with the poliheuristic model of decision are noncompensatory, nonexhaustive, and dimension-based processing. The decisionmaker works "horizontally," or intradimensionally, using the first (and most important) dimension to review alternative after alternative. If necessary, this process continues on to the next dimension(s). Under different noncompensatory strategies (e.g., elimination by aspect, lexicographic, etc.), the review of alternatives along the subsequent dimension(s) may not be exhaustive, that is, may be nonholistic. This means that the decisionmaker may choose an alternative prior to reviewing all the available alternatives along all available dimensions.

What are the implications of the poliheuristic theory for the decision-making processes within the decision board?

- The nonholistic nature of the poliheuristic process is reflected by (1) decisionmakers' reviewing only part of the available information and (2) a selective processing pattern as the decisionmakers evaluate a nonconstant number of items per alternative en route to a choice. Specifically, decisionmakers are expected to view more items on a chosen alternative than on the nonchosen alternatives.
- The poliheuristic model expects the decisionmaker's moves within a decision board to be dimension-based.
- The model is sensitive to changes in the sequence in which *dimensions* of the decision board are examined or presented. It is possible either to accept or reject alternatives along a particular dimension, whereas other alternatives could be chosen or rejected if another dimension were invoked first.
- In correspondence with the "poli" proposition of the poliheuristic model, it is expected that the dimensional and nonholistic processing pattern will be predominant during decision tasks that are cognitively more demanding than during tasks that are less demanding.

The Context and Content of the Matrix

We used two foreign policy scenarios—decision tasks—to introduce four concrete alternatives and four specific dimensions to evaluate these alternatives. One context dealt with a military dispute between two small islands that erupted because of rivalry for control of a large uranium field (see also Geva, DeRouen, and Mintz 1993). Consequently, one nation invaded the other, and foreign citizens were taken as hostages. In this context the decisionmaker was presented with four alternatives: use of force (attacking the invader), containment (setting up a naval blockade), international sanctions, and isolationism (doing nothing). The second scenario dealt with the choice of a site for a new U.S. naval base in the Pacific. The alternatives for this decision were four islands: Nauru, Gilbert, Palau, and Wake.

The dimensions that were employed in both contexts (i.e., the variables affecting the evaluation of each alternative) represent themes found to be relevant in other studies of foreign policy decisions on the use of force (Bueno de Mesquita and Lalman 1990, 1992; James and Oneal 1991; Morgan and Bickers 1992; Ostrom and Job 1986). These dimensions are diplomatic, military, economic, and political.

Following the definition of the four alternatives and four dimensions, we inserted the values (V_{ij}) into the matrix, as illustrated in Figure 5.1. These values consisted of an evaluative descriptive statement and a summarizing numeric value (on a scale from zero to ten).

In a decision task, the value V_{ij} is a summary of the decisionmaker's consideration and deliberation of the utilities of the consequences alternative A_i has on dimension D_j. For instance, the decisionmaker can speculate, on the basis of her stored beliefs (Taber and Steenbergen 1995), what the impact of the use of force on the political dimension would be. She may evaluate the use of force to be a bad move in terms of her public standing in the polls. Converting such a "conclusion" to a ten-point scale, the decisionmaker assigns a low score $V = 1$ or 2, to this alternative on the political dimension. However, the V_{ij} values can stem also from sources external to the decisionmaker. The chief economic adviser, for example, may tell the chief executive that the alternative "do nothing" could benefit the nation's trade deficit, implying a high score ($V_{ij} = 9$) for this alternative on the economic dimension. Naturally, the president may attribute differential weights (importance) to her advisers, and the extent of their influence on

Figure 5.1
Choice of Alternatives on a Given Decision Board
as a Function of the Decision Model

Alternatives

		A_1	A_2	A_3	A_4
Dimensions	**Political**	10	8	6	2
	Economic	6	2	10	8
	Diplomatic	2	8	6	10
	Military	8	6	2	10
Unweighted Evaluation		6.50	6.00	6.00	7.50

the final value of V_{ij} may represent various factors associated with the decisionmaker's susceptibility to influence (e.g., levels of expertise, Fiske, Kinder, and Larter 1983).

The alternatives and their values (utilities) were introduced into our decision board as being provided by chief advisers to the decisionmaker: the chairman of the joint chiefs of staff, the secretary of state, the chief political adviser, and the chief economic adviser. Finally, it should be noted that the assignment of the values to the intersections of the alternatives and dimensions enabled us to differentiate between the poliheuristic model of decisionmaking and other models of foreign policy choice.[8]

In the analysis of results based on this research platform, we assume that different decision tasks and decision contexts affect the extent to which decisionmakers rely solely on the information in the decision board for making a choice. For this reason, we utilized two contexts of decision boards: the choice of a site for a naval base and a choice of international intervention. One distinguishing factor between the two contexts is the extent of the decisionmakers' familiarity with the alternatives, which in turn affects the decisionmakers' dependence on the information in the decision board. In preliminary experiments (Mintz and Geva 1997a, ch. 8) we found that decisionmakers have a priori preferences for the four alternatives in the international intervention task (e.g., a majority of them disliked the "do nothing" option regardless of the type of international scenario). Moreover, postexperimental interviews of the subjects suggested that the a priori preferences in the international intervention scenario led subjects to pay less attention to the decision board in making a final choice, that is, they exhibit "preferences over preferences." These observations are compatible with findings on the effects of familiarity and expertise on decision processes, for example, decreased utilization of information (Fiske, Kinder, and Larter 1983; Mitchell and Beach 1990; Klein 1993). In contrast, in the naval site task, in which none of the decisionmakers has any familiarity with the four alternative islands, decisionmakers lean more heavily on the information provided in the decision board.

In a decision task involving familiar alternatives, we expect decisionmakers to allocate less attention to the information in the decision board. This in turn is expressed by fewer items reviewed and by a smaller proportion of items that are subsequently recalled. Moreover, a familiar scenario is assumed to make the decision task cognitively easier. If this is the case, we can expect more compensatory and alternative-based processing in the less cognitively demanding context than in the scenario involving the unfamiliar choice set.[9]

Finally, as implied by the poliheuristic model, we do assume that different conditions evoke the initiation of different decision strategies (Suedfeld and Tetlock 1992). Just as the decisionmaker's domain (loss vs. gain) is predicted to affect which heuristic is selected (see Mintz and Geva 1997a), so other factors may trigger a choice of a compensatory decision rule rather than a noncompensatory strategy. The format of presentation of the decision matrix (inter-vs. intradimensional) can also affect the choice. We have also noted that numeric presentation of the values (as compared to verbal descriptions) is more likely to promote compensatory processing.

The common denominator of the variables that mediate the onset of decision strategies thus seems to center on the cognitive demands imposed by the decision task. The heavier the demands, the more likely the decisionmaker is to employ simplifying heuristics. In this experiment the variations along the cognitive demands continuum were introduced by: (a) manipulating the familiarity of the choice set (which was described earlier); and (b) introducing the need to justify the decision to the public, which triggers more attention to the information displayed in the decision board (Arkes et al. 1987) and increases the "depth of processing" of the information (see Craik and Lockhart 1972). This increase in the depth of processing is expected to influence the proportion of reviewed items that decisionmakers recall following the decision. Last, in order to increase the "mundane reality" of the experiment (Aronson and Carlsmith 1968), and since many foreign policy decisions are made under time and informational constraints, we subjected all the decisionmakers in this experiment to time pressure: Subjects were told that time was running out, and the decision board screen presented a timer that beeped every fifteen seconds.

METHOD

Subjects

High-ranking national security decisionmakers have participated in different phases of this project (see Geva, Driggers, and Mintz 1996; Mintz and Geva 1997a; Mintz et al. 1997). Here, however, we report results based on the performance of eighty-eight junior and senior undergraduate students. Recruited from a selective leadership development program at the university, the students had demonstrated high academic achievements and leadership qualities. The students were randomly assigned to one of four experimental conditions.

Design

A 2 x 2 between-groups factorial design was employed in the study. The two factors were: (a) Justification of decision (expected vs. not expected); and (b) Decision Task (familiar alternatives vs. unfamiliar alternatives). The dependent variables consisted of several process-tracing parameters of decisionmaking: information acquisition pattern, amount of information acquired, unforewarned free recall of the information acquired during the decision task, and the specific choices subjects made.

The Research Instrument

A 4 (alternatives) x 4 (dimensions) matrix was utilized in this experiment. The decision board was programmed as a SuperCard application for Macintosh. Figure 5.2 portrays the decision board screen. The decision matrix was presented by sixteen information bins (IB) that contained the information pertaining to the evaluation of a given alternative along a specified dimension. This information was presented as a statement followed by a summary evaluation, for example, "Containment of the crisis can prevent the disruption of trade flows to and from the surrounding countries. It also involves fewer investments than the use of force. I would rate this alternative as a 6." Subjects could open any IB by clicking on it with the mouse, but they could view a particular IB only once. After the subjects made their decisions, they clicked on the choice button beneath the corresponding alternative. The computer recorded (1) all the "moves" subjects made on the matrix, (2) the order in which decisionmakers acquired information, (3) the number of items subjects viewed for every alternative and along every dimension, and (4) the amount of time that elapsed since the subjects began the task.

Research Material

We described earlier the two decision tasks that we used in this experiment. The task addressing the unfamiliar alternatives dealt with the choice of a site for a construction of a new naval base in the Pacific. The choice set consisted of four islands that were unknown to all the subjects in this experiment. The task representing the familiar alternatives related to a

Figure 5.2
The Decision Matrix as Displayed on the Monitor

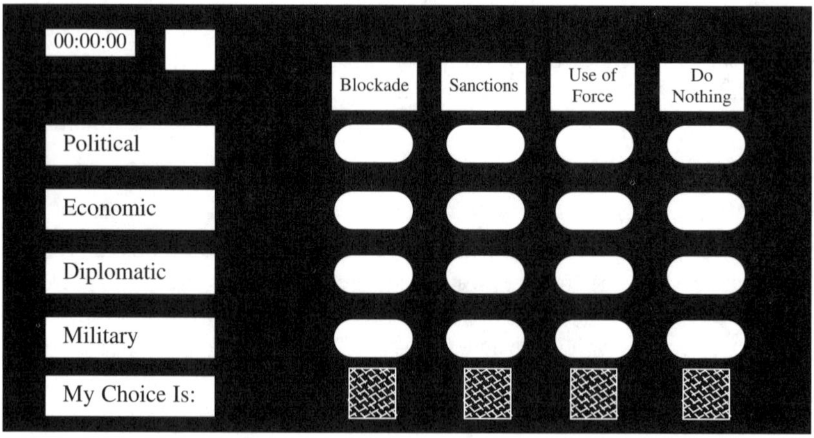

choice among the direct use of force, blockade, sanctions, or doing nothing in an international dispute in which one island invaded its neighboring island and gained control of large uranium fields. Previous experiments (Mintz and Geva 1997a, ch. 8) showed that university students had a priori preferences among these alternatives.

Procedure

The decision board was administered individually—one subject at an experimental session. Prior to performing the foreign policy decision, the subjects took part in a practice session to familiarize them with the decision board platform.[10] Then subjects received a booklet consisting of the background information for one of the two tasks (choice of a site for a naval base or the choice of an intervention policy in the international dispute). They were instructed to make the decision assuming the role of the leader of the nation and to select the best choice among the available alternatives. The instructions to the subjects also mentioned that the "quality of decision you make in the context of the simulation will suggest your ability to comprehend national-level decisionmaking." Previous studies (Ostrom et al. 1980) indicate that portraying a decision task in such terms increases the motivation of the subjects to perform the task seriously, without contaminating or confounding the salience of a particular decisional dimension. Instructions for half the subjects stated that they would have to justify their choices. This statement was omitted from the instructions for the other half. Following this phase, the subjects worked on the computerized decision board. When they had reached a decision, they received a postdecision questionnaire in which they were requested to recall all of the information they reviewed in the decision board (in any order they wished). Upon completion of the experiment, subjects were debriefed about the objectives of the study.

RESULTS

The Information Basis of the Decision

Holistic vs. nonholistic processing. Only 20 percent of the subjects in this experiment reviewed all sixteen information bins accessible on the decision board. Since there was no actual time limit to stop the acquisition of information, the obtained trend is not supportive of holistic processing. On the average, subjects viewed 11.69 items. There was no difference in the number of items they acquired as a function of the different scenarios. These findings are further qualified by the next analysis, which focuses on the differential attention subjects pay to the informational basis in the decision board.

We compared the amount of information subjects viewed on the alternatives they chose and on the alternatives they did not choose. A satisficing strategy would imply that subjects may totally ignore alternatives if a preceding alternative surpasses the satisficing threshold. Yet for the alternatives they reviewed, we would expect a constant amount of information. A maximizing strategy would imply that the subjects would view as many items on a rejected alternative as on the chosen alternative. A noncompensatory principle would imply that subjects would review less information on rejected alternatives than on the chosen alternative. A compensatory process requires the decisionmaker to tally or incorporate the utilities of all the values per alternative and only then to compare the resulting values.

Two analyses were performed to test these decision characteristics. The first analysis compared the number of items viewed on the chosen alternative (n_c) with the number of items viewed of the nonchosen alternatives (n_{nc}), and $n_{nc} = [(N-n_c)/3]$—where N is the total number of items viewed. The split-plot 2 x 2 x 2 ANOVA yielded a significant within-subjects main effect. The decisionmakers viewed significantly more items on their selected alternative $(M = 3.75)$ than on the nonselected alternatives $(M = 2.64)$, $F(1,84) = 99.28$ $p < .0001$. As shown in Table 5.1, this trend was more pronounced in the Justification condition compared to the No Justification condition $[F(1,84) = 3.31$ $p < .07$ for the interaction]. It is as if decisionmakers in the Nonjustification condition do not want to be distracted by counterevidence.[11]

While the results portrayed in Table 5.1 can be evaluated as somewhat incompatible with an expected utility decision strategy, they could still be explained by the operation of a compensatory *satisficing* principle. Hence, fewer items are reviewed in the nonchosen alternatives simply because some nonchosen alternatives were entirely unexplored because the satisficing criterion was surpassed early in the evaluation of the alternatives. To test for the plausibility of this interpretation, we compared the number of items viewed for the chosen alternative (n_c) with n_a, number of items

Table 5.1 Number of Items Viewed on Chosen and Nonchosen Alternatives Under Conditions of "Justification" and "No Justification"

	Chosen Alternative	Other Alternatives
No Justification	3.73	2.82
Justification	3.77	2.46

viewed on alternatives not chosen but considered along at least one dimension. Subjects viewed more of the chosen alternative (M = 3.75) than the average of alternatives viewed but not chosen (M = 2.84). This within-subjects main effect was significant, $F(1,84)$ = 87.13 p < .0001.[12] In sum, decisions were made not on the basis of all the information but rather by utilizing a nonconstant amount of information per alternative. These results refute the plausibility of a satisficing compensatory process and lend support to a noncompensatory, poliheuristic rule.

Recall findings. Following the decision task, subjects were asked to recall the items they reviewed in the decision board. As anticipated, when subjects were expected to justify their decisions, their recall was better (M = 3.41) than when they were not expected to justify their decisions (M = 1.82), $F(1,84)$ = 11.74 p < .001.[13] In addition to supporting the effectiveness of the manipulation of justification, this finding hints that justification increases subjects' attentiveness to the information on the board. Since this attentiveness implies more cognitive demand, it seems logical that subjects concentrated primarily on information on the chosen alternative instead of dividing their attention among all the alternatives. This pattern is more consistent, again, with the poliheuristic model than with the expected utility or cybernetic models.

The ANOVA yielded a significant main effect for the type of the choice set. In the Familiar set of alternatives, subjects recalled fewer items (M = 2.16) than in the nonfamiliar choice set (M = 3.84), $F(1,84)$ = 3.84 p < .055. This finding suggests that subjects paid more attention to the information when the alternatives were unfamiliar than when they were familiar. Hence, the unfamiliar choice set increased the cognitive demands of the decision task.

The Pattern of Information Processing

Alternative vs. dimension-based "moves." We have suggested before that decisionmakers can operate within the decision board in an alternative-based search (vertical) or in a dimensional-based (horizontal) pattern. We applied an information search index devised by Billings and Scherer (1988) to the subjects' moves on the decision board as recorded by the computer. The scoring of the moves followed Billings and Scherer's definition:

> Each move to a new piece of information which was within the same alternative and across dimensions was classified as an interdimensional move (alternatively based), while a move within a dimension and across alternatives was labeled as intradimensional (dimensional based). Moves to both a different alternative and a different dimension were labeled shift. The search pattern variable is defined as the number of alternative

based moves minus the number of dimensional moves divided by the sum of these two numbers (shifts were disregarded from this index). (1988, p. 10)

The index tallies the number of dimensional moves (*d*), alternative moves (*a*), and shifts (*s*) (moves that were neither alternative nor dimensional) and uses the equation $(a - d)/(a + d)$ as a search index. Positive numbers imply more alternative-based moves, while negative numbers express dimensional moves.

A 2 x 2 between groups ANOVA yielded a main effect of the Familiar alternative factor, $F(1,84) = 9.19$ $p < .005$. As expected, in the Unfamiliar alternatives conditions, decisionmakers exhibited less of an alternative-based search pattern ($M = .03$) than in the Familiar alternatives conditions ($M = .44$). In other words, when the decisionmaker is not familiar with the alternatives (and thus the cognitive burden is relatively high), the process is relatively more dimension-based than when the alternatives are relatively known (less cognitive demands).

The above results prompted us to look specifically for one of the common poliheuristic strategies—Elimination by Aspect (EBA). In operational terms, an EBA pattern would imply that after reviewing a certain alternative along a dimension, subjects reject that alternative and therefore do not look at that alternative again, though they continue to review other alternatives on this and other dimensions. Using this definition, we counted the number of such patterns occurring in the four experimental conditions.

Table 5.2   Proportion of Subjects Exhibiting an EBA Search Pattern as a Function of the Experimental Conditions

	Unfamiliar Alternatives	Familiar Alternatives
No Justification	.46	.09
Justification	.46	.41

Table 5.2 shows that 35 percent of the decisionmakers exhibited an EBA decision pattern, thus supporting Abelson and Levi's (1985) findings that different heuristics are employed by decisionmakers. More decisionmakers (46 percent) exhibited EBA-type processing when the choice set was unfamiliar and they had to rely on the information in the decision board than when there were a priori preferences for the relatively familiar alternatives (25 percent). This difference is significant by the *z* test for proportions, $z = 2.30$ $p < .05$ (Langer and Abelson 1972).

The Choice

The specific structure of the decision matrix used in this study has deliberately defined a target alternative that maximizes the utility for the decisionmaker. In the Unfamiliar alternatives scenario, it was Gilbert Island as the site for the new navy base, while in the Familiar alternatives scenario the target alternative was the use of sanctions. A total of 44.4 percent of the subjects (across all experimental conditions) chose the target alternative. Again, the findings fall short of the expectations of the expected utility model. According to Table 5.3, it seems that the "success" of maximizing the choice was higher when the alternatives were familiar and the cognitive demands were low (No Justification). This trend coincides with the poliheuristic claim that under less cognitively demanding conditions there is an increased likelihood for compensatory processing. It should be noted that choosing the target alternative is not necessarily an indication that the decision process proceeded along a maximizing holistic and compensatory route. As many other decision theorists, we accept that a "successful" choice may be made irrespective of the decision strategy (but see Herek, Janis, and Huth 1987). Simple first-order correlations between a "correct" versus "incorrect" choice and several process parameters show that across all experimental conditions deciding for the target alternative is inversely related to the total number of items reviewed ($r = -.23$) but positively related to the number of items viewed along the target alternative ($r = .43$). These results are compatible with key propositions on the use of cognitive shortcuts in the poliheuristic decision theory.

Table 5.3   The Choice of the "Target Alternative" as a Function of the Experimental Conditions

	Unfamiliar Alternatives	Familiar Alternatives
No Justification	.50	.59
Justification	.36	.32

CONCLUSIONS

In this chapter we introduced a new theory of decisionmaking and tested its validity using a new technology—the foreign policy decision board simulator. The results reported in this chapter provide considerable support for the poliheuristic theory of foreign policy choice. Specifically, our findings illustrate that different decision strategies are used en route to a foreign policy choice, and that the adoption of a particular strategy is affected by the cognitive demands imposed by the decision environment. Moreover, the features of the decision environment affect both the decision process and decision outcome. While the results of the present pool of subjects mimic the performance of highly experienced national security decisionmakers, further analyses utilizing empirical process tracing and comparative case studies are needed to cross-validate these patterns of decisionmaking.

NOTES

We thank Uri Geva for his help in programming the foreign policy decision board simulator and Steven B. Redd for research assistance.

1. The leading cognitively based alternative to expected utility is prospect theory (see Kahneman and Tversky 1979; Levy, Chapter 3). Prospect theory is incorporated into and superseded by the poliheuristic theory of decision.

2. This argument is rather obvious in democratic regimes. According to Merritt and Zinnes (1991, p. 221), a certain degree of political support from parts of the ruling elite (or from domestic groups) is also essential for leaders of nondemocratic regimes.

3. Studies of foreign policy decisionmaking have utilized primarily compensatory decisionmaking strategies. Compensatory processes imply that when political leaders choose among alternatives, a high value in one dimension (e.g., the military balance of force) can compensate for a low value in another dimension (e.g., political) for the same decision alternative. Such compensatory models would therefore have difficulty in explaining, for example, the end of U.S. involvement in Vietnam.

4. It is clear that in an infinite data set it would be impossible to show that there is never a level of benefit on a nonpolitical dimension that could compensate for a low score in the political dimension. However, if one were to find favorable circumstances for the use of force internationally and with respect to other domestic factors but unfavorable political circumstances, then a failure to use force would give strong support for a noncompensatory interpretation of the data.

5. The poliheuristic model also allows for changing process heuristics *during* a decision (see Mintz, Geva, Redd, and Carnes 1997).

6. The design of our computerized "process tracer" reflects the ability of decisionmakers to control the inflow of decision-relevant information (i.e., sequential ordering, speed, and quantity). For instance, it has been reported that Saddam Hussein screened out advisers' evaluations that were incompatible with his preferences.

7. Elsewhere we report findings on the consequences of dynamic structures for the decision process and outcome (e.g., concurrent availability of all the alternatives in the choice set, as compared to their sequential emergence or disappearance from the choice set; see Mintz, Geva, Redd, and Carnes 1997).

8. In order to illustrate this structural analysis, we concentrate on numeric values in the matrix presented in Figure 5.1 that demonstrate different choice implications of each decision strategy. A poliheuristic model (in its EBA variant) proposes that the decisionmaker reviews all the alternatives in dimension D_1. If, for example,

a value of five (on a ten-point scale) serves as a cutting-off point, the subject would reject alternative A_4 ($V_{14} = 2$). Then the decisionmaker reviews the remaining alternatives in dimension D_2. According to the values presented in the matrix, alternative A_2 is rejected from further consideration. This leads to the review of the two remaining alternatives (A_1 and A_3) in dimension D_3. Consequently, alternative A_1 is rejected, leaving the decisionmaker with the choice of alternative A_3. In this sequence, processing along dimension D_4 is not necessary for the decision. The lexicographic decisionmaker reviews the alternatives in dimension D_1 to select alternative A_1 as the "best." Since this alternative is not tied to any other alternative, the choice of A_1 can be made at this point, and all the rest of the information is irrelevant to the decision process. This example thus portrays different choices reached on the basis of the *same* information matrix but with different decision strategies.

9. While the distinction between different levels of familiarity with the foreign policy options is warranted in terms of the information-processing perspective, it also has merit in its potential to address differences of experience of chief executives in the international arena.

10. The practice task dealt with the choice of a car out of four domestic brands. The practice task did not include the time pressure component.

11. This trend is in line with recent research on confirmatory biases in information processing in social cognition.

12. Again, this main effect was qualified by the interaction with the justification factor, $F(1,84) = 4.26$ $p < .05$, revealing the same trend as with the previous parameter.

13. Since the number of items each subject opened was not the same, we performed the analysis also on the ratio scores (i.e., the number of items recalled divided by the number of items reviewed). We obtained the same pattern of significant results.

6

The Rationality of Surprise: Unstable Nash Equilibria and the Theory of Moves

Steven J. Brams

It is well known that the order of moves by the players in a game can affect its outcome.[1] In Chicken, for example, the player who moves first (by not swerving) obtains his best payoff, given that the second player responds optimally to the first player's choice (by swerving). This optimal response, however, garners the second player only her next worst payoff, so there is a disadvantage to a player's moving second, rather than first, in Chicken.

Despite the dependence of the outcome on the order of play in many two-person games, most game theoretic models do not make the order of play *endogenous,* that is, the subject of rational calculation by the players.[2] Rather, the rules generally prescribe that one player moves first or the players move simultaneously. In this chapter I begin by assuming that players make simultaneous choices in a 2 x 2 "generic game," which I call the Surprise Game. This game is *generic* in the sense that it subsumes several 2 x 2 strict ordinal games, in which each of the two players has two strategies and is able strictly to rank the resulting four outcomes from best to worst (i.e., there are no ties).

The Surprise Game is defined by two conditions:

1. One player, whom I call Row (R), has a dominant strategy, which guarantees that the game has a unique Nash equilibrium in pure strategies (Hamilton and Slutsky 1993, p. 50, lemma 1);[3]
2. R has an incentive to depart from his dominant strategy and choose his dominated strategy, given that he has the opportunity to move first.[4]

On first blush this seems surprising, because R's dominated strategy is un-conditionally worse than his dominant strategy.[5]

Of the seventy-eight distinct 2 x 2 strict ordinal games (Rapoport and Guyer 1966), R has an incentive to move first in six games, which break down into two classes. In three of the six games (class I), the second player, Column (C), also does better when R moves first, so it is in her interest to allow this to happen.

In the other three games (class II), there is a conflict of interests between the two players, because C does better moving first herself or at least maintaining the status quo of simultaneous play in the 2 x 2 game. Consequently, if the order of play is left endogenous by the rules of the game, then the structure of payoffs in class II games leaves uncertain what will happen.

I have incorporated this ambiguity into the theory of moves, or TOM (Brams 1993, 1994; Brams and Mattli 1993), which adds a dynamic component to classical game theory. Instead of assuming that players choose strategies—either simultaneously or sequentially—in normal-form games (i.e., those given by a payoff matrix), TOM assumes that play begins at outcomes in the matrix, which are called states because they may be only temporary in nature. Players then decide whether to move or not move from these states by making rational calculations (to be described in the fourth section) in order to reach nonmyopic equilibria (NMEs), or far-sighted stable outcomes.

The main theoretical finding of this chapter is that the six 2 x 2 games in which R has an incentive to move first are the only games of the seventy-eight in which a player would, according to TOM, move from a unique dominant-strategy Nash equilibrium. It is in this sense that these equilibria are *unstable:* Each player would, thinking ahead about his or her rational moves and countermoves, move from the Nash equilibrium to an NME that is a different state.[6]

The one-to-one correspondence between games in which the Nash equilibria and NMEs differ, on the one hand, and dominant-strategy games in which who moves first matters, on the other, illustrates how TOM captures order-of-play effects directly in its concept of an NME. This relieves one of the task of having to ask whether, when the order of play is endogenous, the dominant-strategy Nash equilibrium in the 2 x 2 game is unstable. It is unstable if and only if the players would move from this equilibrium to a different NME.

The unexpected tie-in of Nash equilibria that are unstable and those from which players would depart to a different (nonmyopic) state is not just a theoretical issue but also an important empirical consideration. It is reflected in the two real-life cases, generally considered to be examples par excellence of surprise in international politics, that I analyze here. The first is the Japanese surprise attack on Pearl Harbor in 1941, which I model as a class II 2 x 2 game in which Japan had an incentive to seize the initiative by attacking—at the expense of the United States—even though its dominant strategy in the simultaneous-play game was not to attack.

Taking the initiative may involve peaceful as well as warlike actions, as illustrated by the second case, Egyptian president Anwar Sadat's 1977 offer to visit Jerusalem to negotiate a peace treaty directly with the Israelis. I model the situation Sadat and Israeli prime minister Menachem Begin faced as a class I 2 x 2 game in which, unlike the Pearl Harbor game, both players benefited when the player with the dominant strategy (i.e., Sadat) moved first. That abandoning this strategy was risky for Sadat, but *not* irrational, seems borne out by his initial success yet later assassination.

Both the Japanese attack and Sadat's offer were great shocks at the time. I suggest that such surprises might well be defined in terms of a player's (perfectly rational) abandonment of a dominant strategy in favor of a dominated strategy, which in turn induces a countermove on the part of the surprised player to a different state, or NME.[7]

In laying bare the rationality of these moves, TOM makes them explicable and therefore unsurprising, at least in retrospect. Prospectively, I suggest, TOM might be used as a policy tool to help decisionmakers avoid "anticipation failures," caused by incomplete information about what rules are applicable. By making endogenous who moves first, TOM introduces a flexibility into thinking about how different scenarios might arise; by assuming that players think ahead, it provides a calculus for tracing out the dynamic moves they are likely to make over time.

ORDER OF PLAY AND UNSTABLE NASH EQUILIBRIA

The Surprise Game (simultaneous-play version) is shown in Figures 6.1a and 6.1b, in which R has two strategies, s_1 and s_2, and C has two strategies, t_1 and t_2; the payoffs to the players at the resulting four possible outcomes are given by ordered pairs (x_1, x_2), where x_1 is the payoff to R and x_2 the payoff to C.

I show in this section under what conditions the unique dominant-strategy Nash equilibrium in the Surprise Game is vulnerable to order-of-play effects. The conditions for dominance, a Nash equilibrium, and instability are the following:

1. *Dominance.* Without loss of generality, assume that s_1 is R's dominant strategy, so

$$a_1 > d_1; \, b_1 > c_1. \tag{1}$$

That is, whatever strategy C chooses (t_1 or t_2), R prefers his payoffs associated with s_1 to those associated with s_2, making s_1 R's unconditionally better strategy.

Figure 6.1a
Surprise Game (Simultaneous Play)

Column (C)

	t_1	t_2	
s_1	(a_1, a_2)	(b_1, b_2)	◄——Dominant strategy
s_2	(d_1, d_2)	(c_1, c_2)	

Row (R)

Figure 6.1b
Surprise Game (R Moves First)

Column (C)

	t_1/t_1	t_2/t_2	t_1/t_2	t_2/t_1
s_1	(a_1, a_2)	(b_1, b_2)	(a_1, a_2)	(b_1, b_2)
s_2	(d_1, d_2)	(c_1, c_2)	(c_1, c_2)	(d_1, d_2)

Row (R)

Dominant strategy

Key: (x_1, x_2) = (payoff to R, payoff to C)
t_i/t_j: choose t_i if R chooses s_1, t_j if R chooses s_2 (i, j = 1 or 2).
Nash equilibria underscored
Complete ordering for R: $a_1 > d_1 > b_1 > c_1$
Partial ordering for C: $b_2 > a_2$ and $d_2 > c_2$

2. *Nash equilibrium.* Without loss of generality, assume that (b_1, b_2) is the unique Nash equilibrium that is associated with R's dominant strategy of s_1, so

$$b_2 > a_2. \qquad (2)$$

That is, C prefers her payoff at (b_1, b_2) to that which she would receive at (a_1, a_2) if she switched from t_2 to t_1; similarly, R prefers (b_1, b_2) to (c_1, c_2)—and so would not switch from s_1 to s_2—because of the dominance of s_1 assumed in (2) above.

3. *Instability.* To ensure that R benefits by moving first and choosing his dominated strategy of s_2, which is unconditionally worse than s_1, it must be the case that R prefers (d_1, d_2) to the simultaneous-play Nash equilibrium of (b_1, b_2):

$$d_1 > b_1. \tag{3}$$

Also, to ensure that R will induce (d_1, d_2) rather than (c_1, c_2) when he chooses s_2, C must prefer the former outcome to the latter:

$$d_2 > c_2. \tag{4}$$

When inequalities (3) and (4) are both satisfied, the Nash equilibrium, (b_1, b_2), is said to be *unstable*.

Combining inequalities (1) and (3) for R and (2) and (4) for C gives a complete ordering of payoffs for R and a partial ordering for C:

$$\text{R: } a_1 > d_1 > b_1 > c_1; \quad \text{C: } b_2 > a_2 \text{ and } d_2 > c_2. \tag{5}$$

The partial ordering for C admits six different complete orderings:

$$b_2 > a_2 > d_2 > c_2;$$
$$b_2 > d_2 > c_2 > a_2;$$
$$b_2 > d_2 > a_2 > c_2;$$
$$d_2 > c_2 > b_2 > a_2;$$
$$d_2 > b_2 > a_2 > c_2;$$
$$d_2 > b_2 > c_2 > a_2.$$

That is, all six orderings preserve the partial ordering of C. And because they are the only ones to do so, they are exhaustive.

The single strict ordering of payoffs for R and the six strict orderings for C define six strict ordinal games, which are shown in Figure 6.2. In these games, 4 indicates a best payoff, 3 next best, 2 next worst, and 1 worst. Thus the higher the number, the greater the payoff; but because these payoffs are *ordinal,* they indicate only an ordering of outcomes from best to worst, not the degree to which a player prefers one outcome over another. The payoffs to R and C are given as ordered pairs (i, j) in parentheses, where i is the payoff to R and j the payoff to C. The ordered pairs $[u, v]$ in brackets just below the parenthetical pairs will be explained in section four below.[8]

I have grouped the six games into the two classes, I and II, mentioned in the first section of the chapter. In the three class I games, the (d_1, d_2) lower left outcome induced when R moves first and chooses his dominated strategy of s_2 is Pareto-superior—that is, better for both players—to the upper right Nash equilibrium of (b_1, b_2). In the three class II games, neither (d_1, d_2) nor (b_1, b_2) is Pareto-superior to the other outcome.

Before discussing in more detail differences in these two classes of games, I emphasize what they have in common: The Nash equilibrium of (b_1, b_2) in each class is unstable. Specifically, R has an incentive to choose s_2 first, thereby inducing C—by responding optimally—to choose t_1, resulting in (d_1, d_2) rather than the simultaneous-play Nash equilibrium of (b_1, b_2).

Figure 6.2
Six 2 x 2 Strict Ordinal Games Subsumed by
Surprise Game (Simultaneous Play)

Case I: (d_1, d_2) Pareto-superior to Nash equilibrium of (b_1, b_2)

	27 (47)		28 (48)		48 (57)
(4,1)	(2,3)	(4,1)	(2,2)	((4,2))	(2,3)
[3,4]	[3,4]	[3,4]	[3,4]	[4,2]	[3,4]
((3,4))	(1,2)	((3,4))	(1,3)	((3,4))	(1,1)
[3,4]	[3,4]	[3,4]	[3,4]	[3,4]	[3,4]

Case II: (d_1, d_2) not Pareto-superior to Nash equilibrium of (b_1, b_2)

	49 (44)		50 (45)		56 (56)
(4,1)	((2,4))	((4,3))	((2,4))	((4,2))	((2,4))
[2,4]	[3,3]	[4,3]	[4,3]	[4,2]	[3,3]
((3,3))	(1,2)	(3,2)	(1,1)	((3,3))	(1,1)
[2,4]	[2,4]/[3,3]	[4,3]/[2,4]	[2,4]/[4,3]	[2,4]	[2,4]/[3,3]

Key: (x_1, x_2) = (payoff to R, payoff to C) in original game
[x_1, x_2] = [payoff to R, payoff to C] in anticipation game
4 = best; 3 = next best; 2 = next worst; 1 = worst
Nash equilibria underscored in original and anticipation games
NMEs circled in original game

If *both* players have dominant strategies in a 2 x 2 game (e.g., Prisoners' Dilemma), it is never rational for R (or C) to disrupt the unique pure-strategy Nash equilibrium by moving first. To see this, assume, as before, that (b_1, b_2) is the unique Nash equilibrium. If not only R's strategy associated with this equilibrium is dominant, but C's is, too, then in addition to inequality (2), $c_2 > d_2$, which reverses inequality (4) that is necessary for instability.[9]

In class I games, not only would R have an incentive to move first, but C would presumably encourage him to do so in order to benefit herself over what she would obtain at the Pareto-inferior Nash equilibrium, (b_1, b_2). By comparison, this is emphatically not true of the class II games, in which C does better at (b_1, b_2), whereas R does better at (d_1, d_2), which he can induce by moving first.[10]

If R moves first, the game is, technically, not a 2 x 2 game but a 2 x 4 game, in which C has four strategies—contingent on what R does—rather than two. C's strategies may be described as follows:

t_i/t_j: choose t_i if R chooses s_1, t_j if R chooses s_2 (i, j = 1 or 2).

Thus, for example, t_2/t_1 means that C chooses her second strategy (t_2) if R chooses his first strategy (s_1), and C chooses her first strategy (t_1) if R chooses his second strategy (s_2).

Assume R moves first in the 2 x 2 Surprise Game of Figure 6.1a. The 2 x 4 game that results is shown in Figure 6.1b, with each of the four pay-offs in the 2 x 2 game occurring at two different outcomes in the 2 x 4 matrix. For example, a_2 in the 2 x 2 game occurs in the 2 x 4 game when R chooses s_1 and C chooses either t_1/t_1 or t_1/t_2, because the latter two choices both imply that C chooses t_1 when R chooses s_1 in the 2 x 2 game.

Whereas R has a dominant strategy of s_1 in the 2 x 2 game, he has no dominant strategy in the 2 x 4 game. While R's inequality (5) shows that s_1 is better for him than s_2 when C chooses t_1/t_1, t_2/t_2, or t_1/t_2, s_2 is better than s_1 when C chooses t_2/t_1. Hence, s_1 is not unconditionally better for R than s_2. Yet t_2/t_1 for C is *weakly dominant:* It is at least as good, and some-times better, than any of C's other three strategies—whether R chooses s_1 or s_2—according to C's inequality (5).

Assume C chooses her dominant strategy in the 2 x 4 Surprise Game in Figure 6.1b. Anticipating this choice, R would know his best response is to choose s_2, resulting in (d_1, d_2), the unique dominant-strategy Nash equilibrium in *this* game.[11] In other words, there is a reversal of roles when R moves first: Whereas R possesses a dominant strategy in the 2 x 2 game (simultaneous play), C does in the 2 x 4 game (R moves first), leading to a different Nash equilibrium.

The rational choice of (d_1, d_2) in the 2 x 4 game reinforces my earlier contention: If the order of moves is endogenous, R has an incentive to move first. By redefining, in effect, what game is being played, R can in-duce his preferred outcome of (d_1, d_2), because this outcome is the unique dominant-strategy Nash equilibrium in the 2 x 4 game.

C, as I indicated earlier, will have no quarrel with R for moving first in the three class I games in Figure 6.2, because *both* players do better at (d_1, d_2) than (b_1, b_2). In the class II games, by comparison, C will be mo-tivated to preempt R: In the resulting 4 x 2 game (i.e., when C moves first, which is not shown), (b_1, b_2) is the unique dominant-strategy equilib-rium—just as it is in the 2 x 2 game—which C prefers to (d_1, d_2).

The players face a major problem if each thinks he or she can suc-cessfully preempt the other. Then R will choose s_2 when C chooses t_2, re-sulting in (c_1, c_2). This outcome is worse for *both* players than either (b_1, b_2) or (d_1, d_2) in all class II games, wherein precisely this conflict is likely to occur.

This conflict has somewhat the flavor of the game Chicken, whereby each player does better at his or her preferred equilibrium but each courts dis-aster if he or she is not successful in implementing it. But if the players rec-ognize the problem of not coordinating their choices in such a "preemption game"—and there is a compromise outcome that benefits both, as in Chicken, even if it is not as good for each as successful preemption—then perhaps the disaster can be averted.[12]

The analysis so far demonstrates how a preemption problem can crop up, even if a simultaneous-play 2 x 2 game has a unique dominant-strategy Nash equilibrium, when the order of moves is endogenous. But this analysis requires looking separately at 2 x 2 and 2 x 4 games that have the same payoff structures—only the order of moves is different.

I next describe a dynamic approach to the analysis of the stability of equilibria, in which the 2 x 2 game is assumed to be the only game played but under very different rules from those of classical game theory. This approach offers new insight into not only why players might depart from an (unstable) Nash equilibrium but also where they might end up and how they might get there. Thereby TOM makes "surprise" moves both less surprising and more explicable in terms of the dynamics of rational choice.

THE THEORY OF MOVES (TOM)

The starting point of TOM is a payoff matrix, in which the order of play is not specified.[13] In fact, players are assumed not even to choose strategies but instead to move and countermove from outcomes, or states, by looking ahead and using "backward induction" to determine the rationality of both their moves and those of an opponent.

Because game theory assumes that players choose strategies simultaneously,[14] it does not raise questions about the rationality of moving or departing from outcomes—at least beyond an immediate departure, à la Nash. In fact, however, most real-life games do not start with simultaneous strategy choices but commence at outcomes. The question then becomes whether a player, by departing from an outcome, can do better not just in an immediate or myopic sense but, rather, in an extended or nonmyopic sense.

In the case of 2 x 2 games, TOM postulates four rules of play that describe the possible choices of the players at different stages:

1. Play starts at an outcome, called the *initial state,* which is at the intersection of the row and column of a 2 x 2 payoff matrix.
2. Either player can unilaterally switch his or her strategy and thereby change the initial state into a new state in the same row or column as the initial state.[15] The player who switches, who may be either R or C, is called player 1 (P1).
3. Player 2 (P2) can respond by unilaterally switching his or her strategy, thereby moving the game to a new state.

4. The alternating responses continue until the player (P1 or P2) whose turn it is to move next chooses not to switch his or her strategy. When this happens, the game terminates in a *final state,* which is the outcome of the game.

Note that the sequence of moves and countermoves is strictly alternating: First, say, R moves, then C moves, and so on, until one player stops, at which point the state reached is final and therefore the outcome of the game.[16]

The use of the word "state" is meant to convey the temporary nature of an outcome, before players decide to stop switching strategies. I assume that no payoffs accrue to players from being in a state unless it is the final state and therefore becomes the outcome (which could be the initial state if the players choose not to move from it). To assume otherwise would require that payoffs be cardinal rather than ordinal, with players accumulating them as they pass through states. I eschew this assumption in part because I think payoffs to players in most real-life games cannot be quantified and summed across the states visited. More significant, payoffs in the games that most interest me depend overwhelmingly on the final state reached, not on how it was reached. In politics, for example, the payoff for most politicians is not in campaigning, which is arduous and costly, but in winning.

Rule 1 differs radically from the corresponding rule of play in classical game theory, in which players simultaneously choose strategies in a matrix game that determines an outcome. Instead of starting with strategy choices, I assume that players are already in some state at the start of play and receive payoffs from this state if they stay. Basing their choice on these payoffs, they decide, individually, whether or not to change this state in order to try to do better.[17]

To be sure, some decisions are made collectively by players, in which case it would be reasonable to say that they choose strategies from scratch, either simultaneously or by coordinating their choices. But if, say, two countries are coordinating their choices, as when they agree to sign a treaty, the most important strategic question is what individual calculations led them to this point. The formality of jointly signing the treaty is the culmination of their negotiations, which covers up the move-countermove process that preceded it. This is precisely what TOM is designed to uncover.

In summary, play of a game starts in a state, at which players accrue payoffs only if they remain in that state so that it becomes the outcome of the game. If they do not remain, they still know what payoffs they would have accrued had they stayed; hence they can make a rational calculation of the advantages of staying versus moving. They move precisely because they calculate that they can do better by switching states, anticipating a better outcome if and when the move-countermove process finally comes to rest.

Rules 1–4 say nothing about what causes a game to end but only when: Termination occurs when a "player whose turn it is to move next chooses not to switch his or her strategy" (rule 4). But when is it rational not to continue moving or not to move in the first place from the initial state? To answer this question, I posit a rule of rational termination (Brams 1983, pp. 106-107), which has been called "inertia" by Kilgour and Zagare (1987, p. 94). It prohibits a player from moving from an initial state unless doing so leads to a better (not just the same) final state:

5. A player will not move from an initial state if this move
   (i) leads to a less preferred final state (i.e., outcome) or
   (ii) returns play to the initial state (i.e., makes the initial state the outcome).

In the next section I discuss how rational players starting from some initial state use backward induction to determine what the outcome will be.

Condition (i) of rule 5, which precludes moves that result in an inferior state, needs no defense. But condition (ii), which precludes moves to the same state because of cycling back to the initial state, is worth some elaboration. It says that if it is rational, after P1 moves, for play of the game to cycle back to the initial state, P1 will not move in the first place. After all, what is the point of initiating the move-countermove process if play simply returns to square one, given that the players receive no payoffs along the way (i.e., before an outcome is reached)? Not only is there no gain from cycling, but in fact there may be a loss because of so-called transaction costs that players suffer by virtue of making moves that, ultimately, do not change the situation. Therefore it seems sensible to assume that P1 will not trigger a move-countermove process if it only returns the players to the initial state, making it the outcome.

I call rule 5 a *rationality rule* because it provides the basis for players to determine whether they can do better by moving from a state or remaining in it. Still another rationality rule is needed to ensure that both players take into account each other's calculations before deciding to move from the initial state. I call this rule the *two-sidedness rule:*

6. Given that players have complete information about each other's preferences and act according to the rules of TOM, each takes into account the consequences of the other player's rational choices, as as well as his or her own, in deciding whether to move from the initial state or subsequently, based on backward induction. If it is

rational for one player to move and the other player not to move from the initial state, then the player who moves takes *precedence:* That player's move overrides the player who stays, so the outcome is that induced by the player who moves.

Because players have complete information, they can look ahead and anticipate the consequences of their moves. I next show how they use backward induction to do this. In the process, I link order-of-moves effects, due to unstable equilibria (see the second section above), to the results given by TOM, which predicts the moves that players will make from these equilibria.

UNSTABLE NASH EQUILIBRIA AND TOM

I begin by analyzing where the players will end up when the initial state is the unique dominant-strategy Nash equilibrium of (b_1, b_2) in the 2 x 2 Surprise Game (Figure 6.1a).[18]

THEOREM 1. *In the 2 x 2 Surprise Game, (d_1, d_2) is the outcome to which the players will move, according to TOM, from the unique dominant-strategy Nash equilibrium of (b_1, b_2).*
PROOF. There are two cases to consider:

Case 1: R Acts First
If R acts first, the clockwise progression of moves from (b_1, b_2) back to (b_1, b_2)—with the player (R or C) who makes the next move shown below each state in the alternating sequence—is as follows (see Figure 6.1a):

	State 1	State 2	State 3	State 4	State 1
	R	C	R	C	
R starts:	$(b_1, b_2) \rightarrow$	$(c_1, c_2) \rightarrow$	$(\underline{d_1}, \underline{d_2}) \rightarrow\|$	$(a_1, a_2) \rightarrow$	(b_1, b_2)
Survivor:	(d_1, d_2)	(d_1, d_2)	$(\underline{d_1}, \underline{d_2})$	(b_1, b_2)	

The *survivor* is determined by working backward, after a putative cycle has been completed.

Assume the players' alternating moves have taken them counterclockwise from (b_1, b_2) to (c_1, c_2) to (d_1, d_2) to (a_1, a_2), at which point C must decide whether to stop at (a_1, a_2) in state 4 or complete the cycle and return to (b_1, b_2). Given inequality (2), C prefers (b_1, b_2) to (a_1, a_2), so (b_1, b_2) is listed as the survivor below (a_1, a_2): Because C would move the process back to (b_1, b_2) should it reach (a_1, a_2), the players know that if the move-countermove process reaches state 4, the outcome will be (b_1, b_2).

Knowing this, would R at state 3 move to (a_1, a_2)? Given inequality (3), R prefers (d_1, d_2) to the survivor at state 3—namely, (b_1, b_2)—so the answer is no. Hence (d_1, d_2) becomes the survivor when R must choose between stopping at (d_1, d_2) and moving to (a_1, a_2) at state 4—which, as I have just shown, would become (b_1, b_2) once (a_1, a_2) is reached.

At state 2 C prefers moving to (d_1, d_2) to stopping at (c_1, c_2) by inequality (4). Consequently, (d_1, d_2) again is the survivor if the process reaches (c_1, c_2) at state 2. Similarly, at state 1 R prefers the previous survivor, (d_1, d_2), to (b_1, b_2) from inequality (3), so (d_1, d_2) is the survivor at this state as well.

That (d_1, d_2) is the survivor at state 1 means that it is rational for R initially to move to (c_1, c_2) and C subsequently to move to (d_1, d_2). At (d_1, d_2) the process will stop, making (d_1, d_2) the rational choice if R has the opportunity to move first from state 1. That is, after working *backward* from C's choice of completing the cycle or not at state 4, the players can reverse the process and, looking *forward*, determine that it is rational for R to move from (b_1, b_2) to (c_1, c_2) and C to move from (c_1, c_2) to (d_1, d_2), at which point R will stop the move-countermove process at (d_1, d_2). Q.E.D.

Notice that R does better at (d_1, d_2) than at (b_1, b_2), where he could have terminated play at the outset, and C does better at (d_1, d_2) than at (c_1, c_2), where she could have terminated play, given that R moves first. I indicate that (d_1, d_2) is the consequence of backward induction by underscoring this state in the progression; it is the state at which *stoppage* of the process occurs, which I indicate by the vertical line blocking the arrow emanating from (d_1, d_2).

Case 2: C Acts First

If C acts first, the progression of moves from (b_1, b_2) back to (b_1, b_2) is counterclockwise. But this time backward induction seems to leave open which state will be the final survivor. In particular, given that R chooses to complete the cycle at state 4 because $b_1 > c_1$ of inequality (1)—making (b_1, b_2) the survivor at state 4—C's inequality (5) provides no information about which choice C will make at state 3—stay at (d_1, d_2) or move to (c_1, c_2) and thence to (b_1, b_2):

	State 1	State 2	State 3	State 4	State 1
	C	R	C	R	
C starts:	(b_1, b_2) ?	(a_1, a_2) ?	(d_1, d_2) ?	(c_1, c_2) ⟶	(b_1, b_2)
Survivor:				(b_1, b_2)	

This indeterminacy disappears, however, when the consequences of two possibilities at state 3—either (b_1, b_2) survives or (d_1, d_2) survives, depending on whether $b_2 > d_2$ or $d_2 > b_2$—are analyzed:

- (b_1, b_2) survives. Then R will choose (a_1, a_2) at state 2 because of R's inequality (5), and C will choose (b_1, b_2) at state 1 because of inequality (2), so (b_1, b_2) will be the survivor at state 1.
- (d_1, d_2) survives. Then R will choose (a_1, a_2) at state 2 because $a_1 > d_1$ of inequality (1), and C will choose (b_1, b_2) at state 1 because of inequality (2), so (b_1, b_2) will be the survivor at state 1.

In either case (b_1, b_2) will be the outcome when C acts first, which is to say that C will not move from this state. But because I showed in case 1 that R will move from this state and induce (d_1, d_2), (d_1, d_2) will be the outcome because of the precedence of moving over staying (rule 6 in the third section).

Thus the unique Nash equilibrium of (b_1, b_2) in the Figure 6.1a game is not only unstable (section two of this chapter) but also one from which the players would depart and, according to TOM, move to (d_1, d_2). I next consider whether there are any additional 2 x 2 strict ordinal games, apart from the six given in Figure 6.2, that have unique dominant-strategy Nash equilibria from which the players would depart.

THEOREM 2. *The six games in Figure 6.2 are the only 2 x 2 strict ordinal games in which the players will move from a unique dominant-strategy Nash equilibrium. Consequently, these games are the same as those in which order of play, due to instability, matters.*

PROOF. To show that there are no other games among the seventy-eight in which players would move from a dominant-strategy Nash equilibrium, one must show that if either of the necessary conditions for instability fails—inequality (3) or inequality (4)—the backward induction used in the proof of theorem 1 will lead to the players' staying at (b_1, b_2) rather than moving to (d_1, d_2). Consider, first, case 1 when R acts first and the possible failure of each instability condition:

- Inequality (3) is reversed, so $b_1 > d_1$. Then the final survivor at state 1 will be (b_1, b_2) rather than (d_1, d_2).
- Inequality (4) is reversed, so $c_2 > d_2$. Then the next-to-final survivor at state 2 will be (c_1, c_2), which will be displaced as final survivor by (b_1, b_2) at state 1 since $b_1 > c_1$ by inequality (1).

Hence, R will not move from (b_1, b_2) if either inequality (3) or inequality (4) is reversed.

As for C, it is easy to show that the reversal of either inequality does not change the backward-induction analysis in case 2, so C, as before, will not move from (b_1, b_2) with the reversal of either inequality. Therefore only the satisfaction of both inequalities induces the players to move from (b_1, b_2), which are exactly the two conditions that produce the order-of-play effects (i.e., make the dominant-strategy Nash equilibrium unstable). Q.E.D.

Taken together, theorems 1 and 2 demonstrate that order of play matters in 2 x 2 games with unique dominant-strategy Nash equilibria if and only if the players would, according to TOM, move from these equilibria to another state. The state that they would move to is the unique Nash equilibrium in the 2 x 4 game in which R (i.e., the player with the dominant strategy in the 2 x 2 game) moves first and chooses his dominated strategy. For the six games in Figure 6.2, I indicate that the upper right (b_1, b_2) will go into the lower left (d_1, d_2) by putting (d_1, d_2) in brackets, just below (b_1, b_2), in each payoff matrix. In game 27, for example, [3,4] is shown below (2,3) in the upper right cell.

The outcome into which a state goes is the *nonmyopic equilibrium* from that state. NMEs may be viewed as the consequence of both players' looking ahead and making rational calculations of where the move-countermove process will transport them, based on the rules of TOM, from each of the four possible initial states. Backward-induction analysis from each state in game 27 shows that each state will go into (3,4). Thus wherever play starts, the players can anticipate that they will end up at (3,4), making it the unique NME in game 27. This is also true of (3,4) in game 28, but not in game 48, the third class I game. Starting at (4,2) in game 48, the players will not depart from this state, making (4,2) as well as (3,4) an NME in this game.

Like game 48, all games in class II contain at least two NMEs. But some of these NMEs are *indeterminate* because there is a conflict over who will move first. In game 50, for example, if (1,1) is the initial state, [2,4]/[4,3] indicates that when R moves first from (1,1), (2,4) will be the outcome, whereas when C moves first, (4,3) will be the outcome.[19] Because R prefers (4,3) whereas C prefers (2,4), each player will try to hold out longer in order to induce the other player to move first. Who wins in this struggle will depend on which player has "order power"—that is, who can determine the order of moves, starting at (1,1) (Brams 1994, ch. 5).

Every 2 x 2 game contains at least one NME, because from each initial state there is an outcome (perhaps indeterminate) of the move-countermove process. If this outcome is both determinate and the same from every initial state, then it is the only NME; otherwise, there is more than one NME. In game 56 in Figure 6.2, there are three different NMEs, which is the maximum number that can occur in a 2 x 2 strict ordinal game; the minimum, as already noted, is one. All except two of the seventy-eight 2 x 2 games (game 56 and Chicken) have either one or two NMEs.

The four bracketed states of each game in Figure 6.2 define what I call the *anticipation matrix,* with each state in this matrix an NME. Insofar as players choose strategies as if they were playing a game based on this matrix, one can determine which NMEs are Nash equilibria in *this* game and therefore likely to be chosen.[20]

To summarize, where players start in the original games in Figure 6.2—including the unique dominant-strategy Nash equilibria—may not be where they end up, according to TOM. Thus an original game may mask a good deal of instability when the players can move and countermove from states.[21]

I next analyze two real-life cases in which there was a sudden and surprising shift in the apparently dominant strategy of one player to a dominated strategy. Not only is this shift rational when the order of player is assumed endogenous, but it also induces a countershift on the part of the other player. These are precisely the moves predicted by TOM, which benefits one player in the first case and both players in the second case.

TWO CASES OF SURPRISE

The Japanese Attack on Pearl Harbor

There is a mountain of literature on the Pearl Harbor attack of December 7, 1941 (thirty-nine volumes of congressional hearings alone in 1946). To boil down Japanese and U.S. choices to a 2 x 2 game may sound like a heroic if not impossible condensation of the strategic situation that leaders of the two countries faced prior to the surprise attack, the most infamous in history (Schelling 1988, p. xiiv).

In fact, however, Japan's decision one month before the attack was a straightforward one. Planning and training for the attack, which included a war game conducted at the Japanese Naval War College in September 1941, had begun almost a year before the attack occurred. By early November a final decision on whether to proceed with the attack had to be made, so Japan's strategies were attack (A) or don't attack (Ā).

The United States faced no imminent decision before the attack, but earlier decisions had set the stage for the calamitous events that were to follow. In April and May 1940, the Pacific Fleet was moved from San Diego to Pearl Harbor to signal U.S. determination to resist further Japanese expansion, which had begun with the seizure of Manchuria in 1931 and had been followed by the invasion of China six years later. In July 1941, after Japan occupied the southern half of French Indochina, the United States effectively cut off Japanese oil supplies by freezing Japanese assets in the United States and placing an embargo on the export of oil to Japan. At that time Japan had oil reserves that would last only about twelve to eighteen months (Hybel 1986, p. 30).

Japan viewed the oil cutoff with shock and trepidation, giving ammunition to those in the Japanese military who argued for a preemptive naval and air strike on Hawaii. Although U.S. leaders believed the chances of an attack on Pearl Harbor were remote, they did expect *some* military offensive by Japan. On November 24 the chief of naval operations, Admiral Harold Stark, told Admiral Thomas Hart in Manila and Admiral Husband Kimmel on Hawaii that Japanese offensive operations could come soon. On November 27 Stark issued a "war warning" that "an aggressive move by Japan is expected within the next few days." On November 25 President Franklin Roosevelt met with his security advisers and suggested that Japan might launch a surprise attack within the week (Japan had a record of such attacks).[22] Most of the analytic literature on Pearl Harbor seeks to explain the intelligence failure of the United States, which had broken the Japanese diplomatic code before the attack and received numerous (but unassimilated) warnings of an impending attack. Although certain officials took some of these warnings seriously, the "noise" in the system drowned them out (Wohlstetter 1962).[23]

Aggravating this problem before the attack was U.S. preoccupation with the war in Europe and protecting shipping lanes in the North Atlantic. By choosing not to be distracted by developments in Asia, the United States was playing "a delicate game of getting the Japanese to strike the first blow" (Morgan 1983, p. 56), because "national support for a war effort could not be achieved unless Japan committed the first overt act" (Kam 1988, p. 35). Thus the United States chose between the strategies of wait (W) and don't wait ($\overline{W}$), where W means absorbing the first blow—wherever it may come—and $\overline{W}$ means that the United States begins a naval offensive thrust across the Pacific.

As I mentioned, Japan's two strategies were attack (A) and don't attack ($\overline{A}$) Pearl Harbor,[24] which together with the U.S. strategies (W and $\overline{W}$) define a 2 x 2 game. A brief description of the four possible outcomes and the preferences of the players for each is given below (I proceed clockwise from the upper left outcome in Figure 6.3):

1. $\overline{A}\overline{W}$—(4,2). By not attacking the United States when it begins its offensive thrust, Japan gains the advantage of being able to harass and weaken the fleet across the Pacific and then to stage a climactic naval battle—close to home and early in the war, when Japan's relative strength is greatest—yielding it a likely victory, Japan's best outcome (4). I rate this outcome as next worst (2) for the United States because it would be extremely risky for the United States to try to mount an offensive without sufficient time to build up its Pacific forces, especially with major resources being diverted to the European theater.[25]

2. $\overline{A}W$—(2,4). This is the status quo just before the attack, with the United States enjoying its best outcome (4) as it buys time to build up its

Figure 6.3
The Pearl Harbor Game (Game 56)

United States

	Don't Wait ($\overline{W}$)	Wait (W)
Don't Attack ($\overline{A}$)	(4,2) Premature response by U.S.; likely naval victory for Japan in home waters	(2,4) Depletion of Japanese oil reserves; eventual victory for U.S. without major war
Japan Attack (A)	(3,3) War, but with possibility of negotiated settlement	(1,1) Immediate disaster for U.S.; eventual disaster for Japan (in prolonged war)

Key: (i, j) = (payoff to R, payoff to C)
4 = best; 3 = next best; 2 = next worst; 1 = worst
Nash equilibrium underscored
NME, starting at Nash equilibrium, circled

Pacific Fleet. Even though Japan might gain temporary footholds in new territory in the Pacific region without directly attacking the United States, Japan's overall strategic situation deteriorates with the depletion of its oil reserves and the slow but inexorable buildup of Allied forces in the region, giving Japan its next worst outcome (2).

3. AW—(1,1). This is clearly the worst outcome (1) for the United States if its response to the humiliating attack is to do nothing except give the Japanese a free hand to complete their conquests in the Pacific. But because these victories will in the end turn out to be Pyrrhic—certainly once the Allies defeat Hitler and redirect their forces against Japan—I rate this outcome as worst (1) for Japan as well.[26]

4. A$\overline{W}$—(3,3). This is the next best outcome (3) for the United States because its citizens are outraged by the attack on Pearl Harbor and are equipped—psychologically in the beginning and materially in the end—to avenge the attack, including using nuclear weapons in August 1945. This outcome is also viewed by Japanese leaders as next best (3)—certainly better than slow strangulation through the dwindling of oil reserves ($\overline{A}$W)—in part because it offers some prospect that the United States and the Soviet Union would weary of a costly and drawn-out struggle in Asia, resulting in the possibility of a negotiated settlement rather than the "unconditional surrender" that actually occurred (Paul 1994, pp. 67–69).

The most disputable ranking I have given to the four outcomes is (1,1) for AW. Emotionally and psychologically, the attack was a traumatic blow to the United States (hence the ranking of 1), mitigated only in part by the near unanimous declaration of war by Congress on December 8, which moved the outcome toward $A\overline{W}$, though *not* in terms of a military response at the time.[27]

Japan, despite the apparent success of the attack, had good reason to expect defeat in a prolonged war (hence the ranking of 1 for Japan), especially because the delayed military response by the United States (i.e., its choice of W) portended that the Allied counteroffensive in the Pacific would be all the more devastating later. This ominous view was held by both civilian and military leaders in Japan, many of whom foresaw their eventual defeat (Hybel 1986, pp. 32–33). Admiral Isoroku Yamamoto, commander-in-chief of Japan's combined fleet and champion of the attack, put it this way: "Should the war be prolonged for two or three years, I have no confidence in our ultimate victory" (quoted in Wohlstetter 1962, p. 350). Despite Admiral Yamamoto's premonition of the possible catastrophic consequences of the Japanese attack, he became obsessed with eliminating the threat of the U.S. fleet (Morgan 1983, pp. 49–53). Although eight battleships and ten other warships were damaged or destroyed in Pearl Harbor, none of the three aircraft carriers stationed there, which were out to sea, was touched. Such carriers would later prove to be the crucial offensive weapon in the Pacific theater.

That there was internal dissent within the Japanese leadership underscores the problem of modeling a conflict by unitary players. But the rational choices of the players would not change—though the surprise factor would, because Japan would no longer have a dominant strategy of $\overline{A}$—if Japan rated AW as high as 3 or 4.[28]

Notice that the Figure 6.3 game is game 56 in Figure 6.2. When play starts at $\overline{A}W$, TOM predicts that Japan will—as happened—switch to A, and the United States will in turn switch to $\overline{W}$, which it had commenced doing by the time of the Battle of Midway. Japan's move was rational because of the unacceptability of its staying at $\overline{A}W$ and suffering a slow but inevitable exhaustion of its oil supplies.[29] That Japan gambled on a high-risk (dominated) strategy in the 2 x 2 game and lost shows, in retrospect, that Japan's attributing 3 to $A\overline{W}$, while perhaps a reasonable estimate in 1941, was less so in June 1942 (Battle of Midway).

Yet even after the defeat of Germany in May 1945, when it was estimated that the United States would suffer tens of thousands of battle deaths in order to invade and conquer Japan (Bernstein 1991, p. 162), Japan might reasonably have hoped for a negotiated settlement that did not force on it unconditional surrender. The dropping of nuclear bombs on Hiroshima and Nagasaki in August 1945, of course, shattered this hope.

I next turn to a case of diplomatic surprise, the most dramatic of the century (Handel 1981, p. 315), which TOM shows to be a rational move even though it again involves the (surprise) choice of a dominated strategy in a 2 x 2 game. However, this time the outcome benefits both players, not just the initiator of the surprise.

Sadat's Peace Initiative to Israel

The disengagement of forces after the October 1973 Yom Kippur War, engineered by U.S. secretary of state Henry Kissinger, left Israel in control of the Golan Heights of Syria and the Sinai peninsula of Egypt, the same territory it had captured in the Six Day War in June 1967. With no settlement in sight four years after the Yom Kippur War, there seemed every prospect of still another Arab-Israeli war when Anwar Sadat, president of Egypt, reported "thinking along the following lines: Why shouldn't I go to the Israelis directly? Why shouldn't I stand before the Knesset and address the Israelis themselves as well as the whole world, putting forward the Arab cause and stating its dimensions? I conjured up what the reaction might be to such a move, which no one would expect. It would be said that it would be an uncalculated gamble" (Sadat 1984, pp. 104–105).

Although Sadat offered as justification such philosophical musings as "This is my fate" and "The hour is coming, have no doubt" (Sadat 1984, p. 105), it seems that there was considerable calculation behind his gamble, despite his impulsive nature (Handel 1981, pp. 324–325; Silver 1984,

Figure 6.4
The Sadat Initiative Game (Game 27)

Israel

	Cooperate (C)	Don't Cooperate ($\bar{C}$)
Don't Initiate ($\bar{I}$)	(4,1) Premature concessions by Israel; victory for Egypt	(2,3) Status quo: Sinai remains occupied
Egypt		
Initiate (I)	(3,4) Negotiated settlement, but conflict for Egypt with other Arab countries	(1,2) Initiative frustrated, presaging new war

Key: (i, j) = (payoff to R, payoff to C)
4 = best; 3 = next best; 2 = next worst; 1 = worst
Nash equilibrium underscored
NME, starting at Nash equilibrium, circled

p. 177). For one thing, he wanted "to show the Israelis they were dealing with a new style of Arab leadership," not "monsters who wanted only to drive Israel into the sea" (Sadat 1984, p. 105). For another, he was dismayed by the prospect of a reconvening of the Geneva Peace Conference between Israel and its Arab neighbors, which was supported by the superpowers but which Sadat believed was fraught with procedural obstacles and would end in stalemate (Gervasi 1979, pp. 48–54; Handel 1981, pp. 318–320).

After his historic visit to Jerusalem on November 19–21, 1977, Sadat could accurately claim that "the Israeli people themselves became a pressure group in favor of peace" (Sadat 1984, p. 106). As for other Arab leaders, Sadat bitterly remarked that after the Yom Kippur War, "when the entire Arab world made a lot of money out of oil and added to their wealth, Egypt by contrast was drained of its resources" (Sadat 1984, p. 106); indeed, Egypt faced a severe economic crisis in 1976–1977 (Handel 1981, pp. 322–323).

Sadat acknowledged that "we knew we could not fight the United States" (Sadat 1984, p. 107), which would likely side again with Israel if there were another war. More than any other factor, Telhami (1990, p. 13) argues that it was the economic and military power of the United States that moved Egypt from the Soviet toward the U.S. camp and a willingness to negotiate with Israel under U.S. auspices. Israeli leaders also believed that the United States must be a principal participant in the peace process (Stein 1989, p. 179). In addition, Israel's

> military thinking had changed considerably as a result of the 1973 war. Secure borders were still considered vital, but it was recognized that dynamic and mobile warfare could to a large extent compensate for natural borders. . . . As a result of less steadfast American backing, Israel's bargaining position also changed . . . weakened by the Carter administration's more sympathetic policy toward the Arab states and Egypt in particular. (Handel 1981, pp. 265–266)

Thus when Sadat proposed his peace initiative to the Egyptian parliament on November 9, 1977, prime minister Menachem Begin, though caught unprepared, took only four days to extend an official invitation for Sadat to come to Jerusalem "to conduct talks for a permanent peace between Israel and Egypt" (Dayan 1981, p. 75).

Although the "psychological barrier" (Sadat 1978, pp. 300–302) was broken, it was more than psychology that produced what I call the Sadat initiative game (Figure 6.4). Egypt's (Sadat's) choices were to initiate (I) or not initiate ($\overline{\text{I}}$) a lasting peace by visiting Jerusalem, and Israel's (Begin's) choices were to cooperate (C) or not cooperate ($\overline{\text{C}}$) with this initiative. A brief description of the resulting four possible outcomes and the preferences of the players for each is given below (I proceed clockwise from the upper left outcome in Figure 6.4):[30]

1. $\overline{I}C$—(4,1). Israel undermines its bargaining position by being co-operative (presumably, by offering concessions) before Egypt takes the first step and commits itself to a permanent solution to their conflict. (This would be especially damaging to the reputation of Begin, who was the newly elected prime minister from the hawkish Likud Party.) What is worst (1) for Israel is in this case best (4) for Egypt, because any result-ing agreement between the two countries would favor Egypt insofar as it would require fewer concessions from Egypt.

2. $\overline{I}\overline{C}$—(2,3). Without a peace initiative from Egypt or cooperation from Israel, the status quo stays in place. Continuing occupation of the Sinai is next worst (2) for Egypt, whereas it is next best (3) for Israel since its security is ensured, though at a high price.

3. $I\overline{C}$—(1,2). Israel's frustration of Egypt's peace initiative is Egypt's worst outcome (1), because Sadat's big gamble was to no avail. But this outcome is quite unsatisfactory (2) for Israel as well, because it will lose U.S. support and almost surely have to fight another war with Egypt, which will have little recourse to try to regain its lost territory.

4. IC—(3,4). Israel's favorable response to Egypt's peace initiative not only breaks the psychological barrier but also offers a good prospect of permanent peace. With appropriate security guarantees, this is the best out-come (4) for Israel and the next best (3) for Egypt, which will face the wrath of its Arab neighbors and the loss of monetary support from other Arab countries for negotiating a separate peace.

Although Sadat moved first— making the Figure 6.4 game really a 2 x 4 game (see Figure 6.1b) in which (3,4) is the unique dominant-strat-egy equilibrium—it still leaves open the question that both Arabs and Is-raelis (e.g., Fahmy 1983 and Dayan 1981) have struggled to answer: Why did Sadat take the initiative that he did? The answer, I submit, is that it is rational, according to TOM, for Egypt to move to (1,2) and Israel to coun-termove to (3,4). After the peace accords, negotiated at Camp David in September 1978 under heavy pressure from U.S. president Jimmy Carter, were translated into a peace treaty signed in April 1979, it seems fair to say that both players were better off than before Sadat's dramatic visit to Jerusalem.[31]

CONCLUSIONS

I do not pretend that all surprise can be captured in the switch by a player from a dominant to a dominated strategy in the six 2 x 2 games subsumed by the generic Surprise Game. But the two real-life cases of surprise I have analyzed, one involving a belligerent action and the other a peaceful initiative, suggest that such switches may well catch the target completely off guard, generating both shock and surprise.

A move by R from the dominant-strategy Nash equilibrium induces a countermove by C, according to TOM, in the six games. In three games this is to C's benefit as well as R's (both Egypt and Israel in the case of Sadat's visit to Jerusalem), but in the other three games it is only to R's benefit (Japan in the case of Pearl Harbor).[32]

In both standard game theory and TOM, the incentive to move from a unique dominant-strategy Nash equilibrium in a 2 x 2 game has a rational-choice justification. However, the justification in the standard theory is awkward. It requires comparing the Nash equilibrium in the 2 x 2 game with the Nash equilibrium that R can induce if he moves first in a 2 x 4 game. If the equilibrium in the 2 x 4 game is better for R, then R would have an incentive to move first, making the equilibrium in the 2 x 2 game unstable.

TOM, by contrast, does not presume different game forms or a first-moving player. Rather, play starts at outcomes, or states, with the order of moves endogenous. Players move and countermove according to rules of play and rationality rules that enable them to look ahead and anticipate ending up at NMEs from each state.

It turns out that the six 2 x 2 games in which players would move from the dominant-strategy Nash equilibrium to a different state (i.e., NME) are exactly the 2 x 2 games with unstable Nash equilibria, according to the standard theory (shown in theorems 1 and 2). What TOM offers that the standard theory does not is a dynamic and parsimonious rationale for the players' making their moves and countermoves, which were observed in the two empirical cases studied.

The surprises of Pearl Harbor and the Sadat peace initiative stem from thinking that the player with the dominant strategy (Japan and Egypt in the respective cases) would appear to have no incentive to depart from this strategy. But the outcome induced by the other player's best response—that is, the unique Nash equilibrium in the 2 x 2 game—has no equilibrium status, according to TOM, when play starts in this state.

The migration of the players from the Nash equilibrium to a different state is, therefore, not surprising. That there was so much surprise in the empirical cases studied leads me to postulate that even if the games played were games of complete information (i.e., each player knew the other player's strategy choices and preferences for outcomes, as given in Figures 6.3 and 6.4), there was incomplete information about either the rules of play or the rationality rules. Indeed there was probably incomplete information about both player preferences and the rules, but it is the latter kind of incomplete information that has been much less studied, either empirically or theoretically. Because, as I have shown, different rules may generate radically different equilibrium results, it is important to try to ascertain those that are most plausible in a situation.

The rules of TOM, in my opinion, are eminently plausible in many situations. Players often do think more than one step ahead and calculate, on this basis, a series of moves and countermoves that they expect they and an opponent will make. For this reason, I believe, TOM might usefully be employed by policymakers as a decision aid in analyzing consequences of extended play.

Without diminishing the standard explanations for surprise, including lack of warning and noise, it seems to me that a neglected alternative explanation is *anticipation failure*. This occurs when the surprised (myopic) player fails to anticipate the nonmyopic thinking of the other player.[33] In both empirical cases, the myopic players (the United States and Israel) acted very much according to TOM, at least after they got over their initial shock. Had they anticipated the surprise moves of the initiators (Japan and Egypt), however, the myopic players might well have acted differently, though TOM suggests there is not much either player could have done—or would have wanted to do—as counteractions in the two games.

To be sure, the United States could certainly have better prepared for an attack in the case of Pearl Harbor, although it might still have decided to let it happen (for reasons given earlier). In the case of Sadat's peace initiative, Israel would have had no reason to try to undermine it, because Israel, too, benefited from the outcome it induced.

Although thinking along the lines of TOM might well have diminished if not eliminated the surprise in both cases, the course of history would probably not have been drastically altered if the surprise moves had been anticipated. Conceivably, Begin might have tried to steal some of Sadat's thunder, but even this is questionable because Begin's role was already prominent. Also, there is a problem with his making the first move (see note 31).

In the case of the surprise attack on Pearl Harbor, anticipation of the attack raises more interesting questions. Suppose the United States had had sufficient warning to move its battleships and other warships out of the harbor and prepare for an air defense of Hawaii and a counterattack against the Japanese fleet. In order to call off their attack, the Japanese would have had to know of these preparations, which the United States would have had an interest in hiding if it wanted to destroy the Japanese fleet during the attack.[34] In this scenario Japan would have been hobbled earlier, but the eventual outcome (Japan's defeat) would not have changed.

Thus anticipation of a surprise move will not necessarily lead to its cancellation, except, possibly, when the surpriser *knows* his move has been detected (the Japanese commander had standing orders to abort the attack if it was detected by U.S. planes). But even then the surpriser (e.g., Sadat) may still not be deterred from making his move, at least in class I games in which both players benefit from such a move.

NOTES

The author thanks Uri Bar-Joseph, Peter Landweber, Zeev Maoz, and Ben D. Mor for valuable comments on an earlier version of this chapter; and the C. V. Starr Center for Applied Economics for its support.

1. For reviews of the literature on the effects on games outcomes of different rules or protocols, including the timing of moves, see Hirshleifer 1985 and Brams 1994.

2. There are some recent exceptions, including Hamilton and Slutsky 1990, 1993; Rosenthal 1991; and van Damme and Hurkens 1993. Typically, these models allow players in the preplay phase of a game to choose when they will move in the play of the game. However, the choice of when to move applies only to a player's initial strategy choice, whereas the nonmyopic calculations to be developed later assume that players, starting at outcomes, make moves and countermoves that depend on thinking several steps ahead.

3. If neither player has a dominant strategy, there are either multiple Nash equilibria or no Nash equilibria in pure strategies. For example, Chicken has two pure-strategy Nash equilibria; it also has a mixed-strategy equilibrium if the payoffs are not ordinal (as assumed here) but cardinal utilities. In games like Chicken that have multiple Nash equilibria, there is an equilibrium-selection problem, which is the subject of the so-called refinements literature in game theory that seeks to narrow ("refine") the set of Nash equilibria to some proper subset, preferably with only one element (van Damme 1991). By contrast, here I seek not to delimit Nash equilibria, since there is only one in the games studied, but instead to determine when a unique dominant-strategy Nash equilibrium might *not* be chosen.

4. Henceforth I assume R is male and C female.

5. To be sure, R's dominated strategy in the 2 x 2 game is not dominated in the 2 x 4 game that results when R moves first. In fact, it is R's best response to C's (now dominant) strategy in the 2 x 4 game, as I will show in section two. But this rationale for R's switching from his dominant to his dominated strategy in a 2 x 2 game is cumbersome as compared to making the order of moves endogenous in an explicitly dynamic theory.

6. Technically, a Nash equilibrium is not a state but the strategies of players that produce this state. For convenience, however, I will usually identify equilibria—both Nash and nonmyopic—by their state (or payoffs at this state) rather than by the strategy pair that yields this state.

7. Other formal attempts to model surprise include Axelrod 1979b, which analyzes when a surpriser should use a resource for surprise whose value will be nullified or reduced once it is used. But Axelrod's decision theoretic model does not take into account the possible interdependence of decisions between a surpriser and the surprised player in a game, as I do here. In contrast, game theoretic models of deception (Brams 1977; Axelrod 1979a), misperception (Stein 1982), and verification (Brams and Kilgour 1988, ch. 8) do allow for two-sided calculations in games of imperfect or incomplete information, which may give rise to surprise even if the games do not model it directly. By comparison, here surprise arises not from incomplete information about payoffs but rather from incomplete information about the rules of play and rationality rules, discussed later in the chapter.

8. The numbers shown above each game are those given in the classification schemes of Brams 1994 and, in parentheses, Rapoport and Guyer 1966.

9. Specifically, this reversal eliminates R's incentive to move from the Nash equilibrium, because C will not countermove to (d_1, d_2).

10. Maoz and Felsenthal (1987) argue that R must make a self-binding commitment to induce the Pareto-superior (d_1, d_2) outcome in class I games. But this is unnecessary if the order of play is assumed to be endogenous, because it is in C's interest, too, that R move first. By contrast, a credible commitment is much more called for in class II games, which Maoz and Felsenthal do not analyze, because of the players' conflict of interests over the order of play.

11. The outcome (b_1, b_2) associated with the choice of s_1 by R and t_2/t_2 by C is also a Nash equilibrium. Thus (b_1, b_2)'s equilibrium status carries over from the 2 x 2 game, but its selection in the 2 x 4 game is dubious: It would require that R choose a weakly dominated strategy, forsaking his dominant strategy of t_2/t_1, associated with the (d_1, d_2) Nash equilibrium, which gives him a higher payoff than (b_1, b_2) in both class 1 and class 2 games.

12. Game theoretic models of successful deterrence, based on Chicken, are analyzed in Brams 1985 and Brams and Kilgour 1988; see also Zagare 1987 and Powell 1989.

13. The subsequent description of TOM, which also encompasses rules not discussed here that allow for cycling, threats, misperception, and the like, is adapted from Brams 1994, ch. 1.

14. Strategies may allow for sequential choices, as I showed in section two, but the classical theory does not make endogenous who moves first, as TOM does, but instead specifies a fixed order of play (simultaneous or sequential).

15. I do not use "strategy" in the usual sense to mean a complete plan of responses by the players to all possible contingencies allowed by rules 2–4, because this would make the normal form unduly complicated to analyze. Rather, "strategies" refers to the choices made by players that define a state, and "moves" and "countermoves" to their subsequent strategy switches from an initial state to a final state in an extensive-form game, as allowed by rules 2–4. For another approach to combining the normal and extensive forms, see Mailath, Samuelson, and Swinkels 1993.

16. An emendation in the rules of TOM that allows for backtracking would be appropriate in games of incomplete information, wherein players make mistakes that they wish to rectify. For more on possible rules changes under TOM, see Brams 1994.

17. Alternatively, players may be thought of as choosing strategies initially, after which they perform a thought experiment of where moves will carry them once a state is selected. The concept of an "anticipation game," developed later, advances this idea, which might be considered dynamic thinking about the static play of a matrix game. Generally, however, I assume that the term "moves" describes actions, not just thoughts, though I readily admit the possibility of the thought interpretation.

18. Where the players end up depends on the end state, or anchor, from which the backward induction proceeds, which I assume here (for reasons given in section three) is after one complete cycle. This assumption defines a finite extensive-form game, or game tree, to which I apply backward induction.

19. Actually, the result of backward induction by R from (1,1) in game 50 is (3,2) rather than (4,3). But as I argue in Brams 1994, p. 115, n. 20, the players would have a common interest in implementing the Pareto-superior (4,3) to (3,2)

when there is clockwise movement from (1,1). However, the implementation of (4,3) would require a binding commitment on the part of R not to move on from (4,3) to (2,4), which is not assumed possible in noncooperative game theory. I conclude: "I do not see an airtight case being made for either (3,2) or (4,3) as *the* NME from (1,1) when Column moves first, which nicely illustrates the nuances that TOM surfaces that the rules of standard game theory keep well submerged." Incidentally, game 50 is the only game of the 78 2 x 2 strict ordinal games in which this kind of ambiguity about NMEs arises.

20. Because the NMEs in games 27 and 28 are all the same, the strategies of the players in their anticipation games are indistinguishable, making all four states Nash equilibria. In the four other games, s_1 is R's (weakly) dominant strategy; C's best response leads to a unique dominant-strategy Nash equilibrium in each anticipation game. Only in game 49 is the Nash equilibrium in the anticipation game, [2,4], also the Nash equilibrium, (2,4), in the original game.

21. Even the choice of a dominant-strategy Nash equilibrium in the anticipation games offers no assurance that players will stay at this state. Indeed, except for one of the two [4,3] Nash equilibria in the anticipation game of game 50, the players will move from *every* Nash equilibrium in the six anticipation games to some different NME.

22. But naval intelligence discounted the "war warning," and it was expected that attacks would be on "either the Philippines, Thai, or Kra Peninsula [bottleneck of Malaya], or possibly Borneo." These quotations and much of my recounting are drawn from Morgan 1983, pp. 48–57.

23. Some analysts consider such noise ineradicable in a strategic conflict, making surprise attacks inevitable (Kam 1988), whereas others believe that it is not and, consequently, surprise can be significantly reduced (Betts 1982), at least when there is good threat perception and high-quality warning (Levite 1987; but see Bar-Joseph 1988). My view is that surprise becomes less surprising when viewed through the eyes of TOM, which uncovers the rationale for endogenous moves that are ignored in scenarios that postulate a fixed order of moves. Thus warnings that do not fit prescribed scenarios may be rendered more explicable by TOM, ameliorating the problem of noise, which I regard as much a theoretical failure—for want of intellectual tools to anticipate sequences of moves and countermoves—as the usual culprits blamed for detection failures: limited human cognitive abilities, psychological pathologies, problems in information processing, and impediments to organizational coordination.

24. Recall that a Japanese attack was anticipated (see n. 22), but not against Pearl Harbor, which I assume to be the target of attack in the Figure 6.3 matrix.

25. By the time of the Battle of Midway on June 4, 1942, seven months after the Pearl Harbor attack, the balance of forces (and intelligence) in the Pacific had changed, resulting in a decisive victory for Allied forces that spelled the beginning of the end of Japanese dominance in the region.

26. These ratings for the different players are based on different time frames: bad for the United States early, bad for Japan later. In the text I argue shortly that these different perspectives were those of the players at the time. What this game does not address are operational details of when, where, and how an attack might occur (see Kam 1988, pp. 20–21), though in principle such aspects of strategic choice could be incorporated into a more elaborate game theoretic model.

27. Maoz (1990c, pp. 169-192) observes that most surprise attacks in the twentieth century have resulted in the defeat of the attacker, who is typically the militarily weaker player trying to gain an advantage from surprise. A "paradox of

surprise" occurs when the attack leads to the disastrous defeat of the attacker by increasing the victim's resolve and willingness to endure hardships to bring about this defeat. The U.S. response to Pearl Harbor—rage and a burning desire for revenge—certainly fits this pattern, which Japan did not anticipate, hoping instead to stun the United States into paralysis, or at least docility about fighting a protracted war, which would lead to a negotiated settlement (Hybel 1986, p. 32).

28. Note that once Japan moves from $\overline{A}W$ to AW, this higher rating has no effect on the United States' rational countermove from AW to $A\overline{W}$.

29. Contrast this view with Winston Churchill's view that "a declaration of war by Japan could not be reconciled with reason" (quoted in Kam 1988, p. 72), which Kam uses to support his assertion that "surprise attack often works because it violates the rules of rationality." But what are *the* rules of rationality? A major contention of this chapter is that there are different sets of rules, and one set might work better or be more natural (e.g., those of TOM) in a situation than another.

30. After developing this game, I reread Maoz and Felsenthal 1987 and discovered, to my amazement, that they had used exactly the same game to model Sadat's peace initiative. However, their strategies focus on the concrete terms of the eventual peace treaty: for Egypt, to recognize or not recognize Israel; for Israel, to withdraw or not withdraw from the Sinai. They interpret Sadat's visit to Jerusalem as being a self-binding commitment to peace that was made especially credible by its public nature. TOM shows why Sadat moved first and why Begin responded as he did, but it says nothing about why Sadat felt it necessary to create such a public spectacle: Lacking the Israelis' trust, he wanted to convince them with a well-nigh irrevocable commitment to peace.

31. It is worth noting that Israel cannot induce (3,4) by moving first from (2,3) to (4,1), because Egypt would not countermove to (3,4). Thus TOM also explains why it was Egypt, not Israel, that had to seize the initiative that would break the deadlock at (2,3).

32. True, the United States benefited by responding militarily *after* the Japanese attack, but it would have done still better if there had been no attack and Japan, after the depletion of its oil reserves, had been forced to cease its military aggression, which is the Nash equilibrium in the 2 x 2 game.

33. My model, however, is that of a game that incorporates the choices of both players, whereas the surprise literature distinguishes two schools of thought: the "victim's school," whose "central goal is to uncover the factors that constrain a victim's attempt to avert surprise"; and the "surpriser's school," which "seeks to explain the means an actor is likely to use to deceive an adversary" (Hybel 1986, p. 3). A game may be seen as a way of combining these different perspectives in a payoff matrix, which links the strategies and preferences of both the victim and the surpriser.

34. It would have been foolish to pursue the faster Japanese fleet before the attack, which led Admiral Chester Nimitz, who became commander-in-chief of the Pacific Fleet three weeks after the attack, to remark: "It was God's mercy that our fleet was in Pearl Harbor on December 7" (quoted in Mueller 1991/1992, p. 175).

7

A Two-Level Analysis of War and Revolution: A Dynamic Simulation of Response to Threat

Marc V. Simon & Harvey Starr

The complex question of how civil and international conflict are linked has been the focus of significant study in international relations and conflict research for some decades (see Stohl 1980; Levy 1989). We have seen periodic calls for unifying the study of conflict across borders (Tilly 1985) because conflict in the two arenas is both similar in its manifestations and interconnected in its underlying processes. In addition, state decisions in both forms of conflict seek the same goal: security. Most and Starr (1989), Starr (1991a), and Starr and McGinnis (1992) have outlined a framework that captures the "common logic" of decisions states must make as they face the twin threats to security from the domestic and international arenas. In this chapter, which is part of a larger project that explores two-level security management, we examine the effects on state security of factors related to both system structure and policy choice. We outline a model of how states perceive and react to security threats and evaluate the implications of the model using computer simulation.

Our model is based on both rational and cognitive assumptions about how decisionmakers act. For simplicity, we treat governments as unitary rational actors.[1] The unitary actor assumption lends itself to the rational choice/game theoretic framework Tsebelis (1990) discusses as "nested games" and Putnam (1988) as two-level games. Each government faces challenges to security from other governments and domestic opposition groups alike; thus decisionmakers must manage two levels of security and deal with potential trade-offs in addressing threats on each level.

We also apply the ideas set forth in Most and Starr (1989) of opportunity, willingness, substitutability, and "nice laws." Our model allows states

131

to use several alternative policies to achieve security. Furthermore, we stress the willingness of decisionmakers to act; this willingness is necessarily based on how decisionmakers perceive the value of the status quo and the calculations of their adversaries. This emphasis on perception naturally brings cognitive elements into the model (as with other rational models, e.g., Bueno de Mesquita and Lalman 1992).

As in the bounded rationality approach Morrow discusses in Chapter 2, we assume that decisionmakers use cognitive shortcuts to determine when the utility of the status quo (in terms of security) warrants action. We define a set of simple comparisons of a state's capabilities versus risk that prompts action to address an unfavorable imbalance. In Schelling's (1978) terms, these are "micromotives" that drive decision processes. By distinguishing separate "triggers" for domestic and international security, however, we move toward the type of noncompensatory process described by Mintz (1993) and Mintz and Geva (Chapter 5), which posits that decisionmakers make choices by examining different dimensions of utility that may or may not compensate for each other. In particular, we agree with Mintz and Geva that the domestic politics dimension is separate from other considerations.

Our model adds to more standard realist models an awareness that domestic and international security are separate issues and that international security may not compensate for domestic security. However, our basic conclusions challenge a number of realist assumptions. We found that factors relating to decisionmaker choice generally have a greater impact on security than system structure. Domestic legitimacy, a factor ignored in realist models, emerges as central in managing the two-level security games.

AN OVERVIEW OF THE COMMON
LOGIC OF SOCIAL CONFLICT

Our model of the linkage between internal and external security is based on four components of a common logic (see Most and Starr 1989, ch. 5; Starr and McGinnis 1992):

1. C_i, state i's defense capacity against external threats;
2. R_i, the external risks faced by state i in the international system;
3. S_i, state i's domestic defense capacity, that is, the strength of the government in the face of domestic opposition;
4. T_i, the internal risk (threat) to the government from domestic sources.

Each of these components affects the *perceptions* that decisionmakers have of their state's viability or security. Viability is gauged on two levels:

external risk (*R*) and internal threat (*T*), each of which can have political, military, and economic components. Threat and risk are conceptually measured against the state's defense capacities, *C* and *S,* which reflect the military, coercive, economic, and political resources it can bring to bear against external challengers or internal opponents. Figure 7.1 depicts the relationships among the four factors.

Most and Starr (1989, ch. 5) developed sets of inequalities that represent government *i*'s goals. These goals are simply defined: strive to make $C > R$ and $S > T$, and make sure that the magnitude of the *C/R* and *S/T* ratios is maintained or increased over time. When decisionmakers perceive that $C < R$, $S < T$, or that the *C/R* or *S/T* ratios are getting worse over time, they feel vulnerable and take action to remedy the situation. These four ratios are the micromotives discussed above, which if triggered become the motors that drive decision processes.

These triggers, and the decisions that affect them, are linked via the two-level or nested games that decisionmakers play. Decisions to fix a $C < R$ situation have consequences for *S* and *T;* actions taken to lessen an $S < T$ problem may exacerbate a concurrent $C < R$ problem. To sort out these consequences, states must consider the effect of their actions for both domestic opponents and international challengers. Furthermore, those opponents and challengers make their own calculations about the relative utility of the status quo and the likelihood that they might win a war or revolution. International challengers are also faced with *C, R, S,* and *T*

Figure 7.1
Basic C,R,S,T Framework

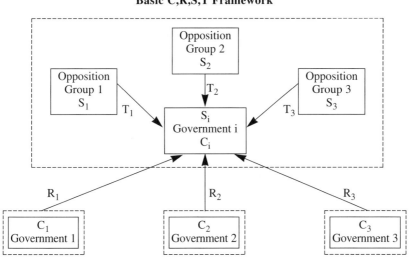

conditions of their own, adding a layer of complexity that makes it hard for decisionmakers to know the full consequences of their policies.

Putnam (1988, p. 427) has addressed this complexity as the "logic of two-level games":

> Neither of the two games can be ignored by central decisionmakers. . . . Each national leader appears at both game boards. . . . *The unusual complexity of this two-level game is that moves that are rational for a player at one board (such as raising energy prices, conceding territory, or limiting auto imports) may be impolitic for that same player at the other board* [emphasis added].

Because of the complexity of the games, decisionmakers might get caught in a series of remedial moves from one arena to another as the feedback from an action in one arena worsens the game in the other. The uncertainty Putnam (1988) and Tsebelis (1990) point out regarding actors' abilities to anticipate successfully the effects of their policies in both arenas raises issues for modeling choice, as Morrow outlines in Chapter 2. To account for this uncertainty, our model assumes that decisionmakers are Bayesian rational actors.[2]

THE THEORETICAL MODEL

Our model, outlined in Figure 7.2, assumes that governments choose between starting a war or maintaining the status quo and that domestic groups choose between intensifying their opposition or supporting the status quo. We assume that governments estimate the probability that other actors are willing to start a war or revolution by comparing the value of the status quo[3] with the value of war or revolution.

In this formulation a government will perceive that another actor is willing to go to war (or revolt) when the value of the status quo at time t is less than or equal to the value of war (or revolution). The government perceives more threat from another actor as (1) the frequency of interaction with that actor increases, (2) the relative capabilities of the actor increase, and (3) the willingness of the other actor to attack increases.[4]

Figure 7.2 summarizes the functional relationships in our theoretical model, which are developed in depth by Starr and McGinnis (1992). Different types of variables are sorted by column in Figure 7.2. Past resource allocation and extraction decisions result in the relative capability levels (C, S) that affect government i's perception of the probabilities (c, s) that j or k can defeat i in a war or revolution. These decisions also lead i to update its model of the goals of other players and the nature of their current relationships. From these models, i evaluates the expected utility that j or

Figure 7.2
Summary of Functional Relationships in the Model

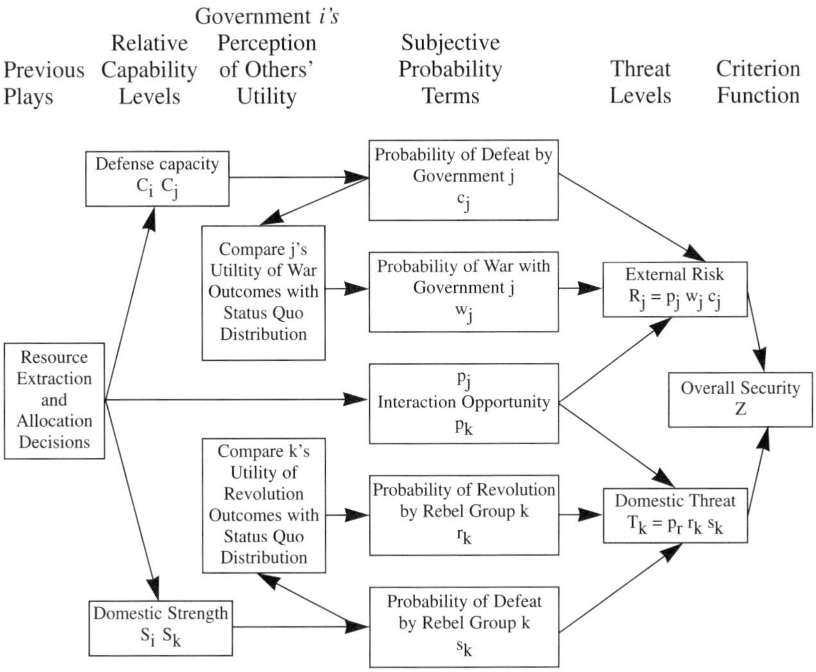

| | Government *i's* | | | | |
| Previous Plays | Relative Capability Levels | Perception of Others' Utility | Subjective Probability Terms | Threat Levels | Criterion Function |

Defense capacity
C_i C_j

Probability of Defeat by Government j
c_j

Compare j's Utiltity of War Outcomes with Status Quo Distribution

Probability of War with Government j
w_j

External Risk
$R_j = p_j\, w_j\, c_j$

Resource Extraction and Allocation Decisions

p_j
Interaction Opportunity
p_k

Overall Security
Z

Compare k's Utility of Revolution Outcomes with Status Quo Distribution

Probability of Revolution by Rebel Group k
r_k

Domestic Threat
$T_k = p_r\, r_k\, s_k$

Domestic Strength
S_i S_k

Probability of Defeat by Rebel Group k
s_k

k would receive from war or revolution and the status quo. Government *i* uses these to derive an assessment of the probability that war or revolution will arise (*w, r*) from each of its relationships. Interaction opportunities (*p*) reflect the relative frequency of interaction between *i* and other states *j* and oppositions *k*. These probability terms combine to form the aggregate external and domestic threat levels (*R, T*) posed by *j* and *k*. Finally, *i* compares its overall capability to threat ratios using some criterion function (*z*) that is used to determine *i*'s reaction to the current status of *C, R, S,* and *T.* We explain in the next section how these steps are implemented in the simulation.

CONSTRUCTING THE COMPUTER SIMULATION

To evaluate this skeletal model and explore its implications, we construct and analyze a computer simulation. We see this step of theoretical explication as a prelude to empirical application of the model to case studies and, perhaps at a later stage, to quantitative data.

We have taken note of the strengths and weaknesses of prior simulation studies (e.g., Cusack and Stoll 1990, 1994; Most and Starr 1989; Salert and Sprague 1980). We understand the limits to what simulations can tell us. However, with complex models that are not easily amenable to empirical or quantitative application, simulations are an initial means of checking whether the model has any internal inconsistencies, as well as exploring the nonobvious implications of the model for potential cases. We use simulation as a type of "plausibility probe" (Eckstein 1975) to determine what sort of empirical work is warranted. We also note the correspondence between the structure and results of the simulation to extant theory and findings, to help demonstrate the broader validity of the simulation.

Defense Capabilities (C), Domestic Strength (S), and Societal Resources (SOC)

Capabilities and strength denote a state's ability to resist external attack (C) or domestic opponents (S). Resources, both tangible and intangible, are extracted by i (from society, allies, or transferred between C and S) and can be applied to either C or S. These capability levels are complements: increases in C bring about increases (at a lower rate) in S and vice versa. Separating C or S allows each to be subject to a law of diminishing marginal returns; thus it costs more to increase C and S the larger they become. From the relative size of C_i and C_j, S_i, and S_k, state i makes some estimate of the likelihood that it would lose a war to j (c_{ij}) or revolution to k (s_{ik}) should that event occur.

To simulate capabilities in a state system, we assign states initial values based on a 100-point scale similar to that used in power indices (Taber 1989). It should be noted that the choice of a metric for C, R, S, and T is not that important since our theoretical model assumes that states are concerned with the C/R and S/T ratios that reflect *relative* capabilities.[5]

Each state in the system is also assigned a pool of societal resources (SOC) from which to extract. The size of this resource base is initially commensurate with the state's overall capabilities. SOC is assumed to grow at a fixed rate (1 percent) based on economic growth, but this growth rate is affected by extraction and allocation decisions, discussed later.

Interaction Opportunities (p) and Willingness (w,r)

We assign each state in the simulation a vector p_{jk} to represent its perception of interaction opportunities with other states (j) and rebel groups (k). These p values reflect i's view of the probability that an issue will arise where j or k might prefer to start a war or revolution with i. P is assumed uniform at the start of our simulation. Thus the systems we model consist of tightly networked sets of frequently interacting states.

Government i must also estimate whether in interactions over such issues, j or k will be *willing* to initiate a war or intensify a revolution. This "probability of willingness" is somewhat affected by the capability ratio between the actors but also by i's opinion of the "disposition" of the other players with regard to risk, hawkishness, and the like.

The domestic context of interaction and willingness is a bit different but still fits within the common framework. The concept of "willingness" is somewhat different for oppositions than for states. Applying the resource-mobilization perspective as the major "rational" explanation for opposition group behavior, rebel groups grow and decay, succeed and fail based on their ability to mobilize resources from society, much as our state i extracts them (Tilly 1978; Oberschall 1973). But rebel groups do not usually "choose" to rebel—they exist to rebel. The rebels are choosing strategies aimed at increasing their control over resources, since this determines the success or failure of their rebellion. If they fail to get resources, their rebellion will cease, regardless of the leadership's willingness to continue. So for oppositions, we conceive of their willingness (r) as willingness to intensify their rebellion, not willingness to rebel. In the simulation, each state is assigned a willingness vector w_{ij} containing its perception that opposing states will initiate war; a similar vector r_{ik} is assigned for the likelihood that existing rebel groups will escalate their rebellion.

Other rational analyses of rebellion (DeNardo 1985) as well as empirical work (Tilly 1978) reveal that government policies and levels of repression do affect the relative success of various rebel strategies of mobilization. This is modeled in our discussion of extraction and allocation decisions below.

Calculations of Risk and Threat

Following Figure 7.2, we use the following formulas for the total risk and threat faced by state i.[6]

$$R_i = \Sigma\, p_{ij} w_{ij} c_{ij}$$
$$T_i = \Sigma\, p_{ik} r_{ik} s_{ik}$$

Each state is assigned C and S values at the start of the simulation; these are used to calculate ratios of state i's capabilities and other states j and rebel groups k. The formulas are normalized to range from zero to one to represent i's view of its likelihood of victory in a war or revolution. Table 7.2 shows formulas and values for all simulation variables.

Conceptually, the three components of risk/threat follow Most and Starr (1989): opportunity (p), willingness (r, w), and power/capabilities (c,

Table 7.1 Baseline Values for Simulation Parameters

	Minor Power	Major Power (where different)
Defense capabilities	C = 50	C = 100
Domestic strength	S = 50	S = 100
Societal resources	SOC = 50	SOC = 100
Interaction opportunity	p = 0.80	
Willingness of major power to attack	w = 0.09	w = 0.06
Willingness of minor power to attack	w = 0.06	w = 0.03
Willingness of rebels to intensify rebellion	r = 0.05	
Initial strength of rebellions	S(reb) = 20	S(reb) = 40
Capabilities ratio: $state_i$-$state_j$ (calculated by simulation)	$c = 1-[C_i/C_i+C_j)]$	
Strength ratio: $state_i$-$rebels_k$ (calculated by simulation)	$s = 1-[S_i/S_i+S_k)]$	
Rebel mobilization rate	V = 0.01	
Probability of extraction for:		
increasing defense capabilities	H = 0.5	
increasing domestic strength	HH = 0.5	
Scapegoating/legitimacy	G = 0.02	
Frequency of ally extraction	E = 0.5	(50% of rounds)

Note: Standard simulation run length 350 rounds; results averaged over 100 runs.

s), which, they argue, is composed of elements of both opportunity and willingness.

DYNAMICS OF THE SIMULATION

Figure 7.2 does not specify the decision rule that states use to address security problems nor the effects of extraction and allocation decisions it takes to improve security. We explain this below and describe how it is implemented in the simulation.

Criterion Function (z)

We have explained how a state arrives at an estimate of the profile of threats it faces, but what does it do about those threats? A state cannot practically eliminate all threats, so what profile of threats should be considered optimal? Perhaps state *i* minimizes the sum of all its threats, but this might produce one very large threat and several small ones or a set of equally menacing medium-sized threats. Most states would rather have the second option. But rather than impose some ideal threat distribution as the goal of state action, we focus on their decision process as implied by bureaucratic politics and realist models of balancing behavior.

Looking at classic treatments of the balance of power, we see that one plausible interpretation of such models is to minimize the maximum threat. That is, the deterrence-based processes upon which the balance of power is built were aimed primarily at stopping drives toward hegemony. For example, in order to achieve the aims represented by the "rules" of Morton Kaplan's (1957) balance-of-power system, the power of the strongest state had to be counterbalanced. Balance-of-power models that were particularly concerned with the role of a "balancer" (almost always identified as Great Britain) also could be interpreted as models that call for the balancer to throw its weight against the most powerful state (or alliance). This would hold for both "power" and "threat." Stephen Walt (1987) argues that states form alliances in response to threat—aggregate power, proximity, offensive capability, and offensive intentions—not simply some measure of power. If Walt is correct that his formulation more adequately captures alliance formation and the dynamics of the balance of power (in terms of both balancing and the bandwagon effect), then we have a solid theoretical foundation for assuming that states move to minimize the maximum threat, looking not only at military capability but at proximity and intention as well (that is, opportunity and willingness).

Moreover, this strategy also minimizes decision costs for actors, consistent with bureaucratic politics and cybernetic models (Steinbruner 1974; Allison 1971) that motivate our assumption that decisionmakers act under bounded rationality. The nature of governments as complex organizations suggests a fairly simple decision rule that requires actors to focus their attention on only a small number of threats at a time, perhaps on only their single most pressing threat.[7] Thus our criterion function is based on the conceptual rule "minimize the maximum threat": State i tries to minimize the maximum value of all external risks (R_j) and domestic threats (T_k).

In the simulation, each government (i) is assigned values of C and S used to calculate the four inequalities that are its "triggers" for action.

1. C_i/R_i
2. $(C_{it}/R_{it}) / (C_{i(t-1)}/R_{i(t-1)})$
3. S_i/T_i
4. $(S_{it}/T_{it}) / (S_{i(t-1)}/T_{i(t-1)})$

Using our "minimize the maximum threat" rule, each state makes extraction and allocation decisions to address its threats. These decisions address the "worst" of the four ratios. Given that more than one may be bad at the same time, we have given priority to ratios (1) and (3), since they represent more of a problem than a one-round deterioration seen in (2) and (4). This rule assumes that government i can rank other governments and rebel groups according to the overall threat they pose and that i will concentrate its attention on reducing the threat posed by the actor most likely to have both the opportunity and willingness to attack and defeat i. However, this rule does not eliminate the strong possibility that efforts to reduce one threat may tend to augment other threats, the essence of the two-level security problem. If states are successful in sequentially reducing their most menacing threat, this might result in a system of equally capable and threatened state—an equal distribution of power. If some states are more successful than others, however, we should see a more accurate system of states with various threat profiles.

Resource Extraction and Allocation

Starr (1994) stresses resource extraction as a key factor in studying the complex nexus between revolution and war. A primary activity of the state is to extract resources in order to exercise authority, protect authority, and satisfy the demands of society. Governments under stress (whether from war or revolution) search for additional resources. Indeed a major theme in the revolution literature is that war weakens legitimacy and promotes opposition and dissent because it forces the government to extend and deepen its extraction of societal resources. The internal extraction of resources may provoke opposition because the increasing demands are not met with increases in benefits or economic performance; they may promote growth in existing rebellions as rebels find it easier to mobilize newly discontented citizens and otherwise gain resources from society. As discussed above, extraction of resources changes the value of the status quo, making resistance to additional extraction efforts increasingly likely.[8]

Yet extraction from society might create a cohesion effect from shared sacrifice in the face of an external (or separatist internal) threat (Stein 1976; Levy 1989). External extraction of resources can lead to "intersections" with other states seeking resources (to use Choucri and North's [1989] term), that is, increased interaction opportunities (p) for generating conflict. It can also lead to more interdependence, predictability, and trust as the mutual gain from trade relations improves both countries' economies. The problem, then, is for governments to maximize the acquisition of resources from society and international actors while minimizing the costs associated with that extraction.

We consider at least two basic possibilities for how extracted resources are used:

1. They can be added to capabilities to deter international or domestic challengers.
2. They can be allocated to those challengers in ways that improve the value of the status quo, thus reducing challengers' willingness to start a war (w) or intensify a rebellion (r).

In essence, we assume that a state either builds capabilities or buys off its potential opponents. Using these methods, government i reshapes the profile of security threats it faces, making some actors more threatening and others less threatening.

The extraction and allocation behavior of rebel groups is quite similar to that of the state, as we can see by applying the resource-mobilization perspective on revolutions and social movements (see also Lichbach 1994).[9] Resources allow oppositions to provide incentives that can overcome the free rider problem and increase mobilization. To the extent that the state can deny opposition groups these resources, oppositions decline in strength. When the balance of resources between state and opposition shifts in favor of the rebels, this also facilitates recruitment and mobilization in the opposition camp, since the plausibility of a rebel victory is greater.

Thus the ability of rebel groups to extract or mobilize resources is the main determinant of their success. Their ability to extract from society is determined by their existing resources and is highly affected by state coercion and the general legitimacy of government. Like states, rebels can extract to build their strength, or they can allocate resources by offering compromise, mitigating their demands, or choosing less violent strategies. Thus like states, oppositions can affect the degree of threat they face.

It should be noted that for simplicity, rebel group policies are represented in the simulation as being reactive to state policies; rebel actions are modeled based on the assumptions from resource-mobilization theory we have outlined.

Extraction and Allocation in the Simulation

Hawks and doves. First, how does a state decide whether to allocate or extract? Drawing on empirical discussions by Ikle (1971) and Barnet (1972), Simon (1991, 1994) has argued that governments have general dispositions toward either hawkish or dovish methods of solving their security problems. For our purposes in the simulation, we label the accommodating states that attempt to "buy off" their foes doves and extracting states that seek to build capabilities hawks. We assign states a hawkishness value (H), a probability used to determine whether they extract or allocate in a given interaction. Since states may treat internal and external threats differently, we assign a separate hawkishness value for international and domestic opponents. If $H_i = 1$, then the state always extracts; $H_i = 0$ means the state always allocates. In practice most states play both strategies ($0 < H < 1$); however, the consequences of extreme hawkishness and dovishness are one factor we examine in the simulation.

Allocation. Allocation involves "spending" capability and strength resources to improve the status quo, making opposing states less willing to go to war and rebel groups less willing to rebel. Therefore an allocation decision directly reduces C_i (or S_i) and also reduces w_{ij} (or r_{ik}), i's perception of j's willingness to go to war (or k's willingness to revolt). The amount of resources "spent" in an allocation decision is arbitrarily set to 3 percent of the current total of C or S; the effect on willingness, w or r, is a 3 percent drop.[10]

An allocation decision also brings domestic economic benefits, since extracting resources to build (military) capabilities is generally taken to be a drag on the economy (see Mintz and Huang 1991; Russett 1990a; Ward, Davis, and Lofdahl 1995; Mintz and Stevenson 1995). To account for this, the allocating state receives the full benefit of a 1 percent rise in societal resources (SOC) given to all states at the end of each round of interactions; the extracting state may receive less. Allocations are made to the state (or rebel group) that currently poses the most risk (or threat), following our "minimize the maximum threat" rule.

Extraction for defense capabilities. Resources can be extracted from domestic strength, society, or allies. In 50 percent of extraction rounds, states extract 1.5 percent of the resources from both S and SOC and add them to C.[11] Transferring resources from S to C worsens the state's S/T ratio but has few important effects beyond this. Societal extraction increases rebel mobilization (1 percent)[12] and reduces the pool of societal resources, which in the absence of extraction is assumed to grow at 1 percent per round.

Also, as noted above, societal extraction produces a further increase or decrease in rebel mobilization depending on the effect of the external threats facing the state. We assign states another dispositional variable (G) to denote the direction and magnitude of change in rebel group strength (S_k) and SOC that results from extraction. This "scapegoating" variable, which we argue is related to government legitimacy, is weighted by the seriousness of the threat faced by the government; thus if C/R is high, the additional effect of extraction on the growth of societal resources is low; if C/R is low, meaning the state faces serious threats to viability, then extraction from society has a greater additional effect on the growth of societal resources.

In 50 percent of extraction rounds, in addition to extraction from S and *SOC*, state i receives a fixed percentage (3 percent) of resources from its closest ally in the system (lowest w_{ik}); i then increases its exposure (p) with that ally by 3 percent[13] and its exposure to all other states in the system by 1 percent, thereby increasing its risk (R). The costs of the extraction to the ally are assumed to be negligible, because while the ally gives up resources, it also may gain from increased cooperation with state i.

Extraction for domestic strength. Extraction to build S involves similar processes and trade-offs as extraction for C. The same fixed percentages of resources can be extracted from external capabilities (C), society (*SOC*), or allies simply by substituting S/T for C/R in the discussion above.

We have now outlined the basic assumptions and formulas used to create the computer simulation of state behavior in the context of two-level security threats. Figure 7.3 provides a detailed overview of its design.

The design of the simulation allows us to create a variety of state systems, with varying numbers of states, major and minor powers, and rebel groups within each state. Each state simultaneously makes extraction and allocation decisions to address its current threat ratios. After all states have acted, new C, R, S, and T values are recalculated for each state in the system.[14]

SIMULATION RESULTS

Our results can be broken down into system-level structural issues and state-level strategy and process issues. We are interested in determining the relative effects of several variables on state security.[15] How does the system size or number of major powers affect security? Do strong states tend to maintain their advantage, or do systems tend toward equal distributions of power? We are curious about the effect of different strategies in general: Does hawkish extraction provide better security than dovish allocation? Under what conditions? Of the many factors we can manipulate in the simulation, which seems to produce the greatest benefits for states seeking security—alliances, legitimacy, low threats of revolution, or hawkish or dovish strategies? Finally, how do particular states survive the problem of simultaneous major threats to viability at the international and domestic level? Do we see oscillating behavior, as states' decisions to increase international security make them vulnerable domestically?

System Level: System Structure and Polarity

System size. We first examined the effect of the size of the system on the likely gain in domestic and international security. In order to assess this,

Figure 7.3
Simulation Flowchart

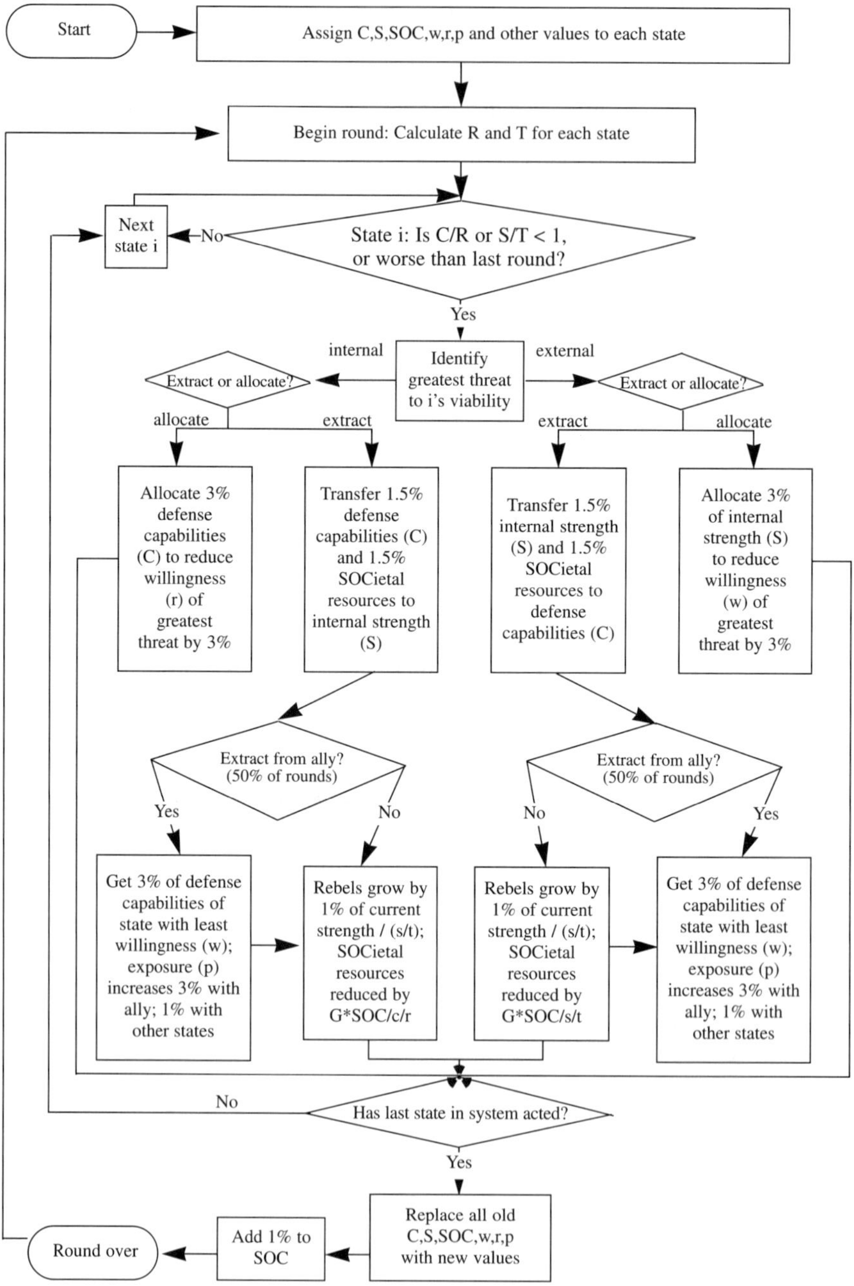
Start
Assign C,S,SOC,w,r,p and other values to each state
Begin round: Calculate R and T for each state
Next state i
No
State i: Is C/R or S/T < 1, or worse than last round?
Yes
internal
Identify greatest threat to i's viability
external
Extract or allocate?
allocate
extract
Extract or allocate?
extract
allocate
Allocate 3% defense capabilities (C) to reduce willingness (r) of greatest threat by 3%
Transfer 1.5% defense capabilities (C) and 1.5% SOCietal resources to internal strength (S)
Transfer 1.5% internal strength (S) and 1.5% SOCietal resources to defense capabilities (C)
Allocate 3% of internal strength (S) to reduce willingness (w) of greatest threat by 3%
Extract from ally? (50% of rounds)
Yes
No
Extract from ally? (50% of rounds)
No
Yes
Get 3% of defense capabilities of state with least willingness (w); exposure (p) increases 3% with ally; 1% with other states
Rebels grow by 1% of current strength / (s/t); SOCietal resources reduced by G*SOC/c/r
Rebels grow by 1% of current strength / (s/t); SOCietal resources reduced by G*SOC/s/t
Get 3% of defense capabilities of state with least willingness (w); exposure (p) increases 3% with ally; 1% with other states
No
Has last state in system acted?
Yes
Replace all old C,S,SOC,w,r,p with new values
Add 1% to SOC
Round over

we created systems where we varied the number of states while holding constant the initial *C/R* and *S/T* ratios as well as the other factors (frequency of extraction vs. allocation, legitimacy, source of extraction, willingness of other states to go to war, etc.) that affect the success of states in seeking security. Initial values of *C/R* (2.4) and *S/T* (1.9) make this a stable system with no state facing a serious initial threat to international or domestic viability.[16] Table 7.1 summarizes our findings.

Three trends emerge from Table 7.1: The more states in the system, the less gain in international security; the more states in the system, the more they gain in domestic security; and the more states in the system, the less the strain on societal resources used to achieve security.

These results are generally consistent with what we would expect in the real world. With more states in the system, it becomes more difficult for a state to manage the array of international threats. Allocation to buy off an adversary has less effect on total risk (*R*), since a state can buy off only one adversary at a time. Furthermore, building capabilities creates less relative gain in security in a larger system because the increase in capabilities is smaller relative to the total capabilities in the system; in addition, building capabilities is more likely to stimulate a counter-buildup in a large state system.[17]

We might have expected states to do better in improving their international security in a large system, since they would have more potential allies (and thus more ally resources) from which to extract. This did not occur, partly because a state extracts from only one ally at a time. Also, in order to hold the initial *C/R* ratios constant across systems, we had to augment the initial level of capabilities of states in the larger systems. For the twenty-state case, each state's initial *C*-value was 105; for the ten-state case, *C* was 50. We conclude that a system with more net capabilities is one in which states have a harder time maintaining security against international threats than a system with fewer capabilities.

The presence of more states in a system helps states reduce domestic threats. For domestic threats, additional states represent only potential ally

Table 7.2 Average Effect of System Size on Security Gains

Size of System	Change in C/R	Change in S/T	Change in SOC	
20 states	−0.35	10.1	−20.9	(−27%)
15 states	−0.18	5.8	−20.7	(−32%)
10 states	0.47	2.3	−18.0	(−36%)
5 states	3.04	−0.11	−18.2	(−51%)
3 states	10.2	−0.63	−18.7	(−62%)

Note: C/R = international security; S/T = domestic security; SOC = societal resources. Initial C/R and S/T ratios were constant across systems.

resources, whereas for international threats they represent both resources *and* additional threats. Domestic security thus improves when the size of the system increases.[18] In contrast, given the two-level logic of security, we might have expected states to do worse against domestic threats in large systems where their international security was more precarious. In fact, this did occur to some extent; subsequent runs demonstrate that states with high levels of international security can indeed more effectively build domestic security.

System polarity. Next we consider the impact of changing polarity on the security gains of states. Figure 7.4 outlines the patterns found using a ten-state system with zero to six major powers. The system size was chosen since it seemed the most neutral with regard to security gains from Table 7.1 above.

Figure 7.4
Security Gain by System Polarity

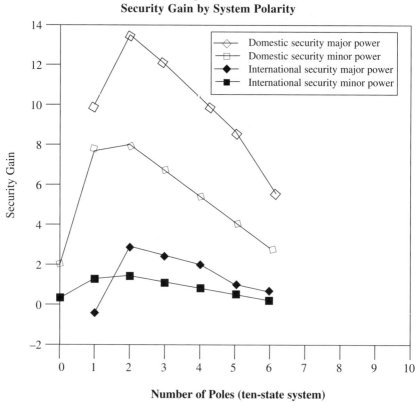

Number of Poles (ten-state system)

Note: Major powers have C, S, SOC = 100; minor powers have C, S, SOC = 50 (see Table 7.2 for standard values).

The trends apparent in Figure 7.4 reflect the conventional wisdom that polarity does matter and that unipolar, bipolar, and multipolar systems are different. The unipolar case is perhaps most striking for its implication that the major power loses international security; in fact this is the worst level of polarity for the major power (supported by the findings in Levy 1985). The result tends to uphold the notion that *hegemons decline,* a theme we have developed elsewhere (Simon and Starr 1996).

Bipolar systems tend to be the best for all states in terms of relative gains in both international and domestic security. This supports the familiar structural argument about the stability of bipolar systems relative to multipolar ones. Given the assumptions of our model, the reasons for this are many. Having more than one major power allows the major powers to form alliances with each other that yield extractable resources. Since the major powers have more resources than minor powers, this helps them gain security. But adding more major powers to a system increases the level of threat to all states. As the number of poles increases in multipolar systems, security gains diminish for both major and minor powers. It appears that the resources made available for extraction by adding major powers are overwhelmed by the additional threat posed by those capabilities as the number of major powers increases.

The stability of bipolar systems is even more striking in the domestic arena. At this point, however, we are unable to determine whether international security helps domestic security or the reverse. This result may indicate that external stability provides more resources for internal control or allocation and thus greater legitimacy. This result is also related to the democratic peace literature that indicates that stable domestic politics can generate stable international relations (see Russett 1993; Bueno de Mesquita and Lalman 1992; Simon and Starr 1995).

Given the results from Table 7.1 and Figure 7.4, we have chosen to use a tripolar, ten-state system as the baseline system from which we measure the effect of changing other variables relevant to states' success in the security game. This system appears to be the most neutral in terms of systemic affects on security.

State Level: State Strategies, Legitimacy, Willingness

Hawks and doves. As Figure 7.5 demonstrates, extraction and allocation strategies have important effects for the individual state and the system as a whole. The left side of Figure 7.5 shows that a hawkish strategy produces increases in security for both major and minor powers. Both achieve significant gains in security and capabilities, to the point where the major power hawk becomes a hegemon and the minor power hawk becomes a major power.

Figure 7.5
Security and Resource Changes in Systems with
One Hawk or One Dove

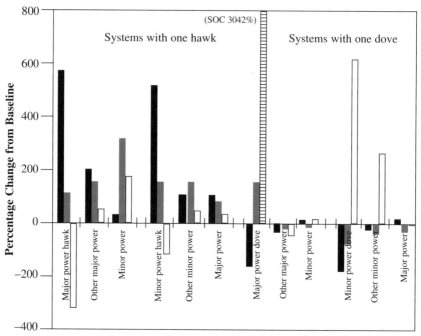

| ■ International security (C/R) change |
| ■ Domestic security (S/T) change |
| □ Societal resource (SOC) change |

Note: Hawks have 90 percent probability of extraction to build capabilities; doves 10 percent.

It is also apparent that the hawkish strategy has some troubling side effects. Hawks gain security at the cost of a severe depletion of societal resources. Further, other (nonhawk) states in the system also register impressive gains in both international and domestic security. In the hegemonic (major hawk) case, they do even better than the hawk in domestic security. Moreover, the other states gain societal resources while the hawk is losing them.

This process conforms extraordinarily well to conventional theories of hegemonic decline (Kennedy 1988; Gilpin 1981). The simulation shows that hegemons provide a stable international environment on which others can free ride; the extraction costs of producing such security eventually drain the hegemon while the free riders are building societal resources and enjoying high domestic security. As we demonstrate elsewhere (Simon and Starr 1996), a hegemon can decline in security and capabilities relative to challenger states solely through the overuse of a hawkish, extractive strategy to address its internal and external threats to security.

Hawkish, extractive strategies also have the effect of causing other states in the system to respond by building capabilities, creating a system with higher overall capabilities than the baseline case (+587 percent in the major hawk system, 326 percent in the minor hawk system). Again, this result conforms to classic descriptions of the security dilemma and balancing strategies (see Maoz [1990c, ch. 8] for an elegant discussion of the paradox of gaining extra power and how it can hurt a state). Systems with doves, on the contrary, produce a lower absolute level of defense capabilities in the system (–40 percent in the major dove system, –95 percent in the minor dove system). Allocative strategies create fewer capabilities for others to extract, making it less necessary and more difficult for other states to extract capabilities from the dove.

Finally, from the results in Figure 7.5 we conclude that dovish strategies tend to work better against domestic opponents than international ones, especially for major powers. This reflects the different effects of extraction in the domestic arena. Building capabilities does deter rebels, but it also increases their mobilization, thereby decreasing societal resources beyond what is extracted initially. As discussed in the following subsection, this problem is exacerbated if the state has low legitimacy.

Since allocation tends to build societal resources rather than deplete them, it seems desirable that states pursue a combination strategy: international extraction and domestic allocation. Figure 7.6 shows the results of "optimal"[19] levels of international extraction and domestic allocation that produce the best effects—security gains in both arenas, plus the flexibility provided by increased levels of societal resources and lesser gains by one's opponents in the system.

Figure 7.6 displays several interesting patterns. First, the domestic security gains achieved by this combination hawk/dove strategy were impressive for both major and minor powers; they exceed those of the pure hawkish and dovish strategies because the hawk/dove strategy maintains international security while providing societal resources that are effective in reducing domestic threats. In addition, the effects of this strategy on other actors in the system are negligible compared to the baseline strategy of 50 percent extraction. Major powers benefit more from the hawk/dove strategy in international security than do minor powers, but the minor hawk/dove still improves relative to other states in the system.[20]

Our conclusion regarding extraction and allocation strategy is that states achieve more security by being dovish to their domestic threats and

Figure 7.6
The International Hawk/Domestic Dove Strategy

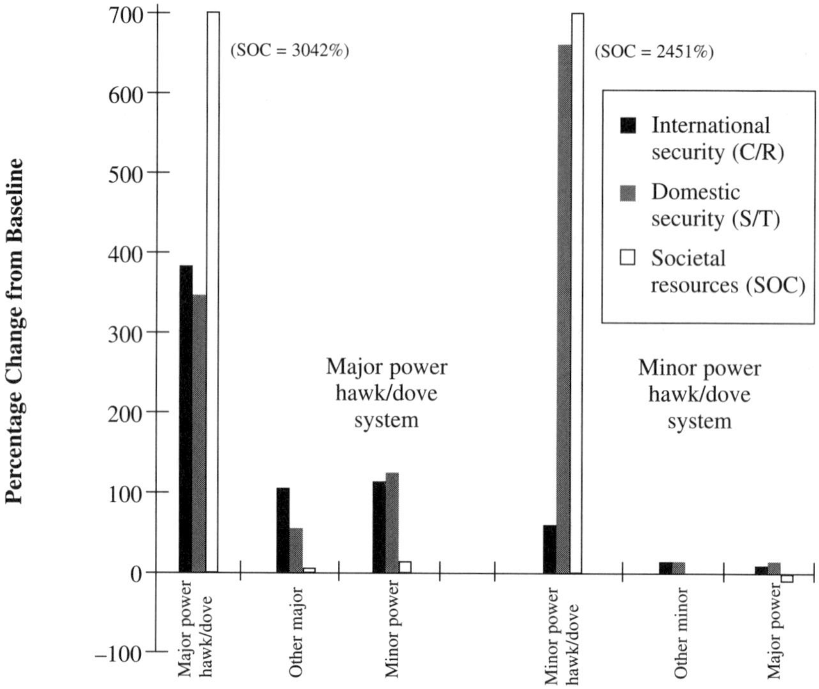

Note: Major hawk/dove extraction probability 80 percent for international threats and 5 percent domestic; minor hawk/dove extraction probability 95 percent international and 5 percent domestic.

hawkish to their international ones. This challenges our earlier assumption that states have a disposition toward hawkishness or dovishness that applies equally to both arenas. Yet it points to another reason why dictatorships may tend to lose viability over time. If a state is extractive both internationally and domestically, it may gain in the short run, but it becomes vulnerable on both fronts because of the strain on societal resources. As Wintrobe's (1990) model notes, eventually it makes economic sense for dictatorships to turn power over to more legitimate, civilian governments that can manage the economy better (and perhaps treat rebels more dovishly); yet in these cases (e.g., Brazil, Argentina, Chile) the military is often bought off by the civilian government's huge defense budgets.[21] This tactic helps keep the military out of domestic affairs and maintains an extractive, hawkish international policy—our hawk/dove strategy.

Legitimacy. As we would expect from the literature on revolution, legitimacy helps a state survive internal threats (see Starr 1994). It is not clear how strong an effect, if any, legitimacy has on international security.[22] Figure 7.7 reports our results.

Recall that we have operationalized legitimacy in the simulation as the effect of extraction on societal resources and rebel group mobilization. When highly legitimate states extract, they receive additional growth in societal resources as societal cohesion increases because of an internal or external threat. Extraction by states with low legitimacy reduces societal resources even beyond the amount extracted as citizens are alienated, grievances are increased, rebels mobilize, and further extraction becomes more difficult.[23] This cohesion or mobilization effect is weighted in the simulation: the greater state security, the less the effect, and vice versa.

Figure 7.7 shows the pronounced effect legitimacy has on the international and domestic security of states in our tripolar system. Legitimacy affects security by providing more societal resources than a state would otherwise have; this allows the state to use those resources either for building capabilities or for allocating to threats (see also Lamborn 1991). It is important to note that the added resources accrue only when a state extracts; thus dovish states gain less than hawkish ones.[24]

Willingness. Another variable that affects state security is the perceived willingness of other states to go to war. Most and Starr (1989, ch. 6) argue that willingness is a more crucial determinant of the frequency of war than system structure. Figure 7.8 shows the effect of changes in perceived willingness on a state's security, both domestic and international. We varied the baseline system's willingness settings by fixed percentages for one major power and then for one minor power and measured the effect on security.

Figure 7.8 reveals that perceived willingness affects the international security gains of both major and minor powers; however, it has a limited affect on minor power domestic security and no effect on major power domestic security. Willingness affects a state's security gains by changing its *C/R* ratio, which becomes worse as a state perceives others as more willing to go to war. These results show that a state's ability to gain security is dependent upon not just its resources, capabilities, and strategies but also its relative security at any point in time. This in part explains why only the minor powers saw any impact on their domestic struggles: They started from a more precarious *C/R* level (1.16 with willingness at +50 percent) than the major powers (6.4 at willingness +50 percent). It is noteworthy that no state began with a *C/R* ratio lower than one; thus we are studying a secure international environment. Even in this case, however, relatively minor changes in willingness produce very different gains in security.

Figure 7.7
The Effect Legitimacy Has on Security and Resources

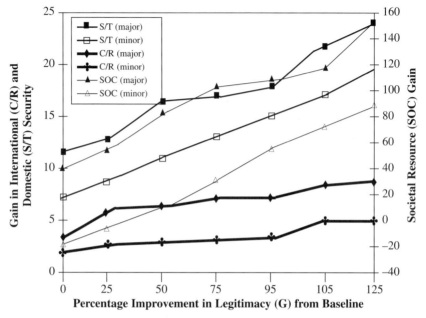

Percentage Improvement in Legitimacy (G) from Baseline

Figure 7.8
The Effect Willingness of Other States to Go to War
Has on Security and Resources

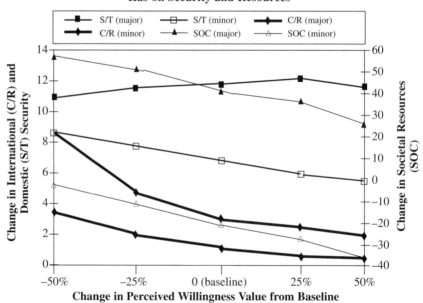

Change in Perceived Willingness Value from Baseline

These results are consistent with models of subjective expected utility in general and conflict spiral–security dilemma models in particular.

Evaluating Effects on Security

We have considered the impact of system size, polar structure, extraction and allocation strategies, legitimacy, and perceived willingness to go to war as factors that affect the security gains of states. Figure 7.9 attempts to illustrate their relative importance in the security game. The data in Figure 7.9 allow us to make only broad generalizations about the relative importance of these factors. It is nearly impossible to measure the effects of "comparable" changes in these variables. The particular baseline system and the relative values of variables may make some factors more significant than others. Still, we try to measure the effect of a 50 percent change in each factor and have found that these broad patterns hold up over a variety of baseline systems.

The size of the system seems most potent for both major and minor powers' *C/R* ratios. The next most potent includes willingness and the extraction strategy. The relative unimportance of system polarity is striking; this adds to Most and Starr's (1989, ch. 6) finding by demonstrating that willingness is more important than polarity for states' international security.[25]

For domestic security, the combination hawk/dove strategy has the most impact for both major and minor powers; legitimacy and polarity are in a second group of important factors. This is surprising in that we had expected legitimacy to be stronger for domestic security. In addition, it is surprising that polarity, a variable relating to system structure, would have a stronger impact on domestic security than on international security. We argue that this greater impact is due to the importance of ally extraction for success against rebellions; yet, as shown by the strength of the hawk/dove strategy, extraction is not the best way to deal with most rebellions. Friedman's (1993) study of Jordan is illustrative; Jordan availed itself of Israeli assistance in 1970 in order to defeat the Palestinians (*and* Syrians).

Regarding the growth of societal resources, for both major and minor powers the combination hawk/dove strategy is most important, with the hawk strategy second and legitimacy third. While again we had expected legitimacy to be stronger, the impact of the combination hawk/dove strategy implies that in the two-level security game, factors involving *choice* and policies over which a government has great control are more influential than factors relating to system structure and the other factors over which states have less or no direct control. This is a powerful statement of the importance of individual and governmental factors in foreign policy over systemic factors. Our conclusion is that states can have great control

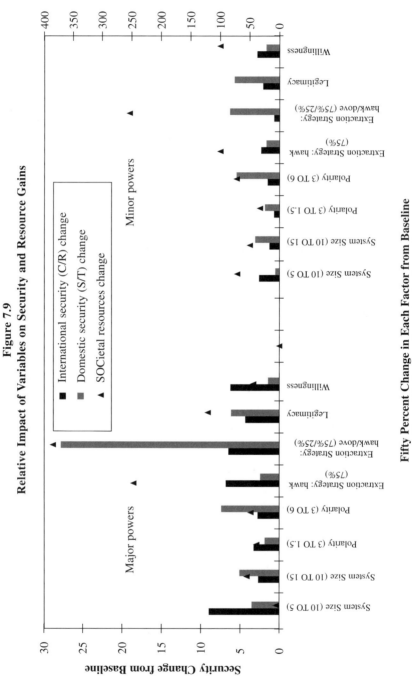

Figure 7.9
Relative Impact of Variables on Security and Resource Gains

over their destinies regardless of the system or the nature of other states and rebellions they face.

This conclusion must yet be tempered with the analysis of states that do not have the luxury of favorable *C/R* and *S/T* ratios as did most of the states in our systems so far. What happens when states are faced with serious threats? How do states play the international and domestic games together? The final section analyzes the course of security games for single states over time.

States with Serious Threats to Viability

To examine the interplay of domestic and international threats to viability, we created states with poor *C/R* and *S/T* ratios (less than one) and observed whether states do in fact make trade-offs between domestic and international viability. We found that this oscillatory behavior is most pronounced in dovish states facing threats to viability.

The enduring existence of states such as Switzerland or Sweden in the face of domestic and/or international threats poses the question of how such states survive over time in the international system. While any state facing threats to viability trades gains in international security for domestic security and vice versa, dovish states have more difficulty since this strategy takes longer to produce international security in the systems we examined.

Figure 7.10
Security and Resources over Time for Weak Dovish State

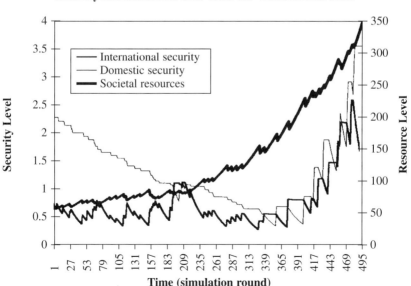

Figure 7.10 pictures a state with domestic security and international insecurity. It begins with *C/R* less than one and *S/T* greater than two. To address its international threats, the state transfers resources from society, domestic strength, and allies. After about 200 rounds, we see that *C/R* finally responds by edging over unity. However, once again reflecting the two-level trade-offs that are central to our arguments, the stress on *S/T* created by reducing domestic strength, as well as the stress of extraction (minimized in this case since the state pursues a dovish strategy) continue to push the *S/T* ratio downward below unity. Fortunately, by this time our state has built enough societal resources to recover in spite of its continued low level of capability and strength.

The key to recovery is the growth of societal resources due to the pursuit of a dovish strategy. In lieu of this strategy, states can also increase societal resources by having the good fortune of high legitimacy (e.g., see Jackman 1993). Barring this, however, if the state uses up its societal resources through too heavy a reliance on extraction (or illegitimacy), it will not recover.

CONCLUSION

We have outlined a theoretical framework for analyzing the impact of two-level security games states play. Applying the theoretical ideas of Most and Starr (1989), Starr and McGinnis (1992), and Starr (1994), we constructed a computer simulation to examine the factors that affect the security of states in various international systems. The simulation helped us to verify the internal consistency of the model by demonstrating that its implications are consistent with much theory and research in international relations, especially that which supplements or fills in gaps left by the inadequacies of realism. It has also produced some interesting results that may have been missed by those focusing on either the domestic or international security game in isolation.

Increasing the size of a system tends to increase domestic viability while making it more difficult for states to remain viable internationally. Bipolar systems proved to be the best environment for all states to improve international and domestic security; unipolar systems are most difficult for major powers seeking to improve international security. While system structure had some effect on international and especially domestic security, we found that the strategic decision of how often to extract versus allocate, what we labeled "hawkishness" and "dovishness," was among the most important ways for states to improve or decay in security. Factors relating to choice, such as hawkishness and the willingness to go to war, were generally more important than the structure of the system in producing security.

States that have serious threats to viability must, in the absence of generous allies, find ways to increase the growth of societal resources or face decline. One important argument that emerges, and that would be all but ignored by realist analyses, is that domestic legitimacy is a core underlying factor crucial for success in the two-level security game (since it directly affects societal resource levels when states extract). Both weak and strong states can survive threats to viability if they can build and maintain a strong societal resource base.

NOTES

A considerable number of people have commented on a set of papers—initially Starr (1990, 1991a, 1991b) and later Starr and McGinnis (1992)—that outline and develop the general concerns, shape, and theoretical foci of the relationships between revolution and war, internal and external conflict. We wish to acknowledge and thank all of these individuals for their input, especially Mike McGinnis, for his participation at various points of this project. Marc Simon also wishes to thank the political science department and the Center for Governmental Research and Public Service at Bowling Green State University for support of this project.

1. Of course we could drop the unitary actor assumption and analyze the security problem as perceived by various factions or individual leaders within that government, but in this chapter we do not address the additional problems of social choice that would arise from this more complex representation.

2. For further justification of this Bayesian approach to game theory, see McGinnis 1991, 1992; McGinnis and Williams 1991, 1992, 1993; Williams and McGinnis 1991.

3. We conceive of the status quo as a dynamic, uncertain relationship whose utility can change over time for each actor. We think of the current utility value of the status quo as a random selection from an overall distribution of possible utility values. The shape of that distribution changes for different types of relationships with different types of actors; for example, allies have a higher mean utility value from their status quo relationships than adversaries.

4. The inspiration for this formulation is our conviction that wars and revolutions do not just "happen" but emerge from some specific situation or issue at a particular point in time. In retrospect we can often separate events that start a conflict from its underlying causes. Those underlying causes are represented as the relationship formalized by the status quo distribution.

5. Likewise, though we began with willingness values of approximately 0.02–0.10 for w and 0.01–0.10 for r, calculated using Correlates of War data for the likelihood that a state will be involved in a nation-month of war in a given year (Small and Singer 1982, pp. 129, 263), this metric is not crucial to our analysis at this stage.

6. In practice these will yield some small fraction between zero and one; to convert them to a metric similar to that which we assign to C and S, we multiply R and T by an appropriate constant (1,000).

7. In reading the memoirs of high-level decisionmakers, one is struck by the extent to which the flow of daily events dictated policy and choice, the limited number of issues that could be attended to at any one time, and the constant attention

to "putting out fires" as they arose. See Kissinger 1979, and especially Acheson 1969.

8. One manifestation of this phenomenon is the reaction to the military draft, as occurred in the New York draft riots during the American Civil War or in the changing levels of resistance to the Vietnam War.

9 . The resource-mobilization perspective explains the growth, decline, success, and failure of opposition groups largely by their success in extracting and utilizing resources. Resources are generally extracted from societal sources but can also be obtained from the state; oppositions with good organization, leadership, ideologies, loyalty, resistance strategies, and coercive resources tend to use their strength to mobilize more resources and thereby increase their resistance.

10. We could complicate the situation by deriving formulas for an "optimal" allocation given the current status of the four ratios, the size of the threat, and so on. However, we argue that states are operating under uncertainty and that the bureaucratic environment of decisionmaking lends itself to incremental decisions (Allison 1971; Lindblom 1959); thus a small, standard allocation increment makes sense.

11. Thus in a typical round, where state i does not extract from allies, it gets roughly a 3 percent boost to C, a value that approximates the 3 percent willingness reduction gained from allocation. Our goal was to make extraction and allocation roughly equivalent in their immediate effect on security, though if ally resources are used, extraction does have an advantage.

12. This 1 percent increase to rebel mobilization is divided by the state's S/T ratio, so that, following resource-mobilization theory, rebels find it more difficult to mobilize when the balance of resources favors the state.

13. This increase is 3 percent of the difference between the current p-value and one; thus interaction opportunities are capped and cannot grow indefinitely.

14. It is important to note that unlike Cusack and Stoll 1990, 1994, the simulation does not count revolutions or wars or allow for the elimination of some states, nor does the simulation dramatically change when any of the four ratios above is less than one. The simulation models states' reactions to threat and the consequences of those reactions in a continuous fashion.

15. Except where noted, the simulation uses standard values for all the parameters in the model. These are listed in Table 7.2.

16 . The simulation was generally limited to 350 rounds in order to maintain some variation in interaction opportunities (at 500 rounds most states had created a maximum exposure to the system, $p = 1$).

17. Returning to the validity of the simulation, this result is fully consistent with the arguments in the literature concerning the level of uncertainty and lack of stability in a multipolar system. Such effects range from Caplow's (1968) discussion of the instability of triads, to the many studies indicating the greater *frequency* of war in multipolar systems (e.g., Haas 1970; Midlarsky 1989), to the broad theoretical analyses indicating the weaknesses of multipolarity compared to bipolarity by theorists such as Waltz (1964, 1979).

18. One might speculate that increased system size also helps domestic security because we have limited the number of rebel groups to two, thereby limiting the potential growth of rebellion. However, the benefits of ally extraction overwhelm this effect. Each extraction to build domestic strength brings about a 1 percent increase in total rebel strength (1 percent for each rebel group—no matter how many groups) and reduces societal resources. Each extraction also increases S by 3 percent of the resources in C and SOC. Combined with this, in 50 percent of the

rounds a state extracts an additional 3 percent of an ally's *C*. Because the state's own *C*, *SOC*, and the ally's *C* are generally larger than the rebels' *S*, the extracting state generally gets more resources from extraction than the rebels do with their 1 percent growth.

19. Optimal values for the likelihood of extraction and allocation were calculated by trial and error, and they represent "optimality" only within the constraints of this tripolar system with all of its particular characteristics.

20. Again, we can find empirical support for the findings generated by the simulation. Friedman (1993, 1994) finds many of these patterns in his case studies of domestic and foreign conflict in Jordan and Iraq since the 1960s.

21. Military expenditure data from the Stockholm International Peace Research Institute (1995, ch. 12) show that for Chile military spending remained high and slightly increased in the five years after a civilian government took power in 1989; for Brazil, military spending sharply increased for five years after the civilian government took over in March 1985 and then began a marked decrease; and for Argentina, military spending remained fairly constant during the 1984–1989 period after the civilian government took power and then notably declined thereafter. This suggests that the hawk/dove strategy may be especially useful for the first few years after a transition from military rule but perhaps not so necessary once civilian control is firmly established.

22. Indeed a major theme in the revolution literature is that war weakens legitimacy and promotes opposition and dissent because it forces governments to extend and deepen extraction of societal resources. As governments seek to take greater resources from society, resistance is generated. Tilly (1975) argues that the extraction of men, supplies, and especially taxes to meet the needs of war promotes resistance from both the masses and elites. War also weakens legitimacy if the government loses (see especially Bueno de Mesquita, Siverson, and Woller 1992). Friedman (1993) demonstrates this in his discussion of Hussein's relationship with the Palestinians after defeat in the 1967 war.

23. For example, Friedman (1994) discusses how, in regard to the Iraqi Kurds, Saddam Hussein retreated from extraction to allocation after the onset of the Iran-Iraq War.

24. An interesting finding not shown in Table 7.4 is that other states in the system are only negligibly affected by the gains in our legitimate state's security and resources. This contrasts to the marked side effects of pure hawkish and dovish strategies on other states in the system. It can be explained in part by the fact that the legitimacy advantage does not affect a state's extractive or allocative behavior, only its capability ratios (see also Bueno de Mesquita and Lalman 1992 and their discussion of hawks and doves and system conflict).

25. It should be noted that the Most and Starr (1989) simulations were constructed from an entirely different framework than those carried out here. They did not use the *CRST* framework and were concerned more with analyzing the relative importance of preponderance/equality of power ratios, system structure, and willingness to go to war with regard to the frequency of war.

Part 3

The Cognitive-Rational Discourse: An Appraisal

8

Decisional Stress, Individual Choice, and Policy Outcomes: The Arab-Israeli Conflict

Zeev Maoz

The debate between cognitive theorists and rational choice theorists on the question of which model best explains actual decisionmaking on war and peace has been as permanent as it has been inconclusive.[1] Indeed in the manner that the issue was framed—are people rational or not?—it is difficult to resolve the problem. In recent years, however, it has been suggested that decision behavior is context-dependent (Maoz 1990b). Specifically, the kind of model (or combination of models) that best characterizes actual decisionmaking is a function of a number of factors. The factors that are said to affect decision behavior vary depending on the level of analysis employed. Certain factors are of major importance at the level of individual choice; others assume a significant role at the group level.

For example, one integrative model of choice behavior (Maoz 1990b, ch. 7) posits that individual decision behavior is affected by situational factors, personality factors, and organizational role. Group behavior is affected by the formal and informal structure of the group, group polarization as seen through the distribution of individual preferences, and situational variables. A key issue in decision analysis concerns the relationship between process and outcome. Specifically, the question is, Which types of decision behaviors are associated with which outcomes? Very few studies have addressed this issue (e.g., Herek, Janis, and Huth 1987; Janis 1989; Maoz and Astorino 1992b). Generally speaking, these studies showed a consistent relationship between rational/analytic decision behavior and decisional outcomes. A similar kind of generalization was made by Bueno de Mesquita and his associates (e.g., Bueno de Mesquita 1981; Bueno de Mesquita and Lalman 1992), who assumed that national decisions on war and peace issues can be seen as if they were made by a unitary rational actor, in order to avoid the paradox of voting that arises in attempting to aggregate individual preferences into social choice functions. However, all these studies were conducted at the group level. Individual decisionmaking was aggregated to generate a group decision process. The outcome of this process was then related to the decisional outcome. The factors affecting individual choices and the relationships between individual choices and national outcomes have not been explored empirically. Accordingly, the aims of this chapter are:

1. To explore how situational factors affect individual choices.
2. To examine the relationship between individual choice behavior and national decision behavior.
3. To assess the extent to which a relationship exists between the strategies of decision employed by individual decisionmakers and the strategies of decision used by national decisionmaking bodies.
4. To the extent that any of the previous questions leads to meaningful conclusions based on empirical evidence, to discuss the implications of these findings for the rational-cognitive debate in international politics.

In order to pursue these aims, I first outline some of the principal theoretical ideas dealing with the factors affecting individual choice and group behavior and the nature of these processes. I then describe a model developed in an earlier study (Maoz 1990b), the theory of international processes (TIP). Third, I discuss the research design and present the empirical findings. Finally, I draw implications for the rational-cognitive debate in international politics.

STRESS AND DECISION BEHAVIOR

The concept of stress is central in cognitive and social psychology. It refers to a situation or a stimulus "that is appraised by the person as taxing or exceeding his or her resources and endangering his or her well-being" (Lazarus and Folkham 1984, p. 19). Typically, stress is equated with threat perception and time pressure (Brecher and Geist 1980; Holsti and George 1975). However, as I have argued elsewhere, opportunities can invoke as much stress as can threats, suggesting that decisional stress is to be seen as "a combination of three factors: perceived threat, perceived opportunity, and time pressure. Threats and opportunities represent motivational antecedents of decision behavior, while time pressure represents practical constraints" (Maoz 1990b, p. 318).

Since the early stages of theoretical analysis of the decisionmaking process, students of foreign policy have emphasized that decision behavior is affected by the components of stress.[2] Both the perceptual definitions of foreign policy crises (cf. Brecher 1993, pp. 2–25) and the early studies of crisis decisionmaking (e.g., Hermann 1969; Holsti 1972) noted that decision performance goes down as threat, surprise, and time pressure go up. Researchers therefore inferred that there exists an inverse relationship between threat perception and decision behavior as well as between time pressure and decision behavior. However, subsequent research, based principally on findings from organizational behavior and cognitive psychology, revealed that reduced decision performance can take place both at very low and very high levels of threat and at very low and very high levels of time pressure. This led to development of the inverse U curve hypothesis, which posits a curvilinear relationship between threat (and time pressure) and decision performance; low decision performance is observed both when decisionmakers perceive little or no threat and when they perceive high levels of threat, while improved decision performance is most likely to be observed when decisionmakers perceive moderate threats (or time pressure).

This hypothesis is predicated on the following logic (Maoz 1990b, ch. 7): At very low levels of threat (or opportunities), decisionmakers treat problems as routine and not sufficiently important to warrant close scrutiny. Time constraints are not high, and decisionmakers tend to do one of two things: They either put the problem aside and deal with issues that are more pressing or resort to routine, cut-and-dried solutions. Thus decisionmaking tends to be noninnovative and incremental.

At very high levels of stress, cognitive functioning is impaired by severe threat and extremely short time spans for solving what seem to be insurmountable problems. The burden of decision often forces decisionmakers to resort to cognitive conflict-reducing mechanisms and oversimplifications designed principally to help decisionmakers cope with their own psychological reactions rather than with the problems they face. Decisionmaking tends to be highly emotional at these levels of stress.

Moderate levels of stress are characterized by sufficient levels of cognitive arousal that demand direct and fairly immediate cognitive attention from the decisionmakers and involve time for careful consideration of options. Because the problems seem important yet not cognitively paralyzing and time is sufficient but pressing, decisionmakers can explore multiple options to process information more efficiently and accurately and to make value trade-offs while evaluating options.

Stress may have different effects on different people. Personality makes a major difference in terms of the ability to cope with the disruptive effects of stress on performance. By and large, however, the performance of most types of people is said to vary with levels of decisional stress in much the same way. For example, it is often hypothesized that the decision behavior of cognitively complex individuals is more adaptive and sophisticated than the decision behavior of cognitively simple people. The tendency of the former type toward rational/analytic decision strategies is more pronounced than that of the latter type. Yet when considered in interaction with decisional stress,

> it is not generally true that highly complex individuals are more predisposed toward analytic choice behavior than cognitively-simple ones across different levels of decisional stress. Cognitively-simple individuals might be more inclined toward analytic choice behavior under medium stress than cognitively-complex individuals would be inclined toward analytic decision making under very low or very high levels of stress. This proposition suggests that, when taking into account the personality types of the decision makers under examination, there will be two parallel inverse U-shaped functions relating decisional stress to decision behavior. The lower function will display the relationship between stress and decision behavior for cognitively-simple individuals and the upper function will display the same relationship for cognitively-complex individuals (Maoz 1990b, p. 334).

Decisional stress is typically said to affect the procedural quality of decision, that is, the kinds of rules decisionmakers employ in order to place themselves into a position of choosing between or among alternatives. Indicators of procedural quality include the number of alternatives explored, the number and nature of outcomes assigned to each alternative, the number of value dimensions used to evaluate alternatives, and the extent to which people use various mechanisms to simplify, downgrade, or eliminate any value conflict invoked by the decision problem. In turn, the procedural quality of decision is said to affect the substantive quality of the decision, that is, the extent to which a given decision yields, on average, acceptable outcomes for the decisionmaker.

In the empirical study of foreign policy, we lack concrete evidence on the relationship between stress (and its components) and substantive decision quality. The attempts to study these relationships have been few and far apart (Saris and Gallhofer 1984; Maoz 1990b, pp. 335–338), and the findings have been mixed at best. The relationships among stress, choice behavior, and substantive quality have not been explored in a quantitative context, to the best of my knowledge.

THEORY OF INTERNATIONAL PROCESSES: AN OVERVIEW[3]

The theory of international processes is composed of four layers that explain how microlevel factors such as individual preferences of political leaders are transformed into macroexplanations of the relations between states. The following is a brief overview of the key ideas of the theory at each of the four layers. The present study emphasizes the first layer of the theory. Maoz and Astorino (1992b) analyze aspects of the third and fourth layers of the theory.

Individual and Group Choices Within States

The first layer of TIP attempts to account for the processes by which individual political leaders choose among varied national policy options. Briefly, we perceive the need to make a decision when an expected or desired state of affairs diverges from the actual one (Burnstein and Berbaum 1983, p. 536). Once this is recognized, the decisionmaker assesses, either explicitly or subconsciously, the threats and opportunities presented by the new situation. The strategies individuals use to diagnose and solve problems are a function of environmental factors (such as decisional stress and the ambiguity of the situation), psychological factors (e.g., cognitive complexity and tolerance of ambiguity), and organizational factors (e.g., the individual's role in the decision group). Thus TIP claims that the kind of decisionmaking model an individual uses to develop preferences over policy options is a function of the interplay of variables on a number of levels.[4]

As noted above, TIP posits an inverse U-shaped relationship between decisional stress and the procedural quality of individual choice. Low and high levels of stress tend to induce defective decision processes; moderate stress levels are associated with high-quality decisionmaking. Similarly, individuals with high levels of cognitive complexity tend, on the average, toward analytic choice behavior, whereas individuals characterized by low cognitive complexity tend toward cognitive decisionmaking behavior. TIP also focuses on substantive differences in decisionmaking behavior resulting from an individual's organizational role. Individual decision processes result not only in the choice of a particular course of action or inaction but in a preference ordering of the various policy options. This ordering of options becomes a key input to group decisionmaking.

The second layer of TIP deals with the aggregation of individual decisionmakers' preferences into a single national policy decision. Group-level perception of the decision situation is some weighted aggregation of individual perceptions. Thus situational and psychological conditions affect group decision processes in much the same way they affect individual decisions. In addition, group decisions are affected by the diversity of individual preferences and by the formal structure of the group. The higher the degree of group polarization, namely, the extent to which group participants differ in their initial preferences over policy options, the higher the quality of group decision. Likewise, the more egalitarian (and the less hierarchical) the formal structure of the decisionmaking group, the more analytic the decision process.[5]

National Choices and International Outcomes

A key argument of TIP is that for two prime reasons well-founded evaluation of individual and group foreign policy making cannot be done at the single-nation level. First, in order to properly assess national decision-making, we must judge the decisions and relate them directly to their outcomes (Herek, Janis, and Huth 1987; Janis 1989). However, the outcomes of national decisions are based on the actions of a number of states; they are *international* in nature. This implies that developing an objective benchmark of decision quality in foreign policy settings requires, at the least, specification of the extent to which decisions taken were the best under the circumstances. This in turn necessitates some objective outline of those circumstances.

In addition, the outcomes of national decisions may be favorable or not depending not only on what those decisions were but also on the simultaneous actions of other actors. It is possible to make a terrible decision but get a favorable outcome because an opponent made an even worse decision. In contrast, some situations are structurally immune to good decisions. Game theory is replete with such pathological cases. Actors playing a single-iteration Prisoners' Dilemma, for example, will get a good outcome if they make bad (irrational) decisions and a bad outcome if they make good (rational) decisions. In the Prisoners' Dilemma, the only "rational" choice of each player is to defect (or betray the other player), regardless of what the other player is expected to do. But this decision does both players in. Each gets his or her second-worst outcome. Had they chosen "irrationally" to cooperate with each other (that is, not to betray), they could have received their second-best outcome, an outcome that is both individually and collectively superior to the "rational" outcome of the game. This clearly suggests that the relationship between "rational" decisionmaking and "good" outcomes is not as straightforward as one may suspect.

Thus the third layer of the theory focuses on the analysis of the relationship between the national policy decisions made by each state and the outcomes of interstate events. The key concept of this analysis is the notion of an international outcome. An international outcome is defined as an intersection of the choices of two or more actors in an interdependent setting. The essence of such an analysis is a comparison between an actor's perception of that outcome and some objective notion of the "real world."[6] The notion of objective reality is a complicated one. It may be subject to biases, and one may even argue that it is impossible analytically to describe objective reality. However, TIP offers such a notion of objective reality based on a combination of actors' self-perceptions. In order to understand the meaning of the concepts of objective and subjective reality, consider the structure of an "international game" as defined by game theory.

TIP uses game theory as a framework for representing both the objective features of an international outcome and its "objective" structure. An international game is defined by four variables: players, alternatives, preferences, and rules of play. The players are the actors involved in an international situation. Alternatives define the courses of action available to each of the players. The intersection of any set of players' alternatives defines a possible outcome in the game. The number of outcomes is simply a product of the number of players and the number of alternatives available to each. Preferences are defined by players over the set of outcomes and represent players' valuation of these outcomes. The valuation of outcomes could be defined in terms of cardinal utility or in terms of ordinal rank ordering of outcomes from best to worst. The rules define the parameters within which the games are played. Rules of play include such issues as simultaneous versus sequential games, games of complete information versus games of incomplete information, single-play versus multiplay games, and so forth. For example, in simultaneous games actors make decisions at the same time and in ignorance of their opponents' decisions; in sequential games one player moves first and the other chooses strategies knowing what the opponent has selected. Games of complete information are those in which the players know the alternatives available to their opponents and the preferences of the opponents over the resulting array of outcomes. In games of incomplete information, the players typically know the alternatives available to their opponents but do not know for sure their opponents' preference orderings of those outcomes. Each of these four elements has a profound impact on how a given game is played and on its outcome.

TIP approaches the task of relating national choices to international outcomes by distinguishing between objective and subjective games. A subjective game describes the decisional situation from a single nation's vantage point. Specifically, in defining a subjective game, TIP attempts to answer five questions regarding an actor's perception of reality:

1. What are my alternatives in a given situation?
2. Who are the other instrumental actors in that situation?
3. What are the alternatives each of the other actors is considering?
4. What are my preferences over the outcomes formed by intersecting my possible choices with the possible choices of other actors?
5. What are each of the other actors' preferences over those outcomes?

This outline of the subjective environment allows one to describe in many but clearly not all cases the structure of a given decision problem and the substantive considerations responsible for a given decision (Maoz 1990b, pp. 423–431).

An objective game is based on a notion that "reality" in situations of decisions under interdependence, wherein each actor's choice depends on the choices of other actors, is made up of the combination of individual self-perceptions. In such situations each individual knows for sure its own preferences over what it perceives to be its own courses of action. However, perceptions of the structure and content of the decision problems of other actors are typically prone to misperception and error. Thus if we collect information about what is known for sure by every participant in a given situation, we can describe objective reality as a juxtaposition of subjective self-perceptions. Specifically, an objective game represents a bird's-eye image of "reality" formed from the researcher's answers to the following questions:

1. Who are the actors involved in a given international outcome?
2. What are the alternatives each perceives to possess?
3. What are the preferences of each of the actors over the union of the set of alternatives identified in the second question above?

The idea here is that what may happen in reality is defined by the courses of action (or inaction) that each actor perceives as available to it. Moreover, while actors may err in attributing alternatives or preferences to other actors, each of them can reliably define its preferences over those outcomes it perceives. These preferences then complete the intersubjective representation of reality.

The objective game can be used to produce a theoretical outcome, that is, the game outcome that we would expect if each national decision had truly been the best possible under the circumstances. In this way we can compare what actors actually did to what they should have done in a particular (objectively defined) situation and explain why and when actual decisions deviate from theoretically defined optimal decisions.[7]

The relationship between national choices and international outcomes is analyzed in terms of the differences between subjective and objective games. This difference both serves to assess the extent to which an actor's perception of reality is accurate and acts as a benchmark for an outcome-based evaluation of national decisions. In other words, in comparing subjective games to objective ones *it is possible to examine the extent to which an actor's actual choice corresponded to the optimal choice it should have made under the "objective" circumstances.* Moreover, this comparison enables us to determine the extent to which the outcome that an actor expected to occur given its subjective game corresponded to the outcome that actually took place.

The Evolution of International Processes

The fourth layer of TIP examines how interstate events come to comprise international processes over time. A central focus of TIP is on the evolutionary dynamics of international processes. The theory identifies two perspectives: ad hoc and strategic decision styles. The ad hoc approach assumes that national decisionmaking processes are motivated by short-term concerns and immediate triggers. Decisionmakers do not have or are unable to apply long-range strategies of international conduct. The ad hoc perspective posits that decisionmakers are motivated by discrepancies between expected and actual outcomes. Two types of discrepancy are observed: positive surprises and negative ones. Positive surprises refer to situations in which actors value actual outcomes more than expected outcomes. In such cases decisionmakers get better outcomes than expected. Negative surprises, in contrast, refer to situations in which the actual outcome is worse than the expected one. We typically expect negative surprises to cause shifts for the better (that is, positively to affect the quality of the national decisionmaking process), whereas by spurring overconfidence, positive surprises or cases of nondiscrepancy can result in reduced decisional quality.

Contrary to the ad hoc approach, the strategic perspective describes a situation in which decisionmakers consistently apply long-term and carefully crafted national strategies to a wide variety of problems and situations. Specific situations prompt national decisions that directly reflect a set of goals that have been operationalized into specific policies. The strategic approach assumes that national preferences do not change readily from one situation or decision to another. Rather, the actor's tactic or the form of its behavior might be varied consistent with the actor's general strategy.[8] I do not examine in detail here this layer of TIP. However, I do make some remarks that relate to the ideas presented above in order to explain some of the more puzzling features of the decisionmaking and bargaining processes that took place in the Middle East in 1970–1973.

In this study I focus on the situational effects on individual choice and group behavior. Specifically, I examine the effects of the three principal situational factors of the theory: threat perceptions, perception of opportunities, and their combined measure decisional stress on the content and structure of individual choice behavior. I also use aggregate measures of substantive decisional quality to assess the relationship between individual decisions and national outcomes. I look at three hypotheses:

1. There exists an inverse U-shaped relationship between any of the situational factors (threat perception, perceptions of opportunity, and time pressure) and decisionmaking behavior: Individuals tend to become increasingly analytic when the values of these variables are moderate and less analytic when the values of these variables are either very low or very high.

2. There exists an inverse U-shaped relationship between stress and decision behavior.

3. There exists a positive association between the path taken by an individual decisionmaker toward a decision and the substantive quality of the outcome of that decision: The more analytic the process, the more adaptive the outcome of that decision.

RESEARCH DESIGN

Data

This study is based on an empirical analysis of 103 decisions made by the top leaders of Egypt, Israel, Jordan, the Palestine Liberation Organization (PLO), Syria, and the United States who dealt with various issues of the Arab-Israeli conflict from 1970 to 1975.[9] In addition this study contains data based on the analysis of thirteen outcomes covering the Yom Kippur War (the war termination decisions and missile crisis, the Egyptian-Israeli and Syrian-Israeli disengagement agreements, and the 1975 Egyptian-Israeli interim agreement). Each of these outcomes is the result of several individual choices and national decisions. A total of eighteen decisionmakers were studied according to the breakdown given in Table 8.1.

Coding and Measures of Decision Behavior

Data for each decision were generated from a detailed questionnaire, a measurement tool I used earlier and have since refined (Maoz 1981, 1986; Maoz and Astorino 1992b). This questionnaire allows systematic structuring of the decisionmaking process at both the individual and group levels. Each decision process was analyzed by two coders who independently filled out the questionnaire. Intercoder reliability levels were reasonably good (in the range of 0.7–0.85) considering the complexity of the questions and the problems of obtaining data from many of these decisions.

Individual Decision Performance Indices

For each decisionmaker and each decision, coders were asked to fill out a search evaluation (SE) matrix consisting in its rows of all alternatives and outcomes perceived by the decisionmaker and in its columns of all the value dimensions used to evaluate these outcomes. The entries in the matrix consisted of the ranking of outcomes in terms of each of these value dimensions. The area of this matrix (number of rows times number of columns) serves as an index of the comprehensiveness of evaluation (CE) of the problem by the decisionmaker. The larger the number of alternatives and outcomes and/or the larger the number of value dimensions a decisionmaker uses

Table 8.1 Individual Decisionmakers and Their Decision Performances

State/Actor	Decisionmaker	Total	Analytic	An.-Cyb.	An.-Cog.	Cybernetic	Cyb.-Cog.	Cognitive
Egypt	Nasser	1	0	1	0	0	0	0
	Sadat	9	6	0	2	0	0	1
Israel	Allon	5	2	1	1	0	0	1
	Begin	2	0	0	0	0	0	2
	Dayan	14	7	2	2	2	0	1
	Eban	8	1	1	2	3	0	1
	Elazar	2	1	0	0	1	0	0
	Gallili	1	0	0	1	0	0	0
	Meir	14	3	2	2	3	0	5
	Rabin	1	0	1	0	0	0	0
Jordan	Hussein	4	2	1	0	0	0	1
PLO	Arafat	2	0	0	0	1	0	1
	Habash	2	0	0	0	0	0	2
Syria	Asad	4	3	0	0	0	0	1
	Jadid	2	1	0	0	0	0	1
United States	Kissinger	13	7	3	1	1	0	1
	Nixon	9	1	1	0	5	1	2
	Rogers	8	1	1	1	0	1	4

The header "Type of Decisional Path" spans the columns Analytic, An.-Cyb., An.-Cog., Cybernetic, Cyb.-Cog., Cognitive.

to evaluate a problem, the more complex the structure of the search evaluation matrix and hence the higher the CE score for that decision.

However, the CE measures only the complexity of the decision problem as the decisionmaker sees it. It does not represent the psychological complexity of the choice problem. The psychological difficulty of making a decision is given by what I have called the trade-off complexity index (TC) (Maoz 1990b). The extent to which outcomes are ranked over the value dimensions represents the extent of trade-off complexity contained in the decisionmaker's perception of the decision problem. I also used measure developed by Maoz (1990b, pp. 237–249) to allow systematic tapping of this complexity (cf. Maoz and Astorino 1992b).

In addition, following the multiple paths to choice (MPC) approach originally proposed by Stein and Tanter (1980) and that I further developed (Maoz 1986, 1990b), I asked coders at each stage of the decision to assess which of the three typical choice models best characterized the stage. On the basis of these assessments, I coded the path to choice that best characterized a given decision, identifying both "pure" (e.g., analytic, cybernetic, cognitive) and "mixed" (i.e., analytic-cybernetic, analytic-cognitive, cybernetic-cognitive) paths.

Independent Variables

Coders also ranked on a three-level scale (low, moderate, and high) the perception of threat, opportunity, and time pressure that the decisionmaker felt while going through the process. Threat perception is defined as an expectation of harm to assets or values of the nation in the absence of action by the decisionmaking unit (Maoz 1990b, p. 86–87). Low levels of threat imply that the decisionmaker foresees little damage to values or assets and/or low probability of damage to existing values or assets. Moderate threat is either a perception of expected loss to important values with a low probability of occurrence or perception of a high probability of loss to moderately important values or assets. High threat represents a high probability of loss to important national values or assets. Opportunity is defined as an expectation of acquisition of new values or assets or enhancement of existing values or assets as a result of action by the decisionmaker (Maoz 1990b, p. 95–96). I also examined a fourth variable, perceived situational ambiguity, or the extent of certainty assigned to the outcomes of a real (or latent) inaction alternative. For this variable, too, values were assessed as low, meaning that actors perceive the probability of certain events as very high (and the probability of complementary events as very low); moderate; and high (when the probability distribution over the expected outcomes of inaction is seen as approaching uniformity). Perceived situational ambiguity was hypothesized (Maoz 1990b, p. 111) to be correlated in a curvilinear fashion (inverse U) with threat perception and in a positive linear fashion with the decision performance variables. In fact the association of ambiguity with threat perception was indeed curvilinear ($m_b =$ 0.88), but only marginally significant ($\chi^2 = 8.95$; $p = 0.06$).

These codings were combined to produce an overall assessment of stress according to the definitions in Maoz (1990, ch. 4). Data were analyzed both on the individual components of decisional stress and on the combined measure of stress. At the group level, I again used the data from an earlier study (Maoz and Astorino 1992b) to measure decisional outcomes. Here I employed the pairwise discrepancy index that examines the extent of misperception of the opponent's preferences to tap the extent to which there exists a gap between a decisionmaker's view of the environment and the "objective" makeup of the environment. I also used two decisional outcome measures that tap the gap between the actual outcome of the decision and (1) the outcome expected by the decisionmaker and (2) the theoretical outcome of the decision, that is, the outcome that should have obtained if everyone made the "right" choice.

FINDINGS

First, I examined the relationships between each of the components of decisional stress and the path to decision taken by decisionmakers. Then I related the stress variable to the decisional path. I conducted this analysis over all decisions, individuals, and states specified in Table 8.1 above. The results are given in Table 8.2.

Table 8.2   Effects of Threat, Opportunity, Time Pressure, and Stress Levels on Decisional Paths

		Type of Decisional Path					
Ind. Var	Level	Analytic	An.-Cyb.	An.-Cog.	Cybernetic	Cyb.-Cog.	Cognitive
Threat	Low	4	2	0	10	2	4
	Med	19	7	6	3	0	6
	High	12	4	6	3	0	13
Statistics: $\chi^2 = 34.11$; $p < .001$; $\nabla = 0.35$; $m_b = 0.77$							
Opportunity	Low	10	6	8	12	2	13
	Med	19	5	5	3	0	4
	High	6	2	1	1	0	6
Statistics: $\chi^2 = 18.59$; $p < .001$; $\nabla = 0.21$; $m_b = 0.85$							
Time Pressure	Low	2	0	3	9	2	5
	Med	17	6	3	5	0	5
	High	16	7	6	2	0	13
Statistics: $\chi^2 = 33.75$; $p < .001$; $\nabla = 0.22$; $m_b = 0.78$							
Perceived	Low	6	2	3	3	2	8
Situational	Med	18	7	6	11	0	8
Ambiguity	High	11	4	3	2	0	6
Statistics: $\chi^2 = 12.66$; $p = .243$; $\nabla = 0.27$; $m_b = 0.70$ (NS)							
Stress	Low	6	3	5	13	2	7
	Med	16	3	1	1	0	2
	High	13	7	6	2	0	14
Statistics: $\chi^2 = 36.44$ $p < .001$; $\nabla = 0.36$; $m_b = 0.89$							

The analysis clearly suggests that all three components of decisional stress as well as the composite stress variable are related to choice behavior in the manner hypothesized above. Specifically, low threat, low opportunity, low time pressure, and low stress are typically associated with cybernetic paths to decisionmaking. This path was hypothesized to characterize routine situations that entail no major significance to decisionmakers. Analytic decision behavior tends to be associated with medium levels of the components of decisional stress as well as with moderate stress levels. At high levels of stress, cognitive decisional paths become quite frequent. However, it is important to note that at high levels of stress, there is a substantial proportion of analytic decisions. This corroborates the findings of the secondary analysis I conducted (Maoz 1990b, pp. 336–337) on the Brecher and Geist (1980) and Dowty (1984) analyses of crisis decisionmaking in Israel (1967 and 1973) and the United States (September 1970). Apparently, there is a substantial degree of analytic decision behavior even under highly stressful conditions. However, one still observes that by and large cognitive or cognitive-rational (or cognitive-cybernetic) paths are the modal categories at high levels of decisional stress. The one variable that does not show any kind of significant relationship with decisional paths is perceived situational ambiguity. The relationship between ambiguity and decisional path is neither linear nor curvilinear.

Table 8.3   Analysis of Variance of Decision Performance Indices by Threat, Opportunity, Time Pressure, and Stress

Dependent Variable	Independent Variable	Level	N	Mean	(SD)	Matrix of Differences			F-Statistic (p value)
SE comprehensiveness	Threat Perception	Low	22	22.09	(9.69)	Med	—		0.729
		Med	43	24.16	(12.59)	High	—	—	(0.49)
		High	38	21.36	(10.14)		Low	Med	
	Opportunity Perception	Low	52	20.98	(11.03)	Low	—		1.572
		Med	35	25.26	(10.66)	Med	—	—	(0.21)
		High	16	22.31	(11.98)	High	Low	Med	
	Time Pressure	Low	23	18.26	(8.77)	Low	*		2.578
		Med	36	24.78	(11.76)	Med	—	—	(0.08)
		High	44	23.19	(11.26)	High	Low	Med	
	Situational Ambiguity	Low	25	17.28	(8.83)	Med	*		4.162
		Med	51	24.49	(11.26)	High	—	*	(0.02)
		High	26	24.42	(11.63)		Low	Med	
	Decisional Stress	Low	37	21.59	(10.27)	Low	—		2.50
		Med	24	27.00	(13.03)	Med	—	*	(0.09)
		High	42	21.07	(10.26)	High	Low	Med	
Trade-off Complexity	Threat Perception	Low	22	0.25	(0.28)	Med	*		5.119
		Med	43	0.42	(0.24)	High	—	*	(0.01)
		High	38	0.28	(0.22)		Low	Med	
	Opportunity Perception	Low	52	0.29	(0.25)	Med	*		3.325
		Med	35	0.41	(0.27)	High	—	*	(0.04)
		High	16	0.26	(0.16)		Low	Med	
	Time Pressure	Low	23	0.25	(0.31)	Med	*		2.873
		Med	36	0.40	(0.22)	High	—	—	(0.06)
		High	44	0.31	(0.23)		Low	Med	
	Situational Ambiguity	Low	25	0.29	(0.26)	Med	—		0.505
		Med	51	0.35	(0.27)	High	—	—	(0.61)
		High	26	0.34	(0.21)		Low	Med	
	Decisional Stress	Low	37	0.30	(0.28)	Med	*		4.563
		Med	24	0.46	(0.22)	High	—	*	(0.01)
		High	42	0.28	(0.22)		Low	Med	

(cont.)

Table 8.3 continued

Dependent Variable	Independent Variable	Level	N	Mean	(SD)	Matrix of Differences		F-Statistic (p value)
Average	Threat	Low	9	0.30	(0.18)	Med	—	4.523
Pairwise	Perception	Med	19	0.27	(0.24)	High	*	*	(0.01)
Discrepancy**		High	15	0.44	(0.27)		Low	Med	
	Opportunity	Low	21	0.31	(0.24)	Med	—	—	0.360
	Perception	Med	14	0.34	(0.34)	High	—	—	(0.70)
		High	8	0.38	(0.26)		Low	Med	
	Time	Low	10	0.30	(0.19)	Med	—	—	2.493
	Pressure	Med	13	0.27	(0.22)	High	—	*	(0.09)
		High	20	0.40	(0.29)		Low	Med	
	Decisional	Low	14	0.28	(0.19)	Med	—	—	6.146
	Stress	Med	12	0.24	(0.24)	High	*	*	(0.01)
		High	17	0.44	(0.27)		Low	Med	
Expected-	Threat	Low	10	−0.14	(0.23)	Med	—	3.359
Actual	Perception	Med	20	0.05	(0.33)	High	—	*	(0.04)
Discrepancy**		High	17	−0.20	(0.31)		Low	Med	
	Opportunity	Low	23	−0.12	(0.36)	Med	—	—	0.382
	Perception	Med	16	−0.05	(0.27)	High	—	—	(0.69)
		High	8	−0.01	(0.29)		Low	Med	
	Time	Low	11	−0.11	(0.22)	Med	—	—	1.529
	Pressure	Med	15	0.04	(0.37)	High	—	—	(0.23)
		High	21	−0.14	(0.31)		Low	Med	
	Decisional	Low	16	−0.06	(0.31)	Med	—	—	1.896
	Stress	Med	13	0.04	(0.28)	High	—	—	(0.16)
		High	18	−0.18	(0.33)		Low	Med	
Theoretical-	Threat	Low	10	−0.14	(0.26)	Med	—	3.384
Actual	Perception	Med	19	0.07	(0.27)	High	—	*	(0.04)
Discrepancy**		High	15	−0.15	(0.25)		Low	Med	
	Opportunity	Low	21	−0.17	(0.29)	Med	*	—	4.513
	Perception	Med	15	−0.03	(0.20)	High	*	—	(0.02)
		High	8	0.11	(0.26)		Low	Med	
	Time	Low	10	−0.19	(0.28)	Med	*	—	4.885
	Pressure	Med	14	0.12	(0.22)	High	—	*	(0.01)
		High	20	−0.11	(0.27)		Low	Med	
	Decisional	Low	16	−0.11	(0.27)	Med	—	—	1.006
	Stress	Med	12	0.04	(0.22)	High	—	—	(0.37)
		High	17	−0.07	(0.32)		Low	Med	

Notes: *Least significant difference multiple comparisons. Difference is significant at $p < 0.05$.
**Aggregate level measures on the group (national level).

It is important to note that the analysis is partial because it does not take into account interindividual differences in coping with stress. These differences may result from the personality attributes of decisionmakers that may interact with the situational variables under examination in the present study.

In Table 8.3 I examine the effects of the situational variables on the substantive aspects of individual choice behavior, as well as on the consequences of decisions. This table shows that the direct effects of the various aspects of decisional stress as well as the combined effects of stress on the substantive measures of decision quality is generally, though not in all cases, consistent with the research hypotheses. In particular, it is evident that the most significant differences are between moderate stress levels and the other two levels rather than between very low and very high stress. Let me elaborate on this. First, the multiple comparison analysis reveals that the differences that are statistically significant are usually between moderate levels of the various situational variables on the one hand and the low or high levels of these variables on the other. Second, the effects of stress on the outcomes of decisions are not consistently significant and considerably less pronounced. From the mean values of the outcome variables (pairwise substantive discrepancy and expected-actual and theoretical-actual discrepancies), it is evident that there may exist a curvilinear relationship between stress and outcome quality, precisely as hypothesized. However, the data do not permit us to specify a direct link between individual choice quality and decisional outcomes because decisional outcomes are based on group performance rather than on the quality of individual decisions. Since this study did not delve into the relationship between individual choice and group decisionmaking, it is possible that the linkage lies at that level.

CONCLUSION

This study provides systematic evidence on the relationship between stress and foreign policy decision performance. From an analysis of 103 decisions made by five international actors (four states and one nonstate entity), the following findings emerge:

1. There exists an inverse U-shaped relationship between threat perception, perception of opportunities, and time pressure and the path to foreign policy decisionmaking: At both low and high levels of the independent variables, decisionmaking tends to become increasingly nonrational. Analytic decisionmaking becomes increasingly typical of decisions made when the levels of threats or opportunities are moderate and when there is some but not unlimited time for decision.
2. The same relationship is observed when the components of stress are combined into an overall measure of decisional stress.

3. The relationship between the various indices of decisional stress and decision performance is maintained both for procedural aspects of the decision (e.g., comprehensiveness of evaluation, type of decisional path) and the substantive aspects such as trade-off complexity.
4. The relationship between situational variables and the outcomes of national decisions is not as strong and as consistent as in the case of individual choice quality. This relationship, too, appears to be curvilinear, but the association between individual perceptions of the situation and decisional quality in terms of the outcomes of national decisions is not robust.

These findings should be viewed as tentative mostly because the framework for analysis is incomplete. It is important to explore the linkages between individual decision behavior and group decision behavior as a way of connecting situational inputs to decision quality and decision quality to decisional outcomes.

The significance of this study lies primarily in revealing the context-dependence of foreign policy decisions. As I have argued elsewhere (Maoz 1990b; Maoz and Astorino 1992a), the study of foreign policy decision-making is characterized by a fundamental debate between proponents of rational choice theory and proponents of extrarational models (e.g., cognitive models, cybernetic models). This debate has sometimes evolved into a zero-sum conflict.[10] Other contributors to this volume (e.g., Morrow, Chapter 2) take a clear stand on one side or the other or attempt to examine competitively which model "best" describes actual decisionmaking (e.g., Mintz and Geva, Chapter 5) or what the implications are of each of the models in terms of state behavior (Zinnes and Muncaster, Chapter 9). I have argued in the past that this competition among different models of decisionmaking did not in fact advance knowledge in the field. It may even have hampered it. The question is not which is the "best" decision-making model. Rather, it is *which model is more likely to be observed under given circumstances.* Following Stein and Tanter (1980) and Brecher and Geist (1980), I think it is unrealistic to expect that a single model, or a single path to choice, would always characterize decisionmaking or even that a given model would provide a "best" prediction of what is actually happening, independent of the circumstances under which the decision is made or the identity of the decisionmaker or the setting of decision. Hence the task should be to identify the precise links between exogenous variables and decisional strategy.

The theory of international processes specifies a set of relationships between situational, personality, and organizational factors on the one hand

and the use of certain decisional models on the other. These hypotheses were derived from the assumptions of the theory itself but were also consistent with ideas of scholars in international relations (e.g., Holsti and George 1975; Brecher and Geist 1980) as well as psychology and organizational behavior.[11]

This chapter is one of the first empirical applications in international relations research of a context-dependent investigation of foreign policy decision processes. The findings corroborate the notion that such processes are situation-specific, but they also reveal that this characteristic does not impede generalization. On the contrary, the findings of this study imply that specifying the links between background conditions and decision strategy would yield significant findings.

In terms of the cognitive-rational debate, my answer to the question of individual rationality in foreign policy decisions is that it depends. This study clearly reveals that decisional stress (and its components) is one of the important determinants of just when and how rational foreign policy decisionmaking can be and which individuals are capable of making good choices. However, as Mor (1993, pp. 6–8) suggests, stress is only one of several factors that affect decisionmaking. Future investigations would have to delve further into the link among multiple exogenous factors and multiple paths to choice.

NOTES

This study was supported by a grant from the U.S. Institute of Peace (USIP). The USIP is absolved, however, from responsibility for any of the ideas expressed herein. A previous version of this chapter was presented at the conference "Decision Making on War and Peace: The Cognitive-Rational Debate," at Texas A&M University, March 10–11, 1994. For their useful comments, I wish to thank Allison Astorino-Courtois, Alex Mintz, Nehemia Geva, and the participants in the conference.

1. See, for example, the January 1989 issue of *World Politics* on deterrence theory.

2. For a comprehensive review of this literature, see Maoz 1990b, chs. 3, 5, and 7. Here I review only the general arguments without going into fine details.

3. This section draws upon Maoz 1990b and Maoz and Astorino 1992b.

4. By "decisionmaking model," I mean a consistent set of procedures and substantive elements of diagnosis of problems, search for and development of policy options, information processing and estimation of future outcomes, appraisal and evaluation of policy options and rules by which individuals and groups choose among these options. TIP considers three possible models of decision: the analytic (rational) model, the cybernetic (bounded rationality, organizational dynamic) model, and the cognitive (affective) model. See Maoz 1990b, pp. 149–303, for a detailed description of these models.

5. An analysis of individual decisionmaking and the aggregation of individual preferences to group decisions is the central issue in a related study just completed.

Some of the issues concerning individual preferences and group choices that are directly relevant to the question addressed herein are discussed in the section on methods, below.

6. Brecher, Steinberg, and Stein (1969); Jervis (1976); Janis and Mann (1977); George (1980); and Vertzberger (1990) have all adopted in one form or another the Frankel's (1963) distinction between the operational and psychological environments. The former represents a notion of "the real world," whereas the latter represents "the world in their [decisionmakers'] mind," to use Vertzberger's terminology. Unfortunately, although there exist many approaches to modeling the structure and content of the psychological environment of decisionmakers, no operational conception of the operational environment has been proposed. TIP, as I show, represents a unique effort at explicit modeling of the operational environment.

7. I use the term "objective game" to describe what a game (defined by players, alternatives, preferences, and rules of play) would look like to an unbiased external observer of a situation who has all the necessary information. In fact, to construct such an "objective" game, such an observer would have to know the view of each actor regarding its own alternatives and its own preferences over the various outcomes. The notion of an objective game is predicated on an assumption that reality is no more and no less than an intersubjective layout of a situation seen from each actor's perspective. See Maoz 1990b, pp. 25–29, 418–421, for a more elaborate exposition of this view. An application of this perspective in the context of enduring international rivalries is given by Maoz and Mor 1996.

8. Those propositions are derived by TIP from a long list of theoretical and empirical studies of foreign policy decisionmaking in which decision processes are linked to the perception of the environment and the perception of the environment is linked to the quality of decisional outcomes. See De Rivera 1968; Brecher, Steinberg, and Stein 1969; Jervis 1976; Janis and Mann 1977; Holsti 1979; Stein and Tanter 1980; Brecher and Geist 1980; George 1980; Janis 1989; Vertzberger 1990 (to name just a few). However, it is amazing to note that with the exception of one study (Herek, Janis, and Huth 1987) no rigorous empirical analysis of these propositions was attempted.

9. Maoz and Astorino 1992b provide details of the forty-four collective decisions made by these actors for the 1970–1973 period.

10. See, for example, the debate on rational versus cognitive models of deterrence (*World Politics,* January 1989, especially Achen and Snidal 1989; Lebow and Stein 1989; George and Smoke 1989; Jervis 1989; Zagare 1990). See also Mor 1993, pp. 1–22; Maoz 1994.

11. For a review of this literature, see Maoz 1990b, chs. 3, 5.

9

Prospect Theory Versus Expected Utility Theory: A Dispute Sequence Appraisal

Dina A. Zinnes & Robert G. Muncaster

Psychologists have debated the viability of expected utility theory as a reasonable model of individual decisionmaking for more than a decade. The most serious challenges were made by Kahneman and Tversky (1979; Tversky and Kahneman 1992), who showed through laboratory experiments that the expected utility model could not account for certain types of decisions. These theorists put forth prospect theory as an alternate decisionmaking model. Although decisionmakers in both models are assumed to optimize over outcomes, the theories differ in their assumptions about the calculus used, in particular the way in which the decisionmaker perceives and utilizes probabilities and utilities. This debate—expected utility versus prospect theory—has recently emerged in the international relations literature.

Bueno de Mesquita's *War Trap* (1981) is, of course, the primary example of an expected utility model of the foreign policy decision to initiate war. Although the original model has undergone a variety of revisions and has recently led to an extensive game model (Bueno de Mesquita and Lalman 1992), the underlying assumptions remain consistent with traditional expected utility theory. While he does not directly challenge these models, Jack Levy (1992a, 1992b) has proposed that international relations researchers take a serious look at prospect theory as a potentially more useful model for understanding foreign policy decisions. Citing a number of historical examples, Levy attempts to show why and how prospect theory could provide a better understanding of international politics.

Which theory, expected utility or prospect theory, is a better explanation for such foreign policy decisions as war initiation remains to be seen.

Absent the luxury of laboratory experiments, comparisons between the foreign policy predictions of the two theories may be difficult to obtain. We can, however, compare the two theories from a different perspective. This chapter asks whether there is a long-run systemic impact of decision-makers operating according to one or the other decision calculus. In other words, within a system of nations, would the systemic consequences differ over an extended sequence of decisions if national leaders were expected utility maximizers versus prospect theorists? Would there be more and larger wars if decisionmakers used one calculus versus the other? Would the structure of the system, say, in terms of the network of hostile and friendly relations be more or less polarized? In short, what are the implications of the two theories over a series of decisions made by a system of optimizing nations?

To answer this question, we need more than a model of decisionmaking. We also need a model of an interacting system of nations within which we can embed the two different decisionmaking processes. We propose to use a model that we have developed to study the evolution of relationships within a system of nations as these relationships evolve over a sequence of disputes involving various subsets of nations. Embedding the two decision calculi in this model of the dispute-to-dispute sequence means that the results of the comparison must be interpreted against this additional theoretical background. We argue, however, that the use of the dispute sequence model is comparable to the use of a laboratory. Like our model, the laboratory is an environment, that is, a set of assumptions, which permits one to examine the implications of the two theories. The difference between laboratory experiments and our use of the dispute sequence is that our decisionmakers are sets of explicit assumptions. Our analyses examine the conclusions, that is, deductions, that would emerge from the dispute sequence model under the two conditions of expected utility and prospect theory. This chapter is, consequently, purely theoretical—a comparison of the deductions of a theory under two different decisionmaking assumptions.

The dispute sequence model has several subcomponents. First, two initial disputants are selected. We call this the initialization problem. Second, the remaining nations must individually decide whether or not to enter the dispute and on which side. This is the joining problem, and this is where we introduce the two decision theories. The decisions of these third-party nations to enter the dispute is modeled either by expected utility theory or by prospect theory. The probabilities and utilities of either calculus are based on the third party's relationships with the two initiating nations, reflecting our basic assumption that what is most important to each nation is its relationships with the other nations in the system: Decisions are based on a "relationship currency." The third part of the model determines what happens in the dispute. This is the conflict problem. A final component, the updating problem, describes how each nation in the system reassesses its relationships with the other nations as a consequence of the dispute, other friendships, and the past history of its relationships.

The dispute sequence model allows us to examine, over a sequence of disputes, the number of nations that join in each dispute and how the network of relationships evolves over time. We can therefore compare the number of nations that join each conflict and the polarization and intensity of hostile or cooperative relationships when nations make the decision to join a conflict based on expected utility theory and prospect theory. This comparison will allow us to assess the long-run significance of these two different decision calculi.

Below we provide the details of our model and describe how the two decision calculi were modeled and inserted into this general model. As will be seen, the model contains significant stochastic components. For this reason, and because of the complexity of the overall model, our analysis of the dispute sequence model under the two different decisionmaking calculi is done using computer simulations. We have recently become aware of the wide variety of meanings attached to the concept "simulation." It is therefore important that the reader understand exactly what we mean by this term in the present context. The results of our simulations must be seen as deductions or solutions from the model under each of the decision conditions. We are *not* generating data. We are *not* generating statistical estimates. The output of our simulations are *consequences,* or conclusions, of our modeling assumptions.

OVERVIEW OF THE DISPUTE SEQUENCE MODEL

The dispute sequence model (Muncaster and Zinnes 1992; Diehl et al. 1993) focuses on internation relationships and captures the way in which those relationships change from one dispute to the next. The relationship between nations x and y is denoted R_{xy} and is taken to be a variable in the range from -1 to 1. A value of 1 indicates that x and y are extremely good friends, while the value -1 indicates that they are bitter enemies. We apply to this variable a superscript that signifies a point in "dispute time." Following the conclusion of the Kth dispute, each nation x, either implicitly or explicitly, reassesses how it feels toward each other nation y and thereby determines a new relationship value $R_{xy}^{(K)}$, the value of the relationship between x and y *following* dispute K.

Figure 9.1 gives a broad overview of the dispute sequence model. It focuses on dispute K and indicates how R_{xy} changes from the beginning to the end of that dispute. The value $R_{xy}^{(K-1)}$ at the left shows that the relationships

Figure 9.1
General Structure of the Dispute Sequence Model

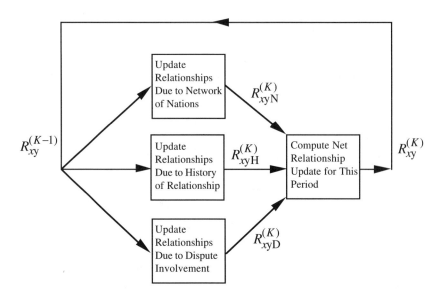

at the end of dispute $K-1$ act as the input for dispute K. Then, following dispute K, a new value $R^{(K)}_{xy}$ is generated. This serves as the input for the next dispute, and so on. In this way a sequence of disputes and an evolving pattern of relationships is created. Figure 9.1 summarizes our assumption that each pair of nations takes into account three different effects in its reassessment of the relationship following dispute K. As the middle box shows, one piece concerns the history of the relationship between x and y. This part of the model determines a new relationship value $R^{(K)}_{xy}$H *given that only the history of the relationship is important.* If x and y were previously friends, in the absence of other effects, they continue to be friends in the future. The second piece, shown by the bottom box, captures the effects of dispute involvement on the relationship between x and y—whether nations did or did not enter the dispute and which side was chosen. This part of the model produces a relationship value $R^{(K)}_{xy}$D, which represents the total reassessment *if only disputes have an impact.* The third part of the calculation, shown in the top box, concerns how each dyad xy relates to all other nations in the system. We call this the network effect, and it produces a new relationship value $R^{(K)}_{xy}$N *that accounts for network effects alone.* This value is determined by the dyad's friendly and hostile relationships with every other nation by utilizing the old rule, "The friend of my friend is my friend; the friend of my enemy is my enemy." We do not describe in detail here the models that generate the updatings due to history and network effects. Because these two submodels are not central to our exploration of the prospect theory–utility theory debate, we reserve them for the appendix to this chapter. The updating model for dispute involvement, in contrast, plays a central role, and we present it in detail.

These three effects—disputes, history, network—do not act in isolation. As represented by the box at the right in Figure 9.1, a simple rule for combining them is needed. The model behind this box is easy to specify, namely, the final relationship value is a weighted sum of the three effects:

$$R^{(K)}_{xy} = \alpha R^{(K)}_{xy\,D} + \beta R^{(K)}_{xy\,H} + \gamma R^{(K)}_{xy\,N}, \qquad (1)$$

where $\alpha + \beta + \gamma = 1$. The weights α, β, and γ are, respectively, the dispute, history, and network percentages by which each effect weighs into the final relationship. In the simulations reported here, these weights are fixed as 96 percent dispute, 2 percent history, and 2 percent network. The high weighting for disputes is chosen deliberately since it is in the dispute part of the model that we implement the models of decisionmaking. These percentages assure that the dispute part of the model has a dominant effect. Previous investigations of the dispute sequence model indicate that the network and history contributions to relationship updating have important long-run effects, even when their overall percentage contributions are small.

We turn now to the dispute involvement component shown in the lower box of Figure 9.1. Figure 9.2 provides an expanded view of this part of the dispute process. Dispute K begins with the selection of two initial disputants i and j. This is the initialization problem. The assumption is that there is a great deal of uncertainty as to precisely which dyad will initiate a dispute. Hence we model the selection process stochastically under the assumption that dyads that are more hostile are more likely to start a conflict. We therefore assign to each dyad xy a probability p_{xy} that it will initiate dispute K. This probability has the form

$$p_{xy} = (1 - R^{(K)}_{xy})^2 / P, \qquad (2)$$

where P is selected so that the sum of these probabilities over all dyads is 1. Note that if the relationship between x and y is near 1 (high friendship), this probability is near 0 and hence it is highly unlikely that xy will be selected. If the relationship is -1 (bitter enmity), p_{xy} is as large as it can get. This captures, then, the idea that enemies are more likely to initiate disputes than friends.

In the next step in the process, shown by the "All Other . . . " box in Figure 9.2, all other nations in the system decide whether or not they will enter the dispute. This is the joining problem. It is here that we insert the decisionmaking calculus, modeling it as a lottery in which the two sides of the dispute are drawn. This lottery is described in greater detail below. The final boxes of Figure 9.2 show how the relationship updatings occur. The

Figure 9.2
General Structure of the Dispute Involvement Submodel

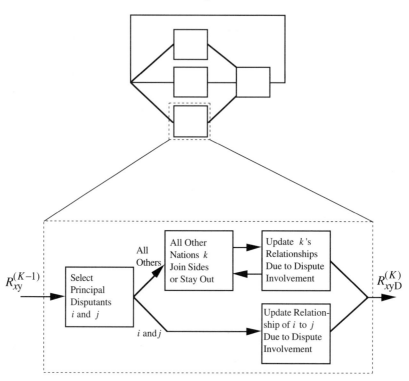

lower of these two boxes involves a model for how the two initial disputants i and j update their relationship because of the dispute. This model
is quite simple:

$$R_{ijD}^{(K)} = \tfrac{1}{2} (R_{ij}^{(K-1)} - 1). \qquad (3)$$

It captures the idea that the relationship between i and j becomes worse.
Specifically, (3) causes this relationship to move from its value at the outset of the dispute to the average of that value and the worst it could be,
namely, -1. The upper box describes the updating for all other nations as a
consequence of their decision to join or not to join. It contains effects of
the type: If a nation should have joined the dispute on i's side because its
level of friendship with i was very high but it stayed out of the dispute,
that nation's relationship with i will suffer a setback. We examine this updating model next.

Figure 9.3 highlights the decision process by teasing apart the two
boxes in Figure 9.2 that involve nation k. The decisionmaking model we

propose involves two pieces: a lottery and a relationship updating. Specifically, the model involves a decisionmaker and the state of the world about which decisions are made. Naturally, these are not disconnected; any decisionmaking calculation must make speculations about how the world works. The decisionmaker then acts on those speculations. The decision rules we use in the lottery weigh the values or utilities of the different relationship updates that can occur depending on which route k takes through the lottery.

Consider briefly the sequence of steps laid out in Figure 9.3. Each third-party nation k must decide between two options: to stay out of the dispute or to enter. If k stays out, its relationships with i and j are updated according to a model reflecting this choice. If k enters the dispute, we postulate that there is a probability p_i^k that it will join i and a complementary probability $p_j^k = 1 - p_i^k$ that it will join j. Thus k tosses a coin weighted with these probabilities and the result determines which side, i or j, it joins. If k joins i, its relationships with i and j are updated in a way that reflects whether or not k *should* have joined one side versus the other. A

Figure 9.3
Substructure of the Model of Dispute Involvement
and Subsequent Relationship Updatings

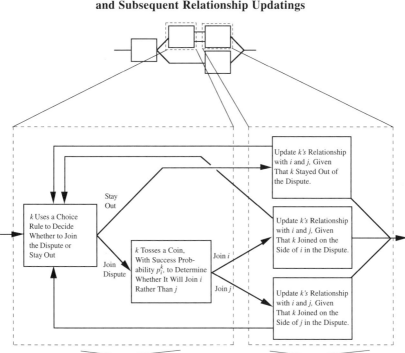

similar updating occurs if k joins j. Note that the final column of boxes in Figure 9.3, where the updatings occur, all feed back into the decisionmaking box for k at the far left. This reflects our assumption that the decisions that are made are influenced by the updating rules to be used, that is, by the state of the world. In our earlier descriptions of the dispute sequence model (Muncaster and Zinnes 1992; Diehl et al. 1993), we indicated that it also contained the conflict problem, a model that determines what actually happens in a dispute. Normally this model would lie between the lottery and the relationship updatings. For this analysis, we have omitted it, preferring for simplicity to make the updating of relationships depend purely on dispute involvement rather than also accounting for dispute outcome.

THE UPDATING MODELS: HOW THE WORLD WORKS

We assume that the relationship updatings characterize how the world in the dispute sequence model actually works. That is, these models describe how relationships actually change as a consequence of being involved in disputes. We also assume that each nation is fully aware of these rules and that decision calculations based on them are reasonable.

Consider first what happens to nation k if it joins the dispute on the side of i. In this case we assume that k's relationship with i improves. A simple way to model this is to shift the value of k's relationship with i upward to the average between this relationship and the best possible relationship with i, namely, 1:

$$R_{ikD}^{(K)} = \tfrac{1}{2}(R_{ik}^{(K-1)} + 1).\tag{4}$$

For comparable reasons, k's relationship with j should decrease, and so we shift it to the average between its previous value and the worst possible relationship value, namely, -1:

$$R_{jkD}^{(K)} = \tfrac{1}{2}(R_{jk}^{(K-1)} - 1).\tag{5}$$

An additional effect is also included here: If k should have joined j because its relationship with j was more positive (or less negative) than its relationship with i, then k should suffer a penalty. It is reasonable to make this penalty proportional to the probability that it should have joined j; the penalty will be largest when p_j^k is 1 and disappear when p_j^k is 0. We therefore modify (5) to include this effect:

$$R_{jkD}^{(K)} = \tfrac{1}{2}(R_{jk}^{(K-1)} - 1) - \tfrac{1}{2}p_j^k(R_{jk}^{(K-1)} + 1).\tag{6}$$

The last factor is constructed so that if p_j^k is 1, that is, k should definitely have joined j but didn't, then the relationship between the two immediately reverts to its worst value, namely, -1.

Similar reasoning is used in the lower box in Figure 9.3 to model the change in k's relationships with i and j under the condition that k joined the dispute on j's side. We can obtain this model from (4) and (6) simply by interchanging i and j.

$$R_{ikD}^{(K)} = \tfrac{1}{2}(R_{ik}^{(K-1)} - 1) - \tfrac{1}{2}p_i^k(R_{ik}^{(K-1)} + 1),$$

$$R_{jkD}^{(K)} = \tfrac{1}{2}(R_{jk}^{(K-1)} + 1). \tag{7}$$

The top box in Figure 9.3 contains our model of what happens to relationships if k stays out of the dispute. We propose three different models, three different worlds within which our decisionmaker could operate. The first we call the true world. In this world the relationships k has with i and j do not change as a result of staying out of the dispute *if* k feels the same toward both i and j, that is, if $R_{ik}^{(K-1)} = R_{jk}^{(K-1)}$. Since k does not favor one over the other, staying out should not affect k's relationships with i and j. In all other cases, we take the change in relationships to be proportional to the relationship difference $R_{ik}^{(K-1)} - R_{jk}^{(K-1)}$. Specifically, we propose the model:

$$R_{ikD}^{(K)} = R_{ik}^{(K-1)} + \tfrac{1}{2}(R_{jk}^{(K-1)} - R_{ik}^{(K-1)}),$$

$$R_{jkD}^{(K)} = R_{jk}^{(K-1)} + \tfrac{1}{2}(R_{ik}^{(K-1)} - R_{jk}^{(K-1)}). \tag{8}$$

The difference terms on the right act either as penalties or rewards. For example, k's relationship with i is penalized if k is a very good friend of i and a bitter enemy of j and yet k does not enter the dispute. In this case i feels that k deserted a friend in need. However, since j has benefited from k's decision to stay out because j does not have k as an additional adversary, the relationship between k and j is rewarded.

The other two worlds are ones in which either prospect theory or expected utility theory is always inconclusive. In the expected utility world, the updating of relationships when k stays out of a dispute is such that an expected utility maximizer would not be able to decide what to do, that is, the utility of staying out of a dispute always equals the expected utility of joining. The conventional assumption in such a case is that the utility maximizer treats both options as equally likely and then selects one randomly. To parallel this, we define a prospect theory world to be one in which the updating of relationships when k stays out is such that a prospect theorist's decisions would be inconclusive and hence result in a toss-up. Here the value of staying out of a dispute always equals the value of joining.

To create these two worlds, we adopt the following updating rules:

$$R_{ikD}^{(K)} = R_{ik}^{(K-1)} + G_k p_i^k,$$

$$R_{jkD}^{(K)} = R_{jk}^{(K-1)} + G_k p_j^k. \tag{9}$$

The quantity G_k represents the overall gain that k sees in its relationships with i and j as a function of staying out of the dispute. As (9) indicates, this gain is distributed to the individual relationships in proportion to the probabilities that k would have joined one nation or the other. If G_k is negative, it represents a loss, but this loss is shared in the same way as for a gain. In an expected utility world, we compute the gain G_k so that the utility of staying out equals the expected utility of joining. In a prospect theory world, we compute G_k so that the value of staying out equals the value of joining. We describe these calculations in detail later, once the decisionmaking problem has been clarified.

One final set of updating rules is needed. These relate to pairs of nations both of which are third parties. So far we have denoted a third party by k; let another be denoted by m. The update rules for the relationship between k and m are the same for all worlds and are quite simple. If either k or m chooses to stay out of the dispute, or both stay out, nothing happens to their relationship *as a result of the dispute:*

$$R^{(K)}_{kmD} = R^{(K-1)}_{km}. \qquad (10)$$

If both k and m enter the dispute, their relationship improves if they are on the same side and deteriorates if they are on opposite sides. We model these increases or decreases as in (4) and (5), that is:

$$R^{(K)}_{kmD} = \begin{cases} \frac{1}{2} \ (R^{(K-1)}_{km} + 1) & \text{if } k \text{ and } m \text{ are on the same side.} \\ \frac{1}{2} \ (R^{(K-1)}_{km} - 1) & \text{if } k \text{ and } m \text{ are on the opposite sides.} \end{cases} \qquad (11)$$

THE DECISION CALCULUS

We are now in a position to introduce a model of the decisionmaker. As Figure 9.3 indicates, the problem confronting a decisionmaker is a lottery, since k must decide whether or not to join the dispute. Moreover, if k joins, it is not certain which side it will join, but it can assess the relative likelihood (i.e., probabilities) of joining one side versus the other and also the utilities (or values) in doing so. Consider first a model of the joining probabilities.

We base our model of the probabilities of joining one side versus the other directly on the relative relationship of k toward one side versus the other. If k has the same relationship with i as it has with j, then the probabilities of joining either i or j should be .5. If k is a strong friend of i and a bitter enemy of j (i.e., $R^{(K-1)}_{ik} = 1$ and $R^{(K-1)}_{jk} = -1$), then the probability of joining i should be 1, and the probability of joining j should be 0. A simple model that captures these effects[1] is

$$p^k_i = \frac{1}{4} \ (2 + R^{(K-1)}_{ik} - R^{(K-1)}_{jk}),$$

$$p^k_j = 1 - p^k_i \ ,$$

$$= \frac{1}{4} \ (2 + R^{(K-1)}_{jk} - R^{(K-1)}_{ik}). \qquad (12)$$

The decisionmaking rules we use here are based on a "relationship currency." Specifically, the relationships that a nation k has with i and j following a dispute carry value or utility for k, with positive relationships having higher utility than negative ones. Moreover, gains in relationships have positive value while losses are negative. Positive relationships are generally associated with stable, predictable behavior, while negative relationships lead to conflict and uncertainty. Consequently, positive relationships are desired over negative ones. Thus we assume that the international system is a collection of nations, *together* with their relationships, and these relationships are of vital importance in predicting how a given nation will respond when placed in a decisionmaking role.

Let the total relationship that k has with i and j be represented by the sum of its separate relationships. Thus we define the initial and final total relationships as

$$R^{\text{initial}} = R_{ik}^{(K-1)} + R_{jk}^{(K-1)};$$
$$R^{\text{final}} = R_{ik\text{D}}^{(K)} + R_{jk\text{D}}^{(K)}. \tag{13}$$

We assume that nation k is fully aware of the various updating calculations that apply to each route through the lottery and that it can therefore base its decision to join the dispute or stay out on those calculations. That is, nation k examines the "worth" of its new total relationship R^{final}, perhaps in comparison with its previous total R^{initial}, and uses this information in its decisionmaking calculus.

As Figure 9.3 indicates, k's updated relationships following a dispute vary with the route k takes through the lottery. From (4) and (6), we get the following new total relationship if k enters the dispute and joins i:

$$R_{k\text{joins }i}^{\text{final}} = \tfrac{1}{2} (R_{ik}^{(K-1)} + 1) + \tfrac{1}{2} (R_{jk}^{(K-1)} - 1) - \tfrac{1}{2} p_j^k (R_{jk}^{(K-1)} + 1),$$
$$= \tfrac{1}{2} \left(R_{jk}^{(K-1)} (1 - p_j^k) + R_{ik}^{(K-1)} + 1 - 1 - p_j^k \right), \tag{14}$$
$$= \tfrac{1}{2} \left(R_{jk}^{(K-1)} p_i^k + R_{ik}^{(K-1)} - p_j^k \right).$$

Similarly, by interchanging i and j in the preceding calculation, we obtain an expression for the new total relationship if k enters the dispute and joins j:

$$R_{k\text{joins }j}^{\text{final}} = \tfrac{1}{2} \left(R_{ik}^{(K-1)} p_j^k + R_{jk}^{(K-1)} - p_i^k \right). \tag{15}$$

If k decides to stay out of the dispute, then the new total relationship of k depends upon the world we are modeling. For the true world, (8) shows that the final total relationship is given by

$$R_{k\text{stays out}}^{\text{final}} = \left(R_{ik}^{(K-1)} + \tfrac{1}{2} (R_{jk}^{(K-1)} - R_{ik}^{(K-1)}) \right) +$$
$$\left(R_{jk}^{(K-1)} + \tfrac{1}{2} (R_{ik}^{(K-1)} - R_{jk}^{(K-1)}) \right), \tag{16}$$
$$= R_{ik}^{(K-1)} + R_{jk}^{(K-1)},$$
$$= R^{\text{initial}}.$$

If we are considering either an expected utility world or a prospect theory world, then from (9) we find that the new total relationship of k is

$$R^{\text{final}}_{k\,\text{stays out}} = R^{(K-1)}_{ik} + G_k p^k_i + R^{(K-1)}_{jk} + G_k p^k_j,$$
$$= (R^{(K-1)}_{ik} + R^{(K-1)}_{jk}) + G_k (p^k_i + p^k_j), \qquad (17)$$
$$= R^{\text{initial}} + G_k.$$

This shows directly that G_k represents the net relationship gain from the beginning to the end of the dispute, given that k did not enter on either side.

If k is an expected utility maximizer, let U denote the function that it uses in determining the utility of its total relationship with i and j. We assume all nations use the same utility function for the simulations conducted here; in a later section we describe the actual function used in the simulations. The utility of staying out of the dispute is the $U(R^{\text{final}}_{k\,\text{stays out}})$. If k chooses to enter the dispute, then we must find the expected utility of the lottery. This is $U(R^{\text{final}}_{k\,\text{joins}\,i})\,p^k_i + U(R^{\text{final}}_{k\,\text{joins}\,j})\,p^k_j$. The decision calculus in this case is as follows: If

$$U(R^{\text{final}}_{k\,\text{stays out}}) < U(R^{\text{final}}_{k\,\text{joins}\,i})\,p^k_i + U(R^{\text{final}}_{k\,\text{joins}\,j})\,p^k_j, \qquad (18)$$

then k will enter the dispute. With the reverse inequality, k will not join the dispute. If there is equality, then staying out and joining are equally likely options, and k selects one at random.

Prospect theory proceeds in a similar fashion but requires that we "frame" the results of the lottery and generally work in terms of gains or losses rather than actual relationship values. That is, a final total relationship level of 1.5 will be assigned one utility value, but how it is *valued* depends on framing. If the initial total relationship is 1 and the lottery results in a gain of .5, the final value is 1.5, but this might be valued differently from a case in which the initial total is −1 and the gain is 2.5, even though the final relationship total is the same. Unfortunately, current discussions of prospect theory do not provide much guidance as to how to frame outcomes, and yet for a simulation study of the type we are pursuing here, we must be explicit. Therefore we introduce a value function $V(x, r)$ with the following interpretation. The argument r is a relationship level about which our value calculation is framed. For the simulations conducted here, it is the total relationship of k toward i and j when the dispute begins. The argument x represents a total relationship gain from the beginning to end of the dispute. It therefore becomes $R^{\text{final}} - R^{\text{initial}}$ in our analysis. Thus $V(R^{\text{final}} - R^{\text{initial}}, R^{\text{initial}})$ gives the value to k of the new relationship it will have after the dispute, framed within the context of its relationship at the outset of the dispute. We must, however, compute this value for each of the possible outcomes in k's lottery. For example, $V(R^{\text{final}}_{k\,\text{stays out}}) - R^{\text{initial}}, R^{\text{intial}})$

is the value to k of not entering the dispute. For the decision calculus of prospect theory, this value is compared with a weighted sum of the values of k's entering the dispute either on the side of i or on the side of j. To simplify the presentation of this rule, let us denote the relationship change $R_{k\,\text{stays out}}^{\text{final}} - R^{\text{initial}}$ by $\Delta R_{k\text{stays out}}$, with a similar notation if k joins i or j. Then the decision rule of prospect theory is: If

$$V(\Delta R_{k\text{ stays out}}, R^{\text{intitial}}) < V(\Delta R_{k\text{ joins }i}, R^{\text{intitial}})$$

$$W(p_i^k) + V(\Delta R_{k\text{ joins }j}, R^{\text{intitial}})\ W(p_j^k), \tag{19}$$

then k values entering the dispute more highly than staying out and so will enter. With the reverse inequality, k will stay out of the dispute. And if there is equality, the decision is a toss-up. W is a weighting function that accounts for the fact that decisionmakers are perceived, in prospect theory, to underestimate probabilities of highly likely events and overestimate probabilities of rare events. Later we describe in detail the weight function W and the value function V used in the simulations.

STRUCTURE OF THE SIMULATIONS

Levy's arguments favoring a prospect theory approach to international decisionmaking used examples that had a special structure that made the implications of prospect theory striking. Each one involved a lottery in which the conventional expected utility calculation yielded no decision, that is, the lottery was a toss-up. By looking at situations in which expected utility theory was inconclusive, a researcher could clearly examine the decisions implied by prospect theory. This strategy, while blatant, served the purpose of illustrating the most divergent properties of expected utility theory and prospect theory.

We pursue a similar strategy here, at least initially. Namely, we consider a decisionmaking model in which expected utility theory yields a toss-up while prospect theory is used to make decisions. Let this be called simulation 1. In the terminology we have introduced here, this simulation describes a prospect theory decisionmaker embedded in an expected utility world. Unlike Levy, however, we construct a second simulation that gives equal emphasis to expected utility theory. In simulation 2 the calculus of prospect theory yields inconclusive decisions while decisions are made on the basis of expected utility theory. This is the case of an expected utility maximizer embedded in a prospect theory world.

Simulations 1 and 2 are constructed to emphasize the differences, as reflected through repeated decisionmaking over a sequence of disputes,

between prospect theory and expected utility theory. However, it is unlikely in the real world that either of these theories yields a tossup, even
approximately, every time. It is entirely possible that in real situations
prospect theory and expected utility theory yield exactly the same decisions at each stage of a simulation, or essentially so. This idea gives rise to
simulation 3 and simulation 4. In simulation 3 k makes decisions according to prospect theory while being embedded in the true world (see updating (8)). In simulation 4 decisions are made according to expected utility
theory, once again in the context of the true world. The comparison between simulations 3 and 4 is therefore especially telling for the ultimate
comparison of the two decisionmaking theories in the setting of international politics.

Simulation 1   *Decisions made via prospect theory in an expected utility*
world. The decision rule in this case is described in (19) where the change
$\Delta R_{k\text{stays out}}$ is computed using the update rule (9). The relationship gain G_k
appearing there is computed so that expected utility theory reduces to a
toss-up. Thus we must have equality in (18). This condition, with the value
of $R_{k\text{stays out}}^{\text{final}}$ given in (17), becomes

$$U(R^{\text{intitial}} + G_k) + U(R_{k\text{ joins } i}^{\text{final}})\, p_i^k + U(R_{k\text{ joins } j}^{\text{final}})\, p_j^k. \tag{20}$$

This equation can always be solved for G_k because it is convention to assume that the utility function U is a strictly increasing function and hence
has a well-defined inverse function U^{-1}. Applying this inverse to both
sides of (20), we are led directly to a formula for G_k:

$$G_k = U^{-1}\left(U(R_{k\text{ joins } i}^{\text{final}})\, p_i^k + U(R_{k\text{ joins } j}^{\text{final}})\, p_j^k \right) - R^{\text{intitial}}. \tag{21}$$

Simulation 2   *Decisions made via expected utility theory in a prospect*
theory world. For this simulation, the decision rule is described by (18).
The total relationship value for staying out, $R_{k\text{stays out}}^{\text{final}}$, that appears there is
given by (17), where G_k is computed so that prospect theory yields a toss-
up. For this, we must arrange that (19) reduce to an equality. We can write
this condition in the form

$$V(G_k, R^{\text{intitial}}) = V(\Delta R_{k\text{ joins } i}, R^{\text{intitial}})\, W(p_i^k) + V(\Delta R_{k\text{ joins } j}, R^{\text{intitial}})\, W(p_j^k). \tag{22}$$

In parallel with our preceding remarks about utility functions, it is conventional to assume that the value function $V(x, r)$ is a strictly increasing
function of x for each choice of the framing variable r. This means that
there is an inverse function $V^{-1}(v, r)$ that transforms values v back into relationship changes x. By applying this inverse function to each side of
(22), we obtain the value

$$G_k = V^{-1}(V(\Delta R_{k\text{ joins } i}, R^{\text{intitial}})\, W(p_i^k) + V(\Delta R_{k\text{ joins } j}, R^{\text{intitial}})\, W(p_j^k), R^{\text{intitial}}). \tag{23}$$

Simulation 3   *Decisions made via prospect theory in a true world.* As with simulation 1, decisions are based on condition (19). But the change $\Delta R_{k\text{stays out}}$ in this case is determined using the true-world updating (16).

Simulation 4   *Decisions made via expected utility theory in a true world.* Decisions in this case are based on the expected utility calculation (18), where, as in simulation 3, the change $\Delta R_{k\text{stays out}}$ is determined using the true-world updating (16).

One of the principal features that these simulations capture is the embedding of a decisionmaking calculus in a dynamic process. Recall that there are two components of the model. The first is the decision that nation k makes as to whether or not it will join the dispute. In simulation 1, for example, nation k makes this decision on the basis of prospect theory in a context in which an expected utility maximizer would not be able to discriminate between the stay out or join options. This piece of the model directly parallels the typical experiments found in the literature on prospect theory. Our model, however, takes the problem one step further. Once k has made the decision either to enter or stay out of the dispute, there is an actual payoff that takes place, that is, k's relationships with the two disputants (and everyone else) are updated. In simulation 1 this updating takes place as if expected utility were the "real world," that is, k's relationships with i and j change as a consequence of its prospect theoretic decision in the expected utility situation. In the experimental settings described in the prospect theory literature, this would be equivalent to having the subject make a decision, giving the subject the money or payoff that would accrue, and then letting that subject go on to the next experiment, similarly constructed so that the lottery versus the sure thing is, in expected utility calculations, a toss-up. Presumably, as the prospect theorist moves from the first experimental setting to the second, the gains or losses in the first help to determine the framing that will take place in the second. This is what is happening in simulation 1. Parallel interpretations apply to the other three simulations. The important point to remember is that the decisionmakers in this model must weigh the virtues of future options, *where decisions made now do indeed affect future behavior.*

UTILITY AND VALUE FUNCTIONS

Let $U(x)$ denote the utility function for a risk-averse decisionmaker. The argument x represents the total relationship k holds for i and j, and therefore we assume U is defined for $-2 \le x \le 2$. The solid curve in Figure 9.4 shows the utility function we use in the simulations. The technical definition we use for U is

$$u = U(x) = \tfrac{1}{2} + x - \tfrac{1}{8}x^2. \tag{24}$$

By solving this equation for x in terms of u, we obtain the inverse function:

$$x = U^{-1}(u) = 4 - \sqrt{20 - 8u}. \tag{25}$$

This is the function that is used in (21) to determine the relationship gain appropriate to an expected utility world. The graph of the inverse function is the dashed curve in Figure 9.4.

Our principal goal here is to compare two theories of decisionmaking. In order for this to be a meaningful enterprise, we need to establish certain uniformities across the two theories that do not compromise their differences. It would be unreasonable, for example, to compare expected utility calculations with prospect theory calculations if utilities were measured in dollars and values were measured in pounds sterling. Even if the units were commensurate, there are more subtle issues. If a person using expected utility calculations assigned a utility of $1 to receiving an apple, it would be unreasonable, for the purposes of comparison, to have that same person assign a value of $1,000 to the receipt of that same apple when using prospect theory. We need to model a single decisionmaker selecting both a utility

Figure 9.4
The Utility Function and Its Inverse

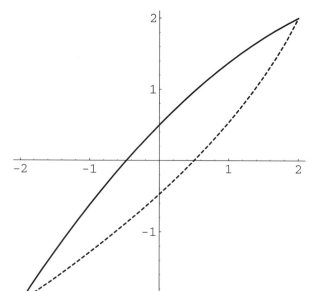

Figure 9.5
The Value Function and Its Inverse

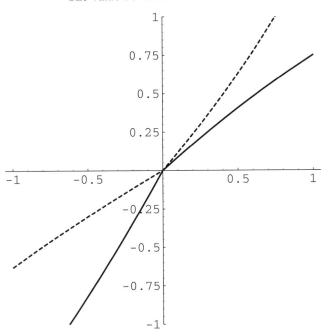

function and a value function in parallel settings. This is done by constructing the value function based on the utility function U given above.

Let r be the total relationship value around which we frame the calculation of values, and let g denote a *gain* in relationship from the value r. The new relationship level is then $x = g + r$. If the gain is positive (i.e., not a loss), prospect theory assumes that the decisionmaker is risk-averse, much as in expected utility theory. It is here that we make a direct connection between the two theories. We assume that a decisionmaker, as prospect theorist, weighs gains in exactly the same way he or she would, as an expected utility maximizer, weigh utilities. That is, the utility of the relationship $g + r$ is $U(g + r)$. If we subtract from this the utility associated with the framing point, that is, $U(r)$, then we obtain a *value* that can be attributed to the gain. Thus, for gain calculations, the value function we use is

$$v = V(g, r) = U(g + r) - U(r),$$
$$= \left(\tfrac{1}{2} + (g + r) - \tfrac{1}{8}(g + r)^2\right) - \left(\tfrac{1}{2} + r - \tfrac{1}{8} r^2\right), \qquad (26)$$
$$= g\left(1 - \tfrac{1}{4} r\right) - \tfrac{1}{8} g^2, \qquad g \geq 0.$$

By solving this equation for g as a function of v (for fixed r), we obtain the inverse value function for positive values:

$$g = V^{-1}(v, r) = 4 - r - \sqrt{(4 - r)^2 - 8v}, \qquad v \geq 0. \qquad (27)$$

Prospect theory assumes that in the realm of losses a decisionmaker is risk-acceptant. A simple way to build this feature into our construction of V is to assume that our decisionmaker is risk-acceptant toward losses *in exactly the same way* that he or she is risk-averse toward gains. That is, if g is negative, then $V(g, r) = -V(-g, r)$. Prospect theory actually says something more about the risk-acceptant side of the value function, namely, that the risk-acceptant portion of the graph of V is steeper than the risk-averse side.[2] We make the risk-acceptant side twice as steep here by using the modified definition:

$$\begin{aligned} v = V(g, r) &= -2V(-g, r), \\ &= -2 \left(-g(1 - \tfrac{1}{4} r) - \tfrac{1}{8} (-g)^2 \right), \qquad\qquad (28) \\ &= g \left(2 - \tfrac{1}{2} r \right) + \tfrac{1}{4} g^2, \qquad\qquad\qquad g < 0. \end{aligned}$$

As a final step, we solve this equation for g as a function of v to obtain the inverse value function for loss calculations:

$$g = V^{-1}(v, r) = - (4 - r) + \sqrt{(4 - r)^2 + 4v}, \qquad v < 0. \qquad (29)$$

Figure 9.5 illustrates the above definitions by showing the value function $V(g, .5)$ (the solid curve) and its inverse $V^{-1}(v, .5)$ (the dashed curve) for values framed about the relationship level .5.

THE PROBABILITY WEIGHT FUNCTION

The probability weight function W appearing in the decision rule (19) embodies the idea that individuals generally overestimate the likelihood of rare events and underestimate highly likely ones. This is one of the principal tenets of prospect theory. In Levy's original paper, this assumption appeared in the form of a graph of the function W. We have selected a definition of W that reproduces his picture. The technical definition is

$$W(p) = \begin{cases} 3.25p - 25p^2 & \text{if } 0 \leq p \leq .05. \\ .059 + .9p - 1.737p^2 + 3.25p^3 - 1.573p^4 & \text{if } .05 \leq p \leq .95. \\ 36 - 75p + 40p^2 & \text{if } .95 \leq p \leq 1. \end{cases} \qquad (30)$$

A graph of W derived from this definition is shown in Figure 9.6.

RESULTS OF THE SIMULATIONS

Our goal here is to compare two settings, namely, international systems in which decisionmakers operate as prospect theorists against international

Figure 9.6
The Probability Weight Function

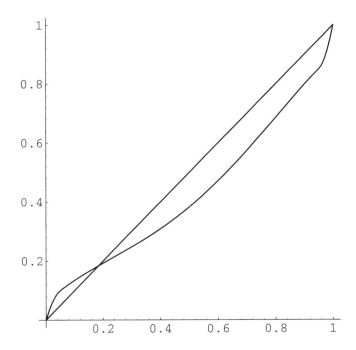

systems in which the decisionmakers operate as expected utility maximizers. We have placed both types of decisionmakers into two types of worlds: a world in which the opposite type of decisionmaker would be unable to make a choice and a so-called true world. These combinations produce four possible scenarios or simulations. The stochastic components of the models make it necessary to run each simulation more than once. A run involves thirty disputes: In each simulation there are thirty different occasions in which two nations are randomly chosen as initial disputants, thirty times when all other nations in the system must decide whether or not to enter the dispute, and so forth. We have elected to run each twenty times and then compile summary information. The simulations reported here contain five nations, so that at each dispute point three nations must determine whether or not they will join the dispute involving the other two.

Our central question is whether an interconnected world of prospect theorists will produce consequences that differ from an interconnected world of expected utility maximizers. Interconnectedness, of course, is meant in terms of positive and negative relationships between the nations

or actors involved. We are specifically interested in three types of consequences. First, is there a difference from one scenario to the next in the
size of disputes, that is, the number of nations involved in each dispute?
Second, do these two decisionmaking calculations produce different degrees of polarization in the system? For example, is a world full of
prospect theorists more likely to be a bipolar world than a world full of expected utility maximizers? Finally, do these two decisionmaking formats
have different effects on the overall intensity of the network of relationships between the nations? That is, does a world full of expected utility
maximizers have more intense relationships (whether positive or negative)
than a world of prospect theorists?

Figures 9.7 through 9.10 illustrate the information we have for a typical run of the four simulations. Each run is characterized by a random
seed. This seed is changed from run to run, but it is held constant across
the four simulations so that the stochastic part of the model can be eliminated, as far as possible, from comparisons across the simulations. By
using a seed for the random number generator, we are able to replicate,
one random number at a time, the effects of making probabilistic choices
at each point in the evolution of the dispute sequence. In all twenty runs,
the initial relationships were selected randomly from the range $-1 \leq R \leq 1$.
This is signified by the "Initial data: 4" statement appearing in the information for each simulation. Since we use the same seed in each run, we
therefore have the same initial relationships in each of the four simulations. Furthermore, as described earlier through equation (1), all simulations were set so that the dispute component was 96 percent, with memory and network effects set at 2 percent each. This permitted maximum
exploration of the impact of the decision calculus.

Consider first the various pieces of information reported in the top
section of Figure 9.7. We note first that the average participants per dispute in this simulation is 2.17. This result is obtained from the graph
shown below the box. This graph indicates how many nations were involved in each of the thirty disputes. As can be seen, there were five nations in the first dispute, three in the second and third disputes, and only
two nations in all the remaining disputes (i.e., nations generally decided
not to enter). Adding the number of nations in each dispute across all disputes and dividing by 30 produces the value of 2.17. Thus Figure 9.7
strongly suggests that prospect theorists functioning in an expected utility
world would primarily decide *not to join the dispute.*

The polarization indices, initial and final, were constructed on the
basis of a theorem in graph theory.[3] These scores reflect the extent to
which the system of five nations is unipolar or bipolar, with 10 being a
completely polar world and -10 reflecting a world in which there is no degree of polarity. The initial polarity score is determined by the initial

Figure 9.7
A Prospect Theorist in an Expected Utility World

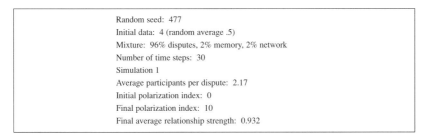

Random seed: 477
Initial data: 4 (random average .5)
Mixture: 96% disputes, 2% memory, 2% network
Number of time steps: 30
Simulation 1
Average participants per dispute: 2.17
Initial polarization index: 0
Final polarization index: 10
Final average relationship strength: 0.932

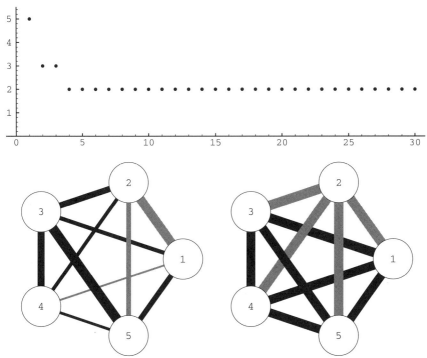

conditions and in Figure 9.7 was 0. This is shown more graphically in the left subfigure in the bottom part of Figure 9.7. The five circles represent the five nations. The black lines indicate friends and gray lines indicate enemies, and the thickness of the lines indicates the intensity of the relationship. As we see in the first configuration, the polarity score of 0 occurs because while nations 3, 4, and 5 are all friends, 3 is also a friend of 2, but 5 is an enemy of 2, and so on. This configuration, then, has some subgroupings that behave as poles, but overall it is not polarized. This is what gives rise to the polarization index of 0. The final polarization score indicates what has happened to the network of relationships following the thirty disputes. We note in Figure 9.7 that the world has become extremely bipolar, as indicated by the score of 10. This is shown at the right in the lower diagram. Here we see that nations 1, 3, 4, and 5 are all friends and that each of these nations is in turn an enemy of nation 2.

The final piece of information shown in Figure 9.7 is the average strength of relationship found by averaging the absolute values of each of the ten relationship bonds. Thus this index taps the extent to which all pairs of nations are concerned (positively or negatively) about each other. A value close to 1 indicates that the nations are all very much involved with one another, either as intense friends or intense enemies. In some sense, this provides an indication of how "connected" the nations are to each other. The prospect theorists in the expected utility world shown in Figure 9.7 are very "connected." Their score is .932.

Let us now compare Figure 9.7 with Figure 9.8. Figure 9.8 portrays the expected utility maximizer in a prospect theory world. Note that the average number of participants has dramatically increased: We have gone from an average of 2.17 participants to an average of 4.47. This is seen even more clearly in the graph given below the box of results; disputes typically involve the entire system of nations. Expected utility maximizers in a prospect theory world are dispute prone. It is interesting, however, to note that the polarization index and relationship index do not differ appreciably between Figures 9.7 and 9.8: In both instances the system has completely polarized and the nations are intensely interconnected, though the configuration of the poles is different.

Figures 9.9 and 9.10 place the prospect theorists and expected utility maximizers, respectively, into a common, so-called true world. In these two simulations, we find that there is not much difference between prospect theory and expected utility with respect to the average number of disputants. In prospect theory the average number of participants per dispute is 2.47, while in expected utility theory the average is slightly higher at 2.67. The polarization indices, however, are drastically different: Prospect theory produces as nonpolar a world as is possible, with a score of −10, while expected utility theory produces a completely bipolar world with a score of 10. The final average relationship strength under prospect theory is .19, indicating that on average these nations do not care much about each other one way or another. Looking at the picture in the lower right corner, we see that while 2 and 3 rather intensely dislike each other and 1 and 5 are relatively hostile, all other bonds are minimal. This result is in contrast to the more interconnected set of nations displayed in Figure 9.10. These expected utility maximizers are generally more concerned about one another, with an average relationship bond strength of .614.

Figure 9.8
An Expected Utility Maximizer in a Prospect Theory World

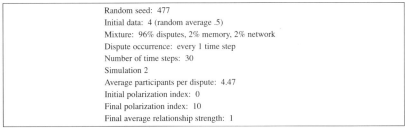

Random seed: 477
Initial data: 4 (random average .5)
Mixture: 96% disputes, 2% memory, 2% network
Dispute occurrence: every 1 time step
Number of time steps: 30
Simulation 2
Average participants per dispute: 4.47
Initial polarization index: 0
Final polarization index: 10
Final average relationship strength: 1

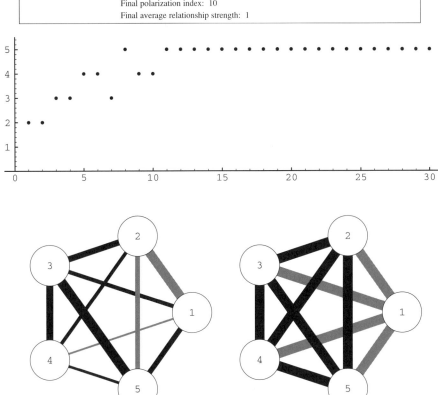

The results just described for Figures 9.7 through 9.10 represent only one of the twenty runs. To see whether these are in some sense "typical," we need to look more generally across runs. These runs are reported in Table 9.1. Under each of the three categories of "Average Number of Participants," "Polarization Score," and "Average Final Relationship," there are four columns representing the four scenarios: Prospect theorists in an

Figure 9.9
A Prospect Theorist in a True World

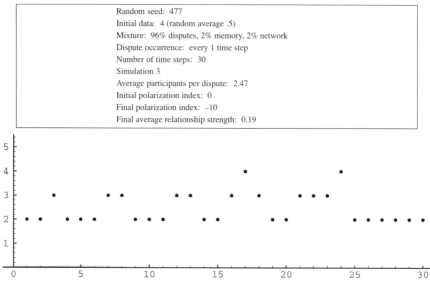

Random seed: 477
Initial data: 4 (random average .5)
Mixture: 96% disputes, 2% memory, 2% network
Dispute occurrence: every 1 time step
Number of time steps: 30
Simulation 3
Average participants per dispute: 2.47
Initial polarization index: 0
Final polarization index: −10
Final average relationship strength: 0.19

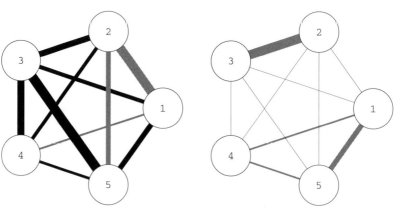

expected utility world, expected utility theorists in a prospect theory world, prospect theorists in a true world, and expected utility theorists in a true world. The random seed in each case is reported at the left. Note that in the third column the polarization scores are reported only in terms of values between 3 and -3. This is because not all values of polarization scores can occur, because of the way the polarization index was created; it can take on only the values[4] of 10, 4, 2, 0, −2, −4, and −10. To

Figure 9.10
An Expected Utility Maximizer in a True World

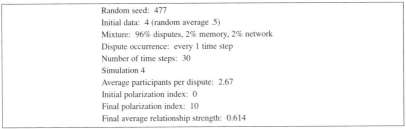

Random seed: 477
Initial data: 4 (random average .5)
Mixture: 96% disputes, 2% memory, 2% network
Dispute occurrence: every 1 time step
Number of time steps: 30
Simulation 4
Average participants per dispute: 2.67
Initial polarization index: 0
Final polarization index: 10
Final average relationship strength: 0.614

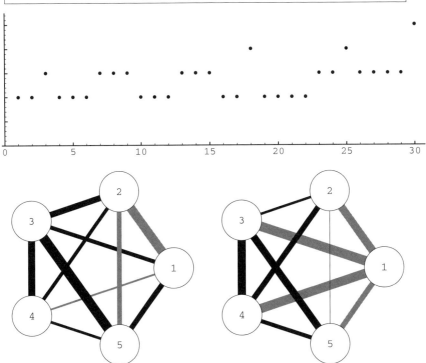

standardize these values, we therefore converted them to 3, 2, 1, 0, –1, –2, and –3.

The values that are of interest are those reported in the final two rows of Table 9.1, the means and standard deviations for each index across the twenty runs. In Figure 9.7 we saw that prospect theorists in an expected utility world tended not to join ongoing disputes. This result continues to hold over the twenty simulation runs, as seen in that the average across simulation runs is 2.477. The standard deviation of .263 suggests relatively few deviations from the average. Similarly, the first column of the second section of Table 9.1 is also consistent with what was found in Figure 9.8. Here the average number of disputants is 4.469, with a standard deviation of .286. Expected utility decisionmakers in a prospect theory world tend to get involved in disputes. In Figures 9.9 and 9.10, we saw that when prospect theory decisionmakers and expected utility maximizers were each put into the same true world, the earlier results tended to disappear. This finding appears to be true across the twenty simulation runs. Thus prospect theorists in a true world are more involved in disputes than they were when embedded in an expected utility world, 2.757 versus 2.477, while expected utility decisionmakers in a true world tend to get less involved in disputes than was the case when they were embedded in a prospect theory world: 3.094 versus 4.469. It should be noted, however, that even in the true world expected utility maximizers are more likely to get into disputes than prospect theory decisionmakers: The average number of prospect theory nations that entered disputes is 2.757, while the average number of expected utility decisionmakers that entered disputes is 3.094.

Both Figures 9.7 and 9.8, however, indicated that after thirty disputes the five nations were highly polarized with very intense relationships. Thus there was little difference between the two types of decisionmakers in the two different worlds with respect to how their relationships evolved. The last two columns of sections 1 and 2 of Table 9.1 indicate that this result generally occurs across all the simulation runs. Recalling that the polarity scores have been standardized to run between −3 and 3, we see that both systems of prospect theorists and expected utility theorists have high polarization scores. Similarly, the intensity of the relationships in both cases is relatively high: .781 and .972.

Looking at the last two sections of Table 9.1, we see that the results obtained for the polarization index and the relationship intensity index in Figures 9.9 and 9.10 are also typical of the other simulations. Thus the average polarization score across the twenty runs for prospect theorists in a true world is −.7 and for expected utility maximizers is .2. In this true world, either decision calculus produces a relatively nonpolarized world. Furthermore, as the last columns of sections 3 and 4 suggest, these nations are considerably less "connected" or intensely involved with one another than was the case in the first two settings: .314 and .472 are the average relationship intensities as compared with .781 and .972. In summary, while the differences for a true world are small, they do suggest that under expected utility calculations there are greater dispute participation, greater polarization, and more intense relationships (both positive and negative) than under the prospect theory decision calculus.

Table 9.1   Summary Results of the Simulations

Run	Seed	Average Number of Participants				Polarization Score				Average Final Relationship			
		1	2	3	4	1	2	3	4	1	2	3	4
1	133	2.400	3.930	2.470	2.970	1	3	2	1	0.604	0.999	0.459	0.497
2	813	2.130	4.800	3.100	3.330	3	3	2	3	0.909	1	0.497	0.709
3	911	2.770	4.300	2.730	3.630	2	3	1	2	0.644	0.992	0.345	0.792
4	111	2.200	4.370	2.770	3.230	3	2	−1	−1	0.914	0.634	0.359	0.362
5	182	2.730	4.930	2.970	3.370	2	3	0	−2	0.633	1	0.275	0.409
6	777	2.830	4.070	2.670	3.170	1	3	−1	1	0.558	0.999	0.227	0.431
7	989	2.270	4.770	3.200	3.300	3	3	−1	−2	0.892	1	0.243	0.384
8	254	2.370	4.800	2.800	3.530	3	3	−2	0	0.893	1	0.281	0.499
9	333	2.770	4.070	2.700	2.800	2	3	−3	−2	0.577	0.997	0.175	0.289
10	455	2.730	4.670	2.670	3.370	2	3	−3	1	0.658	1	0.205	0.603
11	212	2.230	4.500	2.600	2.770	3	3	−2	3	0.919	1	0.415	0.906
12	888	2.130	4.230	2.900	3.070	3	3	−2	−2	0.926	0.824	0.352	0.391
13	190	2.200	4.700	2.770	2.730	3	3	−2	0	0.911	1	0.333	0.3
14	700	2.600	4.230	2.700	2.730	3	3	3	0	0.856	0.987	0.646	0.486
15	924	2.500	4.470	2.770	2.900	3	3	−1	−1	0.873	1	0.202	0.278
16	511	2.700	4.600	2.900	3.130	3	3	−2	1	0.694	1	0.205	0.469
17	602	2.830	4.800	2.500	3.200	3	3	1	−2	0.713	1	0.393	0.291
18	733	2.270	4.270	2.570	2.770	3	3	−1	−2	0.952	1	0.245	0.311
19	402	2.700	4.400	2.870	3.200	3	3	1	2	0.561	1	0.224	0.422
20	477	2.170	4.470	2.470	2.670	3	3	−3	3	0.932	1	0.19	0.614
Avg.		2.477	4.469	2.757	3.094	2.6	2.95	−0.7	0.15	0.781	0.971	0.313	0.472
Std.		0.263	0.286	0.196	0.288	0.68	0.22	1.81	1.84	0.148	0.088	0.122	0.174

APPENDIX:
THE HISTORY AND NETWORK UPDATING MODELS

The history contribution $R^{(K)}_{xy\,\mathrm{H}}$ to relationship updating—the middle box of the column of three in Figure 9.1—is computed using a discounting model based on three steps in the past:

$$R^{(K)}_{xy\,\mathrm{H}} = \frac{R^{(K-1)}_{xy} + aR^{(K-2)}_{xy} + a^2R^{(K-3)}_{xy}}{1 + a + a^2}, \quad 0 \le a \le 1.$$

The parameter a is called the discounting factor. We can view this as saying that the contribution of past history to the current relationship between x and y consists of A percent of the relationship between x and y at time $K - 1$, B percent of the relationship at time $K - 2$, and C percent of the relationship at time $K - 3$. Each of these percentages, $A = 1/(1 + a + a^2)$, $B = a/(1 + a + a^2)$, and $C = a^2/(1 + a + a^2)$, is smaller than its predecessor, and so this history updating model captures a certain sense of fading memory of past relationships.

As mentioned previously, the network contribution $R^{(K)}_{xy\,\mathrm{N}}$—the top box in Figure 9.3—accounts for the old rule, "The friend of my friend is my friend; the friend of my enemy is my enemy." It captures the fact that each nation is a part of a larger network of nations by taking into account friends of friends, and so on. Our use of this rule is an outgrowth of previous work on iternation relationships (Lee, Muncaster, and Zinnes, 1994). The model we use here has the form

$$R^{(K)}_{xy\,\mathrm{N}} = \tfrac{1}{3}\sum_m F(R^{(K-1)}_{xm}, R^{(K-1)}_{my}), \quad F(r, s) = \mathrm{sign}(rs)\sqrt{|rs|},$$

where the sum is over all nations m other than x and y, of which there are three. Thus we have an average over all triads involving x and y. The product $R^{(K-1)}_{xm}R^{(K-1)}_{my}$ is positive, that is, represents a friendship, if x is a friend of m and m is a friend of y ($(+)(+)=(+)$), or if x is an enemy of m and m is an enemy of y ($(-)(-)=(+)$). Similarly $R^{(K-1)}_{xm}R^{(K-1)}_{my}$ is negative and hence represents enmity if x is a friend of m and m is an enemy of y ($(+)(-)=(-)$), or if x is an enemy of m and m is a friend of y ($(-)(+)=(-)$). An average over such products therefore captures the friend-of-my-friend rule for each of the nations m aside from x and y. We use the functional form $F(R^{(K)}_{xm}, R^{(K)}_{my})$ rather than just $R^{(K-1)}_{xm}R^{(K-1)}_{my}$ for technical reasons: $F(x, y)$ behaves exactly like the product xy in regard to sign, but it is not as small in magnitude as xy when applied to relationship variables, that is, variables that lie between -1 and 1.

NOTES

1. The model (12) was found by starting with a simple linear expression $p^k_i = A + BR^{(K-1)}_{ik} + CR^{(K-1)}_{jk}$ for the probability of joining i, and the symmetric relation

$p_j^k = A + BR_{jk}^{(K-1)} + CR_{ik}^{(K-1)}$ for joining j, and then choosing the constants A, B, and C so that the extremes indicated in the text hold.

2. This is just a reflection of the graph of V through the origin.

3. See Theorem 3.1 of Claude Flament's *Applications of Graph Theory to Group Structure* (Englewood Cliffs, N.J.: Prentice-Hall, 1963). Theorem 3.5 is also important, since it, in conjunction with 3.1, shows that a five-nation system is polarized if and only if all three cycles are balanced (i.e., the product of the relationships around any group of three nations is positive). There are 10 three cycles for a five-nation system. The polarization index used here is found by adding the *signs* of all three cycles. A 10 is then the best (polarized), while a –10 is the worst (completely nonpolar).

4. Since the polarization index comes from adding up the signs around each three cycle, one must be careful to account for the fact that different three cycles often have a relationship or connection in common. This is what gives rise to the unusual scale with numerous gaps.

Part 4

Conclusion

10

Decisionmaking on War and Peace: Challenges for Future Research

Nehemia Geva, Steven B. Redd, & Alex Mintz

The preceding chapters have explored how expected utility, prospect theory, the theory of moves, two-level games, and the poliheuristic theory of decisionmaking deal with foreign policy decisions. The general consensus that has emerged among the contributors to this volume is that cognitive and rational approaches to decisionmaking should not be viewed as competing but as complementary. In this final chapter, we take the discourse to the next level by suggesting several new avenues for research on war and peace decisionmaking. The chapter is divided into three sections that represent fundamental issues that scholars of the foreign policy decisionmaking process have not yet seriously addressed: (1) the decision design problem, (2) the impact of a dynamic choice set on strategy selection and choice in foreign policy decisionmaking, and (3) the aggregation of individual preferences into collective decisionmaking in foreign policy situations.

Any review of decisionmaking theories and models should necessarily begin with a discussion of decision matrices. Decision matrices generally take the form of a set of alternatives (options) and a set of dimensions (criteria) upon which alternatives are judged (Mintz 1993). The decision design stage in foreign policy decisionmaking has crucial implications for information processing and choice in international relations. Mitchell and Beach (1990, p. 3) state that "the mechanism that governs admission to the set bears a major responsibility for the eventual decision." Consequently, scholars should devote more attention to the study of the ways in which a given foreign policy decision task originates. Most of the literature begins with the assumption of preexisting policy alternatives and/or evaluative dimensions without investigating how the parameters of the decision task are arrived at in the first place. However, information about how alternatives and dimensions enter into any decision situation and about the origins of the preferences are as important to understanding the foreign policy decisionmaking process as information about how decisions are actually being made.

Second, future models of foreign policy decisionmaking should account for the dynamic nature of the decision environment, an atmosphere constantly changing as events unfold and policy alternatives are added to or disappear from a choice set. The dynamic international environment may affect not only changes in alternatives and dimensions that compose the relevant decision matrix but also the expected utilities associated with each alternative. What ends up being included in the decision problem and the sequence in which decision components are introduced may have profound consequences for the choice that is made. Obviously, if the decisionmaker excludes (or includes) a critical alternative from a choice set, both the process of decisionmaking, which includes the rules by which members of the decision unit aggregate their preferences into a choice, and in turn the decision outcome may be significantly altered.

Finally, research should also focus on the issue of collective decisionmaking that characterizes numerous foreign policy decision situations. The "construction" of the decision matrix is in many cases a reflection of input from multiple players. Moreover, the decision itself may result from complex group dynamics.

DECISION DESIGN

Most studies of foreign policy decisionmaking identify alternatives (options) and dimensions (criteria) and focus on how the decisionmaker operates in order to arrive at an outcome. However, much of the literature fails to determine how alternatives and criteria in a decision matrix emerge. It is important to determine how and why various elements of the decision matrix were included or excluded because this process of "designing" the decision matrix has critical ramifications for information processing, preference ordering, as well as the eventual decision (Billings and Hermann 1994). In essence, decisionmakers must begin by "deciding how to decide" (Anderson 1985). Alternatives and dimensions are either exogenously imposed or endogenously derived or a combination of both. But whether or not the "editing phase" (to use Jack Levy's terminology) of the choice problem accounts for more of the variance in outcomes than does the evaluation of prospects after the decision matrix has been specified is an empirical question.

Several issues concerning decision design and problem representation may affect findings on processes and outcomes. First, it is important to determine the origin of alternatives and preferences. For example, the well-known "preference over preference" effect may result when a given alternative is raised by a prominent player. Second, the ways in which the decision matrix is constructed (e.g., the ordering of alternatives and dimensions and the format in which the utilities across dimensions are represented) may also influence how information is processed as well as which choices are made. Maoz (1990a) has demonstrated that the construction of the decision matrix can provide ample opportunities for political framing and manipulation. Klein (1993) points to evidence that instead of comparing two or more alternatives to each other, many decisionmakers evaluate a single alternative on its own merits and only then decide whether or not to implement it before moving on to other alternatives. Anderson (1983) makes a distinction between comparing four alternatives against one another simultaneously as opposed to separating the four alternatives into groups of two, comparing them within each group, and then making a choice between the surviving alternatives. It is possible, of course, as many similarly structured paradoxes show, that different processes will lead to different outcomes. Finally, there is the possibility that not all alternatives are mutually exclusive, as most models of choice assume. Many alternatives, such as economic sanctions and blockade as well as different military options, are either contingent on the others' implementation or are simply not mutually exclusive.

The decision design issue becomes even more complex when one takes into account that presidents and other national leaders usually do not make important decisions in isolation. Instead, they turn to their advisers for advice and direction, calling for viable options or alternatives and considering the dimensions that each adviser introduces. One can visualize a foreign policy decision unit consisting of a national decisionmaker surrounded by advisers who are responsible for generating feasible alternatives, highlighting the criteria upon which each alternative will be judged, as well as providing evaluations of these alternatives along different dimensions. Thus the decision design problem is often confounded with the issue of collective decisionmaking, which we will return to below.

Stein and Welch (Chapter 4) address the decision design aspect of foreign policy decisionmaking by arguing that some approaches are ill suited to the task of problem representation precisely because they assume away this crucial first step: Actors are already presumed to have a set of alternatives and preferences over possible outcomes (see also Morrow, Chapter 2). Levy's discussion of prospect theory (Chapter 3) points out that it is a theory "of the evaluation of prospects but not a theory of the editing of choices." According to Levy, this is a problem for rational choice approaches as well.

Future research should devote more attention to exploring the origins of the decision matrix: How were the alternatives, dimensions, and preferences of the different actors arrived at? Why was a particular set of alternatives and dimensions included and another set ignored? Were they endogenously derived by the decisionmaker, or were they exogenously imposed? What are the ramifications for a choice based upon the set of dimensions and alternatives employed? The answers to such questions would aid researchers in modeling more realistically and effectively the decisionmaking process and how this process affects choice.

DYNAMIC ENVIRONMENT

Most studies of foreign policy decisionmaking model the decision task as though it were a static event. Researchers typically assume that alternatives and dimensions are available from the outset of a crisis and that they continue to be present throughout the entire decision task. However, history has shown that decisionmaking environments are in a constant state of flux. From the Cuban missile crisis to the Bosnian turmoil, the options available to leaders and the potential ramifications of chosen courses of action change almost on a daily basis (Anderson 1983). Not all alternatives and dimensions are present at the start of a crisis. In such a situation, it would seem that a leader would be hard-pressed to come up with a consistent ranking of preferences over outcomes. Stein and Welch (Chapter 4) note that "few (perhaps none) of the crucial pieces of information necessary to conduct a rational choice theoretic analysis—stakes, preferences, options, costs, benefits, likelihoods—are given by the structure of the interaction but are instead constructed by decisionmakers through processes of introspection, attribution, and estimation." Most cognitive theories of foreign policy decisionmaking have likewise failed to account for dynamic settings of international conflict.

This volume does contain three important studies that account for the dynamic nature in which crises unfold: Brams's work concerning the rationality of surprise and the theory of moves (Chapter 6), Simon and Starr's two-level analysis of revolution and war (Chapter 7), and Zinnes and Muncaster's work on a dispute sequence appraisal (Chapter 9). Brams designed the theory of moves to represent the moves and countermoves that decisionmakers use in response to one another's actions. Brams does assume that players are able to rank a priori their preferences over outcomes, and he models the dynamic nature of conflict by illustrating the foresight of these players and how such strategic thinking affects each player's moves. Specifically, Brams shows that a player can choose a dominated strategy—

a "surprise" move—if the future benefits of such a move outweigh the immediate consequences of moving to a worse state. However, TOM does not explicitly model changes as they occur *during* the decision task; instead, the theory accounts for the possibility of the decisionmaker's changing his or her course of action as a function of the situation and the other player's moves. Similarly, Zinnes and Muncaster assess the implications of expected utility and prospect theory on international disputes. By constantly updating the information that is available to the decisionmaker, the authors dynamically model the propensity of a third party to join an ongoing dispute based upon whether this party is operating under expected utility or prospect theory rules. This innovative approach also accounts for changes between decision tasks but not for those that occur within a given decision task.

Simon and Starr get at the notion of a dynamic environment by varying, in a multilevel computer simulation, the levels of allocation and extraction at both the domestic and international levels to determine the likelihood of war and/or revolution. Simon and Starr simulate the dynamics of domestic-international interactions. They do not explicitly model how these changes tie into foreign policy decisionmaking.

Future research needs to model more realistically the dynamic nature of foreign policy crises as events change and unfold *within* the decision task. In one such experimental example, put forth by Mintz, Geva, Redd, and Carnes (1997), a new alternative is presented to decisionmakers as they are in the midst of the decision task. A subsequent paper by Geva, Redd, and Mintz (1996) examined the consequences of an added dimension or attribute to the decision task during the simulated crisis. In both of these studies, the authors show that information processing, as well as choice, is significantly affected by the dynamic introduction of information into the decision task. It is important to accurately represent the dynamic nature of international conflict, or else we may come to incorrect conclusions about the processes decisionmakers employ as well as how information processing relates to choice.

Several methodologies can be used to study the impact of the dynamic context of political decisionmaking on strategy selection and choice. Lau (1995), for example, used a process-tracing methodology in a study of electoral behavior in a dynamic flow of information. He notes that if anything characterizes political decisions, it is their complexity. According to Lau, "Models of how people decide how to vote fly in the face of scores of studies on how people actually make other types of complex decisions" (p. 189). It would seem that the same can be said about most foreign policy decision situations.

Computational process tracing also allows the researcher to tap into the dynamic processes that decisionmakers employ as well as how these processes affect choice. Taber and Steenbergen (1995), for example, employed computational experimentation to determine what types of decision rules (processes) were the best predictors of choice (outcomes). Through the use of this innovative method, the authors demonstrated that certain rules were more likely to lead to better outcomes than others and that different decision rules or processes were more sensitive than others to changes in information load. It seems reasonable to assume that such a method could and should be used in the field of foreign policy decisionmaking. Computational tracing can help bridge the gap between studies based on process validity and those based on outcome validity.

COLLECTIVE DECISIONMAKING

Although much of the literature on foreign policy decisionmaking assumes a unitary decisionmaking model, Nisbett and Ross (1980) write that most important decisions are made by groups rather than by individuals. Certainly in the foreign policy context, as we have mentioned, decisions are often made by a national leader in consultation with key advisers.

Group members often introduce into the decision process policy alternatives to be considered as part of the overall choice set. They can also highlight certain criteria and objectives for the evaluation of policy. Finally, participants in a group decision typically arrive at the process with certain a priori preferences pertaining to the alternatives in the choice set.

A major problem for scholars of foreign policy decisionmaking is to untie some of the knots that link the explanation of macro-outcomes (foreign policies) in terms of the microbehavior of individual decisionmakers within their groups (Farkas 1996). Our knowledge of how foreign policy decisions are made is limited in part because of the increased complexity associated with the understanding of how individual preferences are aggregated into group decisions. In a well-known study, Arrow showed that the aggregation of individual preferences into a collective decision is not a trivial matter (see also Kreps 1990). Yet the rules of mathematical aggregation of individual preferences into collective choice have received little attention in the IR literature.

However, the rules of aggregation do not necessarily account for intragroup interactions and dynamics that may affect preferences and their consolidation into choice. Moreover, identifying aggregation rules is only part of the story. As Maoz writes (1990a), original preferences may change during group deliberation. For example, studies of the group polarization effect show risky and conservative shifts in group decisionmaking when comparing the individuals' original preferences and the group's final choice (Minix 1982). Thus, a risky shift represents a situation in which the group choice is more extreme in its predisposition to a high-risk alternative than what would have been expected by looking at the mean or median of the distribution of the participants' pregroup deliberation preferences (for an example of group polarization in international relations, see Semmel and Minix 1979).

Groupthink is another phenomenon that reminds us that faulty intra-group processes may hinder vigilant information processes during a decision. Both the risky shift and groupthink phenomena suggest that knowing the a priori preferences of group members and having an arsenal of aggregation models is not always sufficient to predict group choice.

The contribution of group members to the ultimate decision by leaders cannot be viewed merely as adding cognitive ingredients (more alternatives, new dimensions, or preferences and utility estimates for certain outcomes) to the decision process. Instead, a variety of group dynamics (such as risky shifts and groupthink), which are influenced in turn by a host of group characteristics, translates the contribution of the participants into the final outcome, making the whole process quite complex. Understanding the rules of aggregation of individual preferences into collective choice within the context of group dynamics enhances both process validity and outcome validity. Hence the analysis of collective decisionmaking should cover issues associated with the decision design phase (i.e., the construction of the decision matrix) and the choice phase (where a specific policy option is selected).

BEYOND THE DEBATE

Most studies of foreign policy decisionmaking have focused either on the process of decisionmaking or on the outcome of a decision. Although a few studies address both, one or the other is usually chosen as the focal point. The strength of rational choice theory lies in its ability to accurately predict and account for decision outcomes. It does so through the use of deductive assumptions about the processes that decisionmakers use in acquiring information en route to a choice. In contrast, cognitive theorists are generally interested in studying how decisions are actually being made. Thus instead of relying on a priori assumptions about the process of decisionmaking, cognitive theorists attempt to delineate exactly how decisionmakers process information in different contexts and environments. Their key assumption is that decisionmakers do not process information in the same manner in all cases, that is, different decision rules may come into play depending upon the circumstances of each decision task. Devoting more attention to decision design problems, the dynamic context of decisionmaking, and problems associated with collective decisionmaking will help bridge the gap between these "schools" of thought.

Furthermore, by focusing on these challenges, the discipline can move beyond the fractious discourse that has characterized the field thus far. We will be able to more accurately describe and predict foreign policy processes and outcomes and improve our ability to generalize about foreign policy behavior. More important, we may also be able to shed additional light on a process that President John F. Kennedy described as "mysterious because the essence of ultimate decision remains impenetrable to the observer—often, indeed, to the decider himself" (1963, p. xi).

NOTE

The authors of this chapter thank Edward Vogelpohl for research assistance.

References

Abelson, R. P., and A. Levi. 1985. "Decision Making and Decision Theory." In *The Handbook of Social Psychology,* vol. 1, eds. G. Lindzey and E. Aronson. 3rd ed. New York: Random House. Pp. 231–309.

Achen, C. H., and D. Snidal. 1989. "Rational Deterrence Theory and Comparative Case Studies." *World Politics* 41:153–169.

Acheson, D. 1969. *Present at the Creation.* New York: Norton.

Alexander, I. E. 1988. "Personality, Psychological Assessment, and Psychobiography." *Journal of Personality* 56:265–294.

Alexander, I. E. 1990. *Personology: Method and Content in Personality Assessment and Psychobiography.* Durham, N.C.: Duke University.

Allais, M. 1953. "Le Comportement de l'homme rationnel devant le risque: Critique des postulats et axiomes de l'école américaine." *Econometrica* 21:503–546.

Allison, G. T. 1971. *Essence of Decision.* Boston: Little, Brown.

Allport, G. 1958. *The Nature of Prejudice.* Garden City, N.Y.: Doubleday.

Allyn, B. J., J. G. Blight, and D. A. Welch. 1989/1990. "Essence of Revision: Moscow, Havana, and the Cuban Missile Crisis." *International Security* 14:136–172.

Anderson, C. A. 1983. "Abstract and Concrete Data in the Perseverance of Social Theories: When Weak Data Lead to Unshakable Beliefs." *Journal of Experimental and Social Psychology* 19:93–108.

Anderson, C. A., M. R. Lepper, and L. Ross. 1980. "Perseverance of Social Theories: The Role of Explanation in the Persistence of Discredited Information." *Journal of Personality and Social Psychology* 39:1037–1049.

Anderson, P. A. 1983. "Decision Making by Objection and the Cuban Missile Crisis." *Administrative Science Quarterly* 28:201–222.

Anderson, P. A. 1985. "Deciding How to Decide in Foreign Affairs: Decision-Making Strategies as Solutions to Presidential Problems." In *The Presidency and Public Policy Making,* eds. G. C. Edwards III, S. A. Shull, and N. C. Thomas. Pittsburgh: University of Pittsburgh. Pp. 151–172.

Argyris, C., and D. A. Schon. 1978. *Organizational Learning.* Reading, Mass.: Addison-Wesley.

Arkes, H. R., C. Christensen, C. Lai, and C. Blumer. 1987. "Two Methods of Overcoming Overconfidence." *Organizational Behavior and Human Decision Processes* 39:133–144.

Arkin, R., M. Appleman, and J. M. Burger. 1980. "Social Anxiety, Self-Presentation, and the Self-Serving Bias in Causal Attribution." *Journal of Personality and Social Psychology* 38:23–55.

Aronson, E., and J. M. Carlsmith. 1968. "Experimentation in Social Psychology." In *The Handbook of Social Psychology,* vol. 2, eds. G. Lindzey and E. Aronson. 2nd ed. Reading, Mass.: Addison-Wesley. Pp. 1–79.

Arrow, K. 1982. "Risk Perception in Psychology and Economics." *Economic Inquiry* 20:1–9.

Auerbach, Y. 1986. "Turning-Point Decisions: A Cognitive-Dissonance Analysis of Conflict Resolution in Israel–West German Relations." *Political Psychology* 7:533–550.

Axelrod, R. 1976. "The Cognitive Mapping Approach to Decision Making." In *Structure of Decision,* ed. R. Axelrod. Princeton: Princeton University.

Axelrod, R. 1979a. "Coping with Deception." In *Applied Game Theory,* eds. S. J. Brams, A. Schotter, and G. Schwödiauer. Würzburg, Germany: Physica-Verlag. Pp. 390–405.

Axelrod, R. 1979b. "The Rational Timing of Surprise." *World Politics* 31:228–246.

Axelrod, R. 1984. *The Evolution of Cooperation.* New York: Basic Books.

Banks, J. S., and J. Sobel. 1987. "Equilibrium Selection in Signaling Games." *Econometrica* 55:647–662.

Banks, J. S., and R. Sundaram. 1990. "Repeated Games, Finite Automata, and Complexity." *Games and Economic Behavior* 2:97–117.

Bar-Joseph, U. 1988. "Methodological Magic" (review of Levite 1987). *Intelligence and National Security* 3:134–155.

Barnet, R. 1972. *Roots of War.* New York: Atheneum.

Bazerman, M. H. 1983. "Negotiator Judgment." *American Behavioral Scientist* 27:211–228.

Beach, L. R., and T. R. Mitchell. 1978. "A Contingency Model for the Selection of Decision Strategies." *Academy of Management Review* 3:439–449.

Bendor, J., and T. H. Hammond. 1992. "Rethinking Allison's Models." *American Political Science Review* 86:301–322.

Bennett, W. L. 1975. *The Political Mind and the Political Environment.* Lexington, Mass.: Lexington Books.

Berejikian, J. 1995. "Prospect Theory and the 'Gains Dilemma' in International Relations." Paper presented at the annual meeting of the American Political Science Association, Chicago, August 31–September 3.

Bernstein, B. J. 1991. "Eclipsed by Hiroshima and Nagasaki: Early Thinking About Tactical Nuclear Weapons." *International Security* 15:149–173.

Betts, R. K. 1982. *Surprise Attack: Lessons for Defense Planning.* Washington, D.C.: Brookings Institution.

Billings, R., and C. Hermann. 1994. "Problem Re-Representation in Sequential Decisions of Foreign Policy Groups." Paper presented at the annual meeting of the International Society of Political Psychology, Universidad de Santiago, Galicia, Spain, July 12–15.

Billings, R., and S. Marcus. 1983. "Measures of Compensatory and Noncompensatory Models of Decision Behavior: Process Tracing Versus Policy Capturing." *Organizational Behavior and Human Performance* 31:331–352.

Billings, R., and L. Scherer. 1988. "The Effects of Response Mode and Importance on Decision-Making Strategies: Judgment Versus Choice." *Organizational Behavior and Human Decision Processes* 41:1–19.

Binmore, K. 1990. *Essays on the Foundations of Game Theory.* Cambridge, Mass.: Basil Blackwell.

Black, D. 1958. *Voting in Committees and Elections.* Cambridge: Cambridge University.

Blight, J. G. 1990. *The Shattered Crystal Ball: Fear and Learning in the Cuban Missile Crisis.* Savage, Md.: Rowman & Littlefield.

Blight, J. G., B. J. Allyn, and D. A. Welch. 1993. *Cuba on the Brink: Castro, the Missile Crisis, and the Soviet Collapse.* New York: Pantheon.

Blight, J. G., and D. A. Welch. 1990. *On the Brink: Americans and Soviets Reexamine the Cuban Missile Crisis.* New York: Noonday.

Blight, J. G., and D. A. Welch. 1994. "Risking 'The Destruction of Nations': Lessons of the Cuban Missile Crisis for New and Aspiring Nuclear States." *Security Studies* 4:811–850.

Boettcher, W. A. III. 1995. "Context, Methods, Numbers, and Words: Evaluating the Applicability of Prospect Theory to International Relations." *Journal of Conflict Resolution* 39:561–583.

Bradley, G. W. 1978. "Self-Serving Biases in the Attribution Process: A Reexamination of the Fact or Fiction Question." *Journal of Personality and Social Psychology* 36:56–71.

Brams, S. J. 1977. "Deception in 2 x 2 Games." *Journal of Peace Science* 2:171–203.

Brams, S. J. 1985. *Superpower Games: Applying Game Theory to Superpower Conflict.* New Haven, Conn.: Yale University.

Brams, S. J. 1993. "Theory of Moves." *American Scientist* 81:562–570.

Brams, S. J. 1994. *Theory of Moves.* New York: Cambridge University.

Brams, S. J., and D. M. Kilgour. 1988. *Game Theory and National Security.* New York: Basil Blackwell.

Brams, S. J., and W. Mattli. 1993. "Theory of Moves: Overview and Examples." *Conflict Management and Peace Science* 12:1–39.

Brandenburger, A. 1992. "Knowledge and Equilibrium in Games." *Journal of Economic Perspectives* 6:83–101.

Brecher, M. 1993. *Crises in World Politics: Theory and Reality.* New York: Pergamon.

Brecher, M. 1995. "Reflections on a Life in Academe." Paper presented at the annual meeting of the International Studies Association, Distinguished Scholar Panel, Chicago, February 22–25.

Brecher, M., and B. Geist. 1980. *Decisions in Crisis: Israel, 1967 and 1973.* Berkeley: University of California.

Brecher, M., B. Steinberg, and J. Stein. 1969. "A Framework for Research on Foreign Policy Behavior." *Journal of Conflict Resolution* 13:75–101.

Brookshire, D. S., and D. L. Coursey. 1987. "Measuring the Value of a Public Good: An Empirical Comparison of Elicitation Procedures." *American Economic Review* 77:554–566.

Bueno de Mesquita, B. 1981. *The War Trap.* New Haven, Conn.: Yale University.

Bueno de Mesquita, B. 1983. "The Costs of War: A Rational Expectations Approach." *American Political Science Review* 77:347–357.

Bueno de Mesquita, B. 1984. "A Critique of 'A Critique of *The War Trap.*'" *Journal of Conflict Resolution* 28:341–360.

Bueno de Mesquita, B. 1985. "The War Trap Revisited: A Revised Expected Utility Model." *American Political Science Review* 79:156–177.

Bueno de Mesquita, B. 1989. "The Contribution of Expected-Utility Theory to the Study of International Conflict." In *Handbook of War Studies,* ed. M. I. Midlarsky. Ann Arbor: University of Michigan. Pp. 143–169.

Bueno de Mesquita, B., and D. Lalman. 1986. "Reason and War." *American Political Science Review* 80:1113–1129.

Bueno de Mesquita, B., and D. Lalman. 1988. "Empirical Support for Systemic and Dyadic Explanations of International Conflict." *World Politics* 41:1–20.

Bueno de Mesquita, B., and D. Lalman. 1990. "Domestic Opposition and Foreign War." *American Political Science Review* 84:747–765.

Bueno de Mesquita, B., and D. Lalman. 1992. *War and Reason.* New Haven, Conn.: Yale University.

Bueno de Mesquita, B., D. Newman, and A. Rabushka. 1985. *Forecasting Political Events: The Future of Hong Kong.* New Haven, Conn.: Yale University.

Bueno de Mesquita, B., and W. H. Riker. 1982. "An Assessment of the Merits of Selective Nuclear Proliferation." *Journal of Conflict Resolution* 26:283–306.

Bueno de Mesquita, B., R. M. Siverson, and G. Woller. 1992. "War and the Fate of Regimes: A Comparative Analysis." *American Political Science Review* 86:638–646.

Burnstein, E., and M. L. Berbaum. 1983. "Stages in Group Decision Making: The Decomposition of Historical Narratives." *Political Psychology* 4:531–561.

Camerer, C. F. 1990. "Behavioral Game Theory." In *Insights in Decision Making*, ed. R. M. Hogarth. Chicago: University of Chicago. Pp. 311–336.

Camerer, C. F. 1992. "Recent Tests of Generalized Utility Theories." In *Utility Theories: Measurement and Applications*, ed. W. Edwards. Cambridge: Cambridge University. Pp. 207–251.

Camerer, C. F. 1995. "Individual Decision Making." In *The Handbook of Experimental Economics*, eds. J. H. Kagel and A. E. Roth. Princeton: Princeton University. Pp. 587–703.

Campbell, D. T. 1969. "Reform as Experiments." *American Psychologist* 24:409–429.

Caplow, T. 1968. *Two Against One: Coalitions in Triads*. Englewood Cliffs, N.J.: Prentice-Hall.

Carlson, R. 1988. "Exemplary Lives: The Uses of Psychobiography for Theory Development." *Journal of Personality* 56:105–138.

Chan, S. 1984. "Mirror, Mirror on the Wall." *Journal of Conflict Resolution* 28:617–648.

Cho, I., and D. M. Kreps. 1987. "Signaling Games and Stable Equilibria." *Quarterly Journal of Economics* 102:179–222.

Choucri, N. and R. C. North. 1989. "Lateral Pressure in International Relations: Concept and Theory." In *Handbook of War Studies*, ed. M. I. Midlarsky. Ann Arbor: University of Michigan. Pp. 289–326.

Clark, M. S. 1982. "A Role for Arousal in the Link Between Feeling States, Judgments, and Behavior." In *Affect and Cognition: The 17th Annual Symposium on Cognition*, eds. M. S. Clark and S. T. Fiske. Hillsdale, N.J.: Lawrence Erlbaum. Pp. 263–289.

Coleman, J. S. 1992. "Introducing Social Structure into Economic Analysis." In *Decision Making: Alternatives to Rational Choice Models*, ed. M. Zey. Newbury Park, Calif.: Sage. Pp. 265–272.

Conover, P. J., and S. Feldman. 1984. "How People Organize the Political World: A Schematic Model." *American Journal of Political Science* 28:95–126.

Coursey, D. L., J. L. Hovis, and W. D. Schulze. 1987. "The Disparity Between Willingness to Accept and Willingness to Pay Measures of Value." *Quarterly Journal of Economics* 102:679–690.

Cox, J. C., and R. M. Isaac. 1986. "Experimental Economics and Experimental Psychology: Ever the Twain Shall Meet?" In *Economic Psychology: Intersections in Theory and Application*, eds. A. J. and H. W. MacFadyen. Elsevier Science Publishers B. V. Pp. 647–669.

Craik, F. I. M., and R. S. Lockhart. 1972. "Levels of Processing: A Framework for Memory Research." *Journal of Verbal Learning and Voting Behavior* 11:671–676.

Crawford, V. P. 1990. "Equilibrium Without Independence." *Journal of Economic Theory* 50:127–154.

Crocker, J. 1981. "Judgment of Covariation by Social Perceivers." *Psychological Bulletin* 90:272–292.

Crocker, J., D. B. Hannah, and R. Weber. 1983. "Person Memory and Causal Attributions." *Journal of Personality and Social Psychology* 44:55–66.

Cusack, T., and R. J. Stoll. 1990. *Exploring Realpolitik*. Boulder, Colo.: Lynne Rienner.

Cusack, T., and R. J. Stoll. 1994. "Collective Security and State Survival in the Interstate System." *International Studies Quarterly* 38:33–59.

Dacey, R. 1992. "Risk Attitude, Punishment, and the Intifada." Discussion paper, Martin Institute for Peace Studies and Conflict Resolution, University of Idaho.

Dawes, R. M. 1992. "The Fundamental Attribution Error: An Important Psychological Factor in Crisis Decision Making." In *New Perspectives for a Changing World Order*, ed. E. Arnett. Washington, D.C.: American Association for the Advancement of Science.

Dayan, M. 1981. *Breakthrough: A Personal Account of the Egypt-Israel Peace Negotiations*. New York: Knopf.

De Bondt, W., and R. Thaler. 1985. "Does the Stock Market Overreact?" *Journal of Finance* 40:793–808.

De Bondt, W., and R. Thaler. 1990. "Stock Market Volatility: Do Security Analysts Overreact?" *American Economic Review* 80:52–57.

De Bondt, W., and R. Thaler. 1994. "Financial Decisionmaking in Markets and Firms: A Behavioral Perspective." Cambridge, Mass.: National Bureau of Economic Research. Working paper 4777.

DeNardo, J. 1985. *Power in Numbers*. Princeton: Princeton University.

De Rivera, J. H. 1968. *The Psychological Dimension of Foreign Policy*. Columbus, Ohio: Merrill.

DeRouen, K. 1993. "The Political Economy of the U. S. Use of Force." Ph.D. dissertation, Department of Political Science, Texas A&M University.

Diehl, P. F., R. Muncaster, D. Zinnes, and G. Goertz. 1993. "Political Shocks in Rivalry Processes." Paper presented at the North American meeting of the Peace Science Society (International), Syracuse, New York.

Dixon, W. J. 1993. "Democracy and the Management of International Conflict." *Journal of Conflict Resolution* 37:42–68.

Dixon, W. J. 1994. "Democracy and the Peaceful Settlement of International Conflict." *American Political Science Review* 88:14–32.

Dowty, A. 1984. *Middle East Crisis: U.S. Decision Making in 1958, 1970, and 1973*. Berkeley: University of California.

Ebbesen, E. B., and V. J. Koncini. 1980. "On the External Validity of Decision-Making Research: What Do We Know About Decisions in the Real World?" In *Cognitive Processes in Choice and Decision Behavior*, ed. T. S. Wallsten. Hillsdale, N.J.: Lawrence Erlbaum.

Eckstein, H. 1975. "Case Study and Theory in Political Science." In *Handbook of Political Science*, eds. F. Greenstein and N. Polsby. Reading, Mass.: Addison-Wesley.

Elster, J. 1986. "Introduction." In *Rational Choice*, ed. J. Elster. New York: New York University. Pp. 1–33.

Enzle, M. E., and D. Shopflocher. 1978. "Instigation of Attribution Processes by Attributional Questions." *Personality and Social Psychology Bulletin* 4:595–599.

Erber, R., and S. T. Fiske. 1984. "Outcome Dependency and Attention to Inconsistent Information." *Journal of Personality and Social Psychology* 47:709–726.

Etzioni, A. 1992. "Normative-Affirmative Factors: Toward a New Decision-Making Model." In *Decision Making: Alternatives to Rational Choice Models*, ed. M. Zey. Newbury Park, Calif.: Sage. Pp. 89–111.

Fahmy, I. 1983. *Negotiating for Peace in the Middle East*. Baltimore: Johns Hopkins University.

Farkas, A. 1996. "Evolutionary Models in Foreign Policy Analysis." *International Studies Quarterly* 40:343–361.

Farnham, B. 1992. "Roosevelt and the Munich Crisis: Insights from Prospect Theory." *Political Psychology* 13: 205–235.

Farnham, B., ed. 1994. *Avoiding Losses/Taking Risks: Prospect Theory and International Conflict*. Ann Arbor: University of Michigan.

Fearon, J. D. 1994. "Signaling Versus the Balance of Power and Interests: An Empirical Test of a Crisis Bargaining Model." *Journal of Conflict Resolution* 38: 236–269.

Fearon, J. D. 1995. "Rationalist Explanations for War." *International Organization* 49:379–414.

Fishburn, P. C., and G. A. Kochenberger. 1979. "Two-Piece Von Neumann–Morgenstern Utility Functions." *Decision Sciences* 10:503–518.

Fiske, S. T. 1981. "Social Cognition and Affect." In *Cognition, Social Behavior, and the Environment*, ed. J. Harvey. Hillsdale, N.J.: Lawrence Erlbaum. Pp. 227–264.

Fiske, S. T. 1982. "Schema-Triggered Affect: Applications to Social Perception." In *Affect and Cognition: The 17th Annual Symposium on Cognition*, eds. M. S. Clarke and S. T. Fiske. Hillsdale, N.J.: Lawrence Erlbaum. Pp. 55–78.

Fiske, S. T. 1986. "Schema-Based Versus Piecemeal Politics: A Patchwork Quilt, but Not a Blanket, of Evidence." In *Political Cognition*, eds. R. R. Lau and D. O. Sears. Hillsdale, N.J.: Lawrence Erlbaum. Pp. 41–53.

Fiske, S. T., D. R. Kinder, and W. M. Larter. 1983. "The Novice and the Expert: Knowledge-Based Strategies in Political Cognition." *Journal of Experimental Social Psychology* 19:381–400.

Fiske, S.T., and S. L. Neuberg. 1990. "A Continuum of Impression Formation from Category-Based to Individuating Processes: Influence of Information and Motivation on Attention and Interpretation." In *Advances in Experimental Social Psychology*, ed. M. P. Zanna. New York: Academic Press. Pp. 1–74.

Fiske, S. T., and S. E. Taylor. 1991. *Social Cognition*. 2nd ed. New York: McGraw-Hill.

Ford, K. J., N. Schmitt, S. L. Schechtman, B. M. Hults, and M. L. Doherty. 1989. "Process Tracing Methods: Contributions, Problems and Neglected Research Questions." *Organizational Behavior and Human Decision Processes* 43:75–117.

Frankel, J. 1963. *The Making of Foreign Policy: An Analysis of Decision Making*. London: Oxford University.

Freedman, L., and E. Karsh. 1991. "How Kuwait Was Won: Strategy in the Gulf War." *International Security* 16:5–41.

Freedman, L., and E. Karsh. 1993. *The Gulf Conflict 1990–91*. Princeton: Princeton University.

Friedman, G. 1993. "Multi-Level Social Conflict and External Efforts at Self Help: Jordanian Foreign Policy, 1963–1970." M.A. thesis, Department of Political Science, University of New Mexico.

Friedman, G. 1994. "Opportunity and Willingness, Two-Level Social Conflict and Balance of Threat: Iraqi Kurd–Iraqi Government Relations, 1974–1984." Manuscript, Department of Government, University of South Carolina.

Friedman, M. 1953. *Essays in Positive Economics*. Chicago: University of Chicago.

Frisch, D. 1993. "Reasons for Framing Effects." *Organizational Behavior and Human Decision Processes* 54:399–429.

Funder, D. C. 1987. "Errors and Mistakes: Evaluating the Accuracy of Social Judgment." *Psychological Bulletin* 101:75–90.

Garthoff, R. L. 1989. *Reflections on the Cuban Missile Crisis*. Rev. ed. Washington, D.C.: Brookings Institution.

Geanakoplos, J. 1992. "Common Knowledge." *Journal of Economic Perspectives* 64:53–82.

George, A. L. 1980. *Presidential Decisionmaking in Foreign Policy: The Effective Use of Information and Advice*. Boulder, Colo.: Westview.

George, A. L. 1983. *Bridging the Gap: Theory and Practice in Foreign Policy*. Washington, D.C.: United States Institute of Peace.

George, A. L. 1986. "The Impact of Crisis-Induced Stress on Decision Making." In *The Medical Implications of Nuclear War*, eds. F. Solomon and R. Q. Marsten. Washington, D.C.: National Academy. Pp. 529–552.

George, A. L., and J. L. George. 1956. *Woodrow Wilson and Colonel House*. New York: John Day.

George, A. L., and R. Smoke. 1989. "Deterrence in Foreign Policy." *World Politics* 41:170–182.

Gervasi, F. 1979. *The Life and Times of Menahem Begin: Rebel to Statesman*. New York: Putnam.

Gettys, C. F., C. W. Kelley III, and C. R. Peterson. 1973. "The Best Guess Hypothesis in Multistage Inference." *Organizational Behavior and Human Performance* 10:364–373.

Geva, N., K. R. DeRouen, and A. Mintz. 1993. "The Political Incentive Explanation of Democratic Peace: Evidence from Experimental Research." *International Interactions* 18:215–229.

Geva, N., R. Driggers, and A. Mintz. 1996. "Effects of Ambiguity on Strategy and Choice in Foreign Policy Decision Making: An Analysis Using Computerized Process Tracing." Paper presented at the annual meeting of the American Political Science Association, San Francisco, August 29–September 1.

Geva, N., and A. Mintz. 1993. "The Experimental Analyses of Conflict Processes Project: Preliminary Findings." *International Studies Notes* 18:15–20.

Geva, N., and A. Mintz. 1994. "Framing the Options for Peace in the Middle East." Paper presented at the annual conference of ECAAR-Israel, "The Political Economy of Peace in the Middle East," Haifa, Israel, June 20.

Geva, N., S. B. Redd, and A. Mintz. 1996. "Structure and Process in Foreign Policy Decision Making: An Experimental Assessment of Poliheuristic Propositions." Paper presented at the annual meeting of the International Studies Association, San Diego, California, April 16–20.

Gilpin, R. 1981. *War and Change in World Politics*. Cambridge: Cambridge University.

Gochman, C. S. 1993. "The Evolution of Disputes." *International Interactions* 18:49–76.

Gollwitzer, P. M., W. B. Earle, and W. G. Stephan. 1982. "Affect as a Determinant of Egotism: Residual Excitation and Performance Attributions." *Journal of Personality and Social Psychology* 43:702–709.

Green, D., and I. Shapiro. 1994. *Pathologies of Rational Choice Theory: A Critique of Applications in Political Science*. New Haven, Conn.: Yale University.

Grether, D. M., and C. R. Plott. 1979. "Economic Theory of Choice and the Preference Reversal Phenomenon." *American Economic Review* 69:623–638.

Grofman, B. 1993. *Information, Participation and Choice: An Economic Theory of Democracy in Perspective.* Ann Arbor: University of Michigan.

Gronn, P. 1993. "Psychobiography on the Couch: Character, Biography, and the Comparative Study of Leaders." *Journal of Applied Behavioral Science* 29:343–358.

Haas, M. 1970. "International Subsystems: Stability and Polarity." *American Political Science Review* 64:98–123.

Hamilton, J. H., and S. M. Slutsky. 1990. "Endogenous Timing in Duopoly Games: Stackelberg or Cournot Equilibria." *Games and Economic Behavior* 2:29–46.

Hamilton, J. H., and S. M. Slutsky. 1993. "Endogenizing the Order of Moves in Matrix Games." *Theory and Decision* 34:47–62.

Handel, M. I. 1981. *The Diplomacy of Surprise: Hitler, Nixon, Sadat.* Cambridge: Center for International Affairs, Harvard University.

Harsanyi, J. C. 1973. "Games with Randomly Disturbed Payoffs: A New Rationale for Mixed-Strategy Equilibrium Points." *International Journal of Game Theory* 2:1–23.

Harsanyi, J. C., and R. Selten. 1988. *A General Theory of Equilibrium Selection.* Cambridge: MIT.

Hart, P. 1991. "Irving L. Janis: Victims of Groupthink." *Political Psychology* 12:247–278.

Hartman, R. S., M. J. Doane, and C. Woo. 1991. "Consumer Rationality and the Status Quo." *Quarterly Journal of Economics* 106:141–162.

Hedberg, B. 1981. "How Organizations Learn and Unlearn." In *Handbook of Organizational Design*, vol. 1, eds. P. C. Nystrom and W. H. Starbuck. New York: Oxford University. Pp. 3–27.

Herek, G., I. Janis, and P. Huth. 1987. "Decision Making During International Crises: Is Quality of Process Related to Outcome?" *Journal of Conflict Resolution* 31:203–226.

Hermann, C. F. 1969. *Crises in Foreign Policy.* New York: Free Press.

Hermann, M. G. 1974. "Leader Personality and Foreign Policy Behavior." In *Comparing Foreign Policies: Theories, Findings, and Methods*, ed. J. N. Rosenau. New York: Sage.

Hermann, M. G. 1980. "Explaining Foreign Policy Behavior Using the Personal Characteristics of Political Leaders." *International Studies Quarterly* 24:7–46.

Hermann, M. G., and C. W. Kegley Jr. 1995. "Rethinking Democracy and International Peace: Perspectives from Political Psychology." *International Studies Quarterly* 39:511–533.

Hershey, J. C., and P. J. H. Schoemaker. 1980. "Prospect Theory's Critical Reflection Hypothesis: A Critical Examination." *Organizational Behavior and Human Performance* 25:395–418.

Higgins, E. T., and J. A. Bargh. 1987. "Social Cognition and Social Perception." In *Annual Review of Psychology* 38, eds. M. R. Rosenzweig and L.W. Porter. Palo Alto, Calif.: Annual Reviews.

Hirshleifer, J. 1985. "Protocol, Payoff, and Equilibrium: Game Theory and Social Modelling." Working paper 366, Department of Economics, University of California, Los Angeles.

Hirt, E. R., and S. J. Sherman. 1985. "The Role of Prior Knowledge in Explaining Hypothetical Events." *Journal of Experimental Social Psychology* 21:519–543.

Holsti, O. R. 1972. *Crisis, Escalation, War.* Montreal: McGill University.

Holsti, O. R. 1979. "Theories of Crisis Decision Making." In *Diplomacy: New Approaches in History, Theory and Policy*, ed. P. G. Lauren. New York: Free Press. Pp. 99–136.

Holsti, O. R. 1989. "Crisis Decision-Making." In *Behavior, Society, and Nuclear War*, vol. 1, eds. P. E. Tetlock, J. L. Husbands, R. Jervis, P. C. Stern, and C. Tilly. New York: Oxford University. Pp. 8–84.

Holsti, O. R., and A. George. 1975. "The Effects of Stress on the Performance of Foreign Policy-Makers." In *Political Science Annual: An International Review*, ed. C. P. Cotter. Indianapolis: Bobbs-Merrill. Pp. 255–319.

Holsti, O. R., C. North, and R. Brody. 1968. "Perception and Action in the 1914 Crisis." In *Quantitative International Politics*, ed. J. D. Singer. New York: Free Press. Pp. 123–158.

Holsti, O. R., C. North, and R. Brody. 1969. "The Management of International Crisis: Affect and Action in American-Soviet Relations." In *Theory and Research on the Causes of War*, eds. D. G. Pruitt and R. C. Snyder. Englewood Cliffs, N.J.: Prentice Hall. Pp. 62–79.

Hoyenga, K. B., and K. T. Hoyenga. 1984. *Motivational Explanations of Behavior: Evolutionary, Physiological and Cognitive Ideas.* Monterey, Calif.: Brooks/ Cole.

Hybel, A. R. 1986. *The Logic of Surprise in International Conflict.* Lexington, Mass.: Lexington Books.

Ikle, F. C. 1971. *Every War Must End.* New York: Columbia University.

Iyengar, S. 1991. *Is Anyone Responsible? How Television Frames Political Issues.* Chicago: University of Chicago.

Iyengar, S., and W. J. McGuire. 1993. *Explorations in Political Psychology.* Durham, N.C.: Duke University.

Jackman, R. W. 1993. *Power Without Force.* Ann Arbor: University of Michigan.

James, P., and J. R. Oneal. 1991. "Influences on the President's Use of Force." *Journal of Conflict Resolution* 35:307–332.

Janis, I. 1982. *Groupthink: Psychological Studies of Policy Decisions and Fiascoes.* New York: Houghton Mifflin.

Janis, I. 1989. *Crucial Decisions: Leadership in Policymaking and Crisis Management.* New York: Free Press.

Janis, I. L., and L. Mann. 1977. *Decision Making: A Psychological Analysis of Conflict, Choice and Commitment.* New York: Free Press.

Jervis, R. 1976. *Perception and Misperception in International Politics.* Princeton: Princeton University.

Jervis, R. 1978. "Cooperation Under the Security Dilemma." *World Politics* 30:167–214.

Jervis, R. 1986. "Cognition and Political Behavior." In *Political Cognition,* eds. J. R. R. Lau and D. O. Sears. Hillsdale, N.J.: Lawrence Erlbaum. Pp. 319–336.

Jervis, R. 1989. "Rational Deterrence: Theory and Evidence." *World Politics* 41(2): 183–207.

Jervis, R. 1991/1992. "The Future of World Politics: Will It Resemble the Past?" *International Security* 16:39–73.

Jervis, R. 1992. "Political Implications of Loss Aversion." *Political Psychology* 13:187–204.

Jervis, R., R. N. Lebow, and J. G. Stein. 1985. *Psychology and Deterrence.* Baltimore: Johns Hopkins University.

Johnson, E. J. 1988. "Expertise and Decision Under Uncertainty: Performance and Process." In *The Nature of Expertise*, eds. M. T. H. Chi, R. Glaser, and M. J. Farr. Hillsdale, N.J.: Lawrence Erlbaum.

Jones, B. 1994. *Reconceiving Decision-Making in Democratic Politics: Attention, Choice and Public Policy.* Chicago: University of Chicago.

Jones, E. E., and R. E. Nisbett. 1972. "The Actor and Observer: Divergent Perceptions of the Causes of Behavior." In *Attribution: Perceiving the Causes of Behavior*, eds. E. E. Jones, D. E. Kanouse, H. H. Kelley, R. E. Nisbett, S. Valins, and B. Weiner. Morristown, N.J.: General Learning. Pp. 79–94.

Jungermann, H. 1983. "The Two Camps on Rationality." In *Decision Making Under Uncertainty*, ed. R.W. Scholz. Amsterdam: Elsevier.

Kahneman, D., J. L. Knetsch, and R. H. Thaler. 1990. "Experimental Tests of the Endowment Effect and the Coase Theorem." *Journal of Political Economy* 98:1325–1348.

Kahneman, D., J. L. Knetsch, and R. H. Thaler. 1991. "The Endowment Effect, Loss Aversion, and Status Quo Bias." *Journal of Economic Perspectives* 5: 193–206.

Kahneman, D., P. Slovic, and A. Tversky, eds. 1982. *Judgment Under Uncertainty: Heuristics and Biases.* Cambridge: Cambridge University.

Kahneman, D., and A. Tversky. 1972. "Subjective Probability: A Judgment of Representativeness." *Cognitive Psychology* 3:430–454.

Kahneman, D., and A. Tversky. 1973. "On the Psychology of Prediction." *Psychological Review* 80:237–251.

Kahneman, D., and A. Tversky. 1979. "Prospect Theory: An Analysis of Decision Under Risk." *Econometrica* 47:263–291.

Kahneman, D., and A. Tversky. 1984. "Choices, Values and Frames." *American Psychologist* 4:341–350.

Kam, E. 1988. *Surprise Attack: The Victim's Perspective.* Cambridge: Harvard University.

Kaplan, Morton. 1957. *System and Process in International Politics.* New York: Wiley.

Kelley, H. H. 1967. "Attribution Theory in Social Psychology." In *Nebraska Symposium on Motivation*, vol. 15, ed. D. Levine. Lincoln: University of Nebraska. Pp. 192–238.

Kelley, H. H. 1972. *Causal Schemata and the Attribution Process.* Morristown, N.J.: General Learning.

Kennedy, J. F. 1963. "Forward." In *Decision-Making in the White House*, ed. T. C. Sorensen. New York: Columbia University. Pp. xi–xiv.

Kennedy, P. 1988. *The Rise and Fall of the Great Powers: Economic Change and Military Conflict from 1500 to 2000.* New York: Random House.

Khong, Y. F. 1992. *Analogies at War: Korea, Munich, Dien Bien Phu, and the Vietnam Decisions of 1965.* Princeton: Princeton University.

Kilgour, M., and F. Zagare. 1993. "Asymmetric Deterrence." *International Studies Quarterly* 37:1–27.

Kim, W., and J. D. Morrow. 1992. "When Do Power Shifts Lead to War?" *American Journal of Political Science* 36:896–922.

King, G., R. O. Keohane, and S. Verba. 1994. *Designing Social Inquiry: Scientific Inference in Qualitative Research.* Princeton: Princeton University.

Kinglake, A.W. 1863. *The Invasion of the Crimea: Its Origin and an Account of Its Progress Down to the Death of Lord Raglan.* Edinburgh: W. Blackwood and Sons.

Kissinger, H. 1979. *White House Years*. Boston: Little, Brown.

Klein, G. A. 1980. "Automated Aids for the Proficient Decision Maker." In *IEEE Transactions on Systems, Man, and Cybernetics*. New York: IEEE. Pp. 301–304.

Klein, G. A. 1989. "Recognition-Primed Decisions." In *Advances in Man-Machine System Research*, vol. 5, ed. W. B. Rouse. Greenwich, Conn.: JAI. Pp. 47–92.

Klein, G. A. 1993. "A Recognition-Primed Decision (RPD) Model of Rapid Decision Making." In *Decision Making in Action: Models and Methods*, eds. G. A. Klein, J. Orasanu, R. Calderwood, and C. E. Zsambok. Norwood, N.J.: Ablex. Pp. 138–147.

Knetsch, J. L. 1989. "The Endowment Effect and Evidence of Nonreversible Indifference Curves." *American Economic Review* 79:1277–1284.

Knetsch, J. L., and J. A. Sinden. 1984. "Willingness to Pay and Compensation Demanded: Experimental Evidence of an Unexpected Disparity in Measures of Value." *Quarterly Journal of Economics* 99:507–521.

Knetsch, J. L., and J. A. Sinden. 1987. "The Persistence of Evaluation Disparities." *Quarterly Journal of Economics* 102:691–695.

Kowert, P. A., and M. G. Hermann. 1994. "Who Takes Risks? Prospect Theory and Leadership in International Bargaining." Paper presented at the annual meeting of the International Society for Political Psychology.

Kren, G. M., and L. H. Rappoport, eds. 1976. *Varieties of Psychohistory*. New York: Springer.

Kreps, D. M. 1982. *Game Theory and Economic Modeling*. New York: Oxford University.

Kreps, D. M. 1990. *A Course in Microeconomic Theory*. Princeton: Princeton University.

Kreps, D. M., and R. Wilson. 1982. "Reputation and Imperfect Information." *Journal of Economic Theory* 27: 253–279.

Kruglanski, A.W. 1980. "Lay Epistemologic-Process and Contents: Another Look at Attribution Theory." *Psychology Review* 87:70–87.

Kruglanski, A.W. 1986. *Basic Processes in Social Cognition: A Theory of Lay Epistemology*. New York: Plenum.

Kruglanski, A.W., and I. Ajzen. 1983. "Bias and Error in Human Judgment." *European Journal of Social Psychology* 13:1–44.

Kugler, J. 1984. "Terror Without Deterrence: Reassessing the Role of Nuclear Weapons." *Journal of Conflict Resolution* 28:470–506.

Kuhl, J. 1986. "Motivation and Information Processing: A New Look at Decision Making, Dynamic Change, and Action Control." In *Handbook of Motivation and Cognition: Foundations of Social Behavior*, eds. R. M. Sorrentino and E. T. Higgins. New York: Guilford.

Kuhn, T. S. 1970. *The Structure of Scientific Revolutions*. 2nd ed. Chicago: University of Chicago.

Kuklinski, J. H., R. C. Luskin, and J. Bolland. 1991. "Where Is the Schema? Going Beyond the 'S' Word in Political Psychology." *American Political Science Review* 85:1341–1356.

Kulik, J. A. 1983. "Confirmatory Attribution and the Perpetuation of Social Beliefs." *Journal of Personality and Social Psychology* 44:1171–1181.

Lahti, P., and P. Mittelstaedt, eds. 1987. *Symposium on the Foundations of Modern Physics 1987: The Copenhagen Interpretation 60 Years After the Como Lecture, Joensuu, Finland, 6–8 August, 1987*. Singapore: World Scientific.

Lakatos, I. 1970. "Falsification and the Methodology of Scientific Research Programs." In *Criticism and the Growth of Knowledge*, eds. I. Lakatos and A. Musgrave. Cambridge: Cambridge University. Pp. 91–196.

Lakatos, I. 1978. *The Methodology of Scientific Research Programmes.* Vol. 1. Cambridge: Cambridge University.

Lamborn, A. C. 1991. *The Price of Power.* Boston: Unwin Hyman.

Lane, R. E. 1959. *Political Life: Why People Get Involved in Politics.* Glencoe, Ill.: Free Press.

Langer, E., and R. Abelson. 1972. "The Semantics of Asking a Favor: How to Succeed in Getting Help Without Really Dying." *Journal of Personality and Social Psychology* 24:26–32.

Lanzetta, J. T. 1955. "Group Behavior Under Stress." *Human Relations* 8:29–52.

Larson, D. W. 1985. *The Origins of Containment: A Psychological Explanation.* Princeton: Princeton University.

Lasswell, H. 1948. *Power and Personality.* New York: Norton.

Lau, R. R. 1995. "Information Search During an Election Campaign: Introducing a Processing-Tracing Methodology for Political Scientists." In *Political Judgment,* eds. M. Lodge and K. M. McGraw. Ann Arbor: University of Michigan. Pp. 179–205.

Lau, R. R., and D. O. Sears. 1986. "Social Cognition and Political Cognition: The Past, the Present, and the Future." In *Political Cognition,* eds. R. R. Lau and D. O. Sears. Hillsdale, N.J.: Lawrence Erlbaum. Pp. 347–366.

Laurikainen, K.V., and C. Montonen, eds. 1993. *Symposia on the Foundations of Modern Physics 1992: The Copenhagen Interpretation and Wolfgang Pauli, Helsinki, Finland, June–August 1992.* Singapore: World Scientific.

Lazarus, R. S., and S. Folkham. 1984. *Stress, Appraisal, and Coping.* New York: Springer.

Lebow, R. N. 1981. *Between Peace and War: The Nature of International Crisis.* Baltimore: Johns Hopkins University.

Lebow, R. N. 1985. "Miscalculation in the South Atlantic: The Origins of the Falklands War." In *Psychology and Deterrence,* eds. R. Jervis, R. N. Lebow, and J. G. Stein. Baltimore: Johns Hopkins University. Pp. 89–124.

Lebow, R. N. 1993. "Deterrence and Threat Assessment: The Lessons of 1962 and 1973." Paper presented to the conference on strategic warning, National War College, Fort McNair, September 27–28.

Lebow, R. N., and J. G. Stein. 1989. "Rational Deterrence Theory: I Think, Therefore I Deter." *World Politics* 61:208–234.

Lebow, R. N., and J. G. Stein. 1993. "Afghanistan, Carter, and Foreign Policy Change: The Limits of Cognitive Models." In *Diplomacy, Force, and Leadership: Essays in Honor of Alexander L. George,* eds. D. Caldwell and T. J. McKeown. Boulder, Colo.: Westview.

Lebow, R. N., and J. G. Stein. 1994. *We All Lost the Cold War.* Princeton: Princeton University.

Lee, S. C., R. G. Muncaster, and D. A. Zinnes. 1994. "The Friend of My Enemy Is My Enemy: Modeling Triadic International Relationships." *Synthese* 100:333–358.

Levite, A. 1987. *Intelligence and Strategic Surprises.* New York: Columbia University.

Levy, J. S. 1985. "The Polarity of the System and International Stability: An Empirical Analysis." In *Polarity and War,* ed. A. N. Sabrosky. Boulder, Colo.: Westview. Pp. 41–66.

Levy, J. S. 1989. "The Diversionary Theory of War: A Critique." In *Handbook of War Studies,* ed. M. I. Midlarsky. Ann Arbor: University of Michigan. Pp. 259–288.

Levy, J. S. 1992a. "An Introduction to Prospect Theory." *Political Psychology* 13:171–186.

Levy, J. S. 1992b. "Prospect Theory and International Relations: Theoretical Applications and Analytical Problems." *Political Psychology* 13:283–310.

Levy, J. S. 1994. "Learning and Foreign Policy: Sweeping a Conceptual Minefield." *International Organization* 48:279–312.

Levy, J. S. 1996a. "Hypotheses on the Framing of Decisions." Paper presented at the annual meeting of the International Studies Association, San Diego, Calif., April 16–20.

Levy, J. S. 1996b. "Loss Aversion, Framing, and Bargaining: The Implications of Prospect Theory for International Conflict." *International Political Science Review* 17:179–195.

Levy, J. S. 1997. "Prospect Theory, Rational Choice, and International Relations." *International Studies Quarterly* 41 (March): 87–112.

Lichbach, M. I. 1994. *The Rebel's Dilemma*. Ann Arbor: University of Michigan.

Lichtenstein, S., and P. Slovic. 1971. "Reversals of Preference Between Bids and Choices in Gambling Decisions." *Journal of Experimental Psychology* 89:46–55.

Lindblom, C. E. 1959. "The Science of Muddling Through." *Public Administration Review* 19:79–88.

Linville, P. W. 1982a. "Affective Consequences of Complexity Regarding the Self and Others." In *Affect and Cognition: The 17th Annual Symposium on Cognition*, eds. M. S. Clark and S. T. Fiske. Hillsdale, N.J.: Lawrence Erlbaum. Pp. 79–109.

Linville, P.W. 1982b. "The Complexity-Extremity Effect and Age-Based Stereotyping." *Journal of Personality and Social Psychology* 42:193–211.

Loomes, G., and R. Sugden. 1982. "Regret Theory: An Alternative Theory of Rational Choice Under Uncertainty." *Economic Journal* 92:805–824.

Machina, M. J. 1982. "'Expected Utility' Analysis Without the Independence Axiom." *Econometrica* 50:277–323.

Machina, M. J. 1987a. "Choice Under Uncertainty: Problems Solved and Unsolved." *Journal of Economic Perspectives* 1:121–154.

Machina, M. J. 1987b. "Decision-Making in the Presence of Risk." *Science* 236:537–543.

Machina, M. J. 1989. "Dynamic Consistency and Non–Expected Utility Models of Choice Under Uncertainty." *Journal of Economic Literature* 27:1622–1668.

Mailath, G. J., L. Samuelson, and J. Swinkels. 1993. "Extensive Form Reasoning in Normal Form Games." *Econometrica* 61:273–302.

Majeski, S. J., and D. J. Sylvan. 1984. "A Critique of *The War Trap*." *Journal of Conflict Resolution* 28:316–340.

Mandel, R. 1986. "Psychological Approaches to International Relations." In *Political Psychology*, ed. M. G. Hermann. San Francisco: Jossey-Bass. Pp. 251–278.

Mandler, G. 1975. *Mind and Emotion*. New York: John Wiley.

Maoz, Z. 1981. "The Decision to Raid Entebbe: Decision Analysis Applied to Crisis Behavior." *Journal of Conflict Resolution* 25:677–707.

Maoz, Z. 1983. "Resolve, Capabilities, and the Outcomes of Interstate Disputes, 1816–1976." *Journal of Conflict Resolution* 27:195–229.

Maoz, Z. 1986. "Multiple Paths to Choice: An Approach for the Analysis of Foreign Policy Decision Making." In *Text Analysis Procedures for the Study of*

Decision Making, eds. I. N. Gallhofer, W. E. Saris, and M. Melman. Amsterdam: Sociometric Research Foundation. Pp. 69–96.

Maoz, Z. 1990a. "Framing the National Interest: The Manipulation of Foreign Policy Decisions in Group Settings." *World Politics* 43:77–110.

Maoz, Z. 1990b. *National Choices and International Processes.* Cambridge: Cambridge University.

Maoz, Z. 1990c. *Paradoxes of War: On the Art of National Self-Entrapment.* Boston: Unwin Hyman.

Maoz, Z. 1994. "Waging War, Waging Peace: Decision Theoretic Contributions to Peace Research." In *Psychological Perspectives on War and Peace,* ed. K. Larsen. Beverly Hills: Sage.

Maoz, Z., and A. Astorino. 1992a. "The Cognitive Structure of Peacemaking: Egypt and Israel, 1970–78." *Political Psychology* 13:647–662.

Maoz, Z., and A. Astorino. 1992b. "Waging War, Waging Peace: Decision Making and Bargaining in the Arab-Israeli Conflict, 1970–1973." *International Studies Quarterly* 36:373–399.

Maoz, Z., and D. S. Felsenthal. 1987. "Self-Binding Commitments, the Inducement of Trust, Social Choice, and the Theory of International Cooperation." *International Studies Quarterly* 31:177–200.

Maoz, Z., and B. D. Mor. 1996. "Enduring International Rivalries: The Early Years." *International Political Science Review* 17:141–160.

Maoz, Z., and B. Russett. 1993. "Normative and Structural Causes of Democractic Peace." *American Political Science Review* 87:624–638.

Markus, H., and R. B. Zajonc. 1985. "The Cognitive Perspective in Social Psychology." In *The Handbook of Social Psychology,* vol. 1, eds. G. Lindzey and E. Aronson. 3rd ed. New York: Random House. Pp. 137–230.

Maslow, A. H. 1970. *Motivation and Personality.* 2nd ed. New York: Harper & Row.

McDermott, R. 1992. "The Failed Rescue Mission in Iran: An Application of Prospect Theory." *Political Psychology* 13:237–264.

McGinnis, M. D. 1991. "Richardson, Rationality, and Restrictive Models of Arms Races." *Journal of Conflict Resolution* 35:443–473.

McGinnis, M. D. 1992. "Bridging or Broadening the Gap? A Comment on Wagner's 'Rationality and Misperception in Deterrence Theory.'" *Journal of Theoretical Politics* 4:443–457.

McGinnis, M. D., and J. T. Williams. 1991. "Configurations of Cooperation: Correlated Equilibria in Coordination and Iterated Prisoner's Dilemma Games." Paper presented at the North American meeting of the Peace Science Society (International), Ann Arbor, Michigan, November 15–17.

McGinnis, M. D., and J. T. Williams. 1992. "A Model of Domestic Coalitions and International Rivalry." Paper delivered at the conference "Linkage Politics and International Conflict," University of California, Davis, May.

McGinnis, M. D., and J. T. Williams. 1993. "Policy Uncertainty in Two-Level Games: Examples of Correlated Equilibria." *International Studies Quarterly* 37: 29–54.

McInerney, A. 1992. "Prospect Theory and Soviet Policy Towards Syria, 1966–1967." *Political Psychology* 13:265–282.

Mehra, R., and E. Prescott. 1985. "The Equity Premium: A Puzzle." *Journal of Monetary Economics* 15:145–161.

Mendelson, S. E. 1993. "Internal Battles and External Wars: Politics, Learning, and the Soviet Withdrawal from Afghanistan." *World Politics* 45:327–360.

Merritt, R. I., and D. A. Zinnes. 1991. "Democracies and War." In *On Measuring Democracy*, ed. A. Inkeles. New Brunswick, N.J.: Transaction Books. Pp. 207–234.

Midlarsky, M. I. 1989. "Hierarchical Equilibria and the Long-Run Instability of Multipolar Systems." In *Handbook of War Studies*, ed. M. Midlarsky. Ann Arbor: University of Michigan. Pp. 55–81.

Miller, D. T. 1976. "Ego-Involvement and Attributions for Success and Failure." *Journal of Personality and Social Psychology* 34:901–906.

Miller, D. T., S. A. Norman, and E. Wright. 1978. "Distortion in Person Perception as a Consequence of Need for Effective Control." *Journal of Personality and Social Psychology* 36:598–602.

Minix, D. A. 1982. *Small Groups and Foreign Policy Decision-Making*. Washington, D.C.: University Press of America.

Mintz, A. 1993. "The Decision to Attack Iraq: A Noncompensatory Theory of Decision Making." *Journal of Conflict Resolution* 37:595–618.

Mintz, A., and N. Geva. 1993. "Why Don't Democracies Fight Each Other? An Experimental Study." *Journal of Conflict Resolution* 37:484–503.

Mintz, A., and N. Geva. 1997a. *The Poliheuristic Theory of Decision: A Noncompensatory Approach to Foreign Policy Decision Making*. Mimeo.

Mintz, A., and N. Geva. 1997b. "A Prospect-Based Analysis of War Termination." In *New Directions in the Study of International Conflict, Crisis, and War*, eds. F. Harvey and B. Mor. New York: Macmillan.

Mintz, A., N. Geva, S. B. Redd, and A. Carnes. 1995. "The Effect of Dynamic and Static Choice Sets on Decision Strategy: An Analysis Utilizing the Decision Board Platform." *American Political Science Review* 91 (September).

Mintz, A., and C. Huang. 1991. "Guns Versus Butter: The Indirect Link." *American Journal of Political Science* 35:738–757.

Mintz, A., and R. Stevenson. 1995. "Defense Expenditures, Economic Growth, and the 'Peace Dividend.'" *Journal of Conflict Resolution* 39:283–305.

Mitchell, T. R., and L. R. Beach. 1990. "'. . . Do I Love Thee? Let Me Count . . .' Toward an Understanding of Intuitive and Automatic Decision Making." *Organizational Behavior and Human Decision Processes* 47:1–20.

Moe, T. M. 1979. "On the Scientific Status of Rational Models." *Journal of Political Science* 23:215–243.

Monroe, K. R., ed. 1991. *The Economic Approach to Politics: A Critical Reassessment of the Theory of Rational Action*. New York: HarperCollins.

Monroe, K. R. 1995. "Psychology and Rational Actor Theory." *Political Psychology* 16:1–21.

Mor, B. D. 1993. *Decision and Interaction in Crisis: A Model of International Crisis Behavior*. Westport, Conn.: Praeger.

Morgan, P. 1983. "Examples of Strategic Surprise in the Far East." In *Strategic Military Surprise: Incentives and Opportunities*, eds. K. Knorr and P. Morgan. New Brunswick, N.J.: Transaction Books. Pp. 43–76.

Morgan, T. C. 1994. *Untying the Knot of War: A Bargaining Theory of International Crises*. Ann Arbor: University of Michigan.

Morgan, T. C., and K. Bickers. 1992. "Domestic Discontent and the External Use of Force." *Journal of Conflict Resolution* 36:25–52.

Morgan, T. C., and R. K. Wilson. 1990. "The Spatial Model of Crisis Bargaining: An Experimental Test." Paper presented at the annual meeting of the International Society of Political Psychology, Washington, D.C., June 11–14.

Morrow, J. D. 1988. "Social Choice and System Structure in World Politics." *World Politics* 41:75–97.

Morrow, J. D. 1989a. "Capabilities, Uncertainty, and Resolve: A Limited Information Model of Crisis Bargaining." *American Journal of Political Science* 33:941–972.

Morrow, J. D. 1989b. "A Twist of Truth: A Reexamination of the Effects of Arms Races on the Occurrence of War." *Journal of Conflict Resolution* 33:500–529.

Morrow, J. D. 1994. *Game Theory for Political Scientists*. Princeton: Princeton University.

Most, B. A., and H. Starr. 1989. *Inquiry, Logic and International Politics*. Columbia: University of South Carolina.

Mueller, D. C. 1993. "Democracy: The Public Choice Approach." In *Democracy and Decision: The Pure Theory of Electoral Preference,* eds. G. Brennan and L. E. Lomasky. Cambridge: Cambridge University.

Mueller, J. E. 1991/1992. "Pearl Harbor: Military Inconvenience, Political Disaster." *International Security* 16: 172–203.

Mueller, J. E. 1992. "American Public Opinion and the Gulf War: Trends and Historical Comparisons." Paper presented at the Midwest Political Science Association meeting.

Muncaster, R. G., and Zinnes, D. A. 1992. "A Model of Dispute Processes. Phase I: The Dynamics of Internation Relationships." Paper presented at the North American meeting of the Peace Science Society (International), Pittsburgh.

Myers, D. G., and H. Lamm. 1976. "The Group Polarization Phenomenon." *Psychological Bulletin* 83:602–627.

Nalebuff, B. 1991. "Rational Deterrence in an Imperfect World." *World Politics* 43:313–335.

Neale, M. A., and M. H. Bazerman. 1985. "The Effects of Framing and Negotiator Overconfidence on Bargaining Behaviors and Outcomes." *Academy of Management Journal* 28:34–49.

Neale, M. A., V. L. Huber, and G. B. Northcraft. 1987. "The Framing of Negotiations: Contextual Versus Task Frames." *Organizational Behavior and Human Decision Processes* 39:228–241.

Neale, M. A., and G. B. Northcraft. 1991. "Behavioral Negotiation Theory: A Framework for Conceptualizing Dyadic Bargaining." *Research in Organizational Behavior* 13:147–190.

Neisser, U. 1980. "On 'Social Knowing.'" *Personality and Social Psychology Bulletin* 6:601–605.

Neustadt, R. E., and E. R. May. 1986. *Thinking in Time: The Uses of History for Decision-Makers*. New York: Free Press.

Newell, A., and H. A. Simon. 1972. *Human Problem Solving*. Englewood Cliffs, N.J.: Prentice-Hall.

Nielson, S. L., and S. G. Sarason. 1981. "Emotion, Personality, and Selective Attention." *Journal of Personality and Social Psychology* 41:945–960.

Niou, E. M. S., and P. C. Ordeshook. 1990. "Stability in Anarchic International Systems." *American Political Science Review* 84:1207–1234.

Niou, E. M. S., P. C. Ordeshook, and G. F. Rose. 1989. *The Balance of Power: Stability in International Systems*. New York: Cambridge University.

Nisbett, R. E., and L. Ross. 1980. *Human Inference: Strategies and Shortcomings of Social Judgment*. Englewood Cliffs, N.J.: Prentice-Hall.

Nye, J. S., Jr. 1987. "Nuclear Learning and U.S.-Soviet Security Regimes." *International Organization* 41:371–402.

Oberschall, A. 1973. *Social Conflict and Social Movements*. Englewood Cliffs, N.J.: Prentice-Hall.

Ostrom, C., and B. Job. 1986. "The President and the Political Use of Force." *American Political Science Review* 80:541–566.

Ostrom, T., J. H. Lingle, J. B. Pryor, and N. Geva. 1980. "Cognitive Organization of Person Impressions." In *Person Memory: The Cognitive Bases of Impressions*, eds. R. Hastie, T. M. Ostrom, E. B. Ebbesen, R. J. Wyer Jr., D. L. Hamilton, D. E. Carlston. Hillsdale, N.J.: Lawrence Erlbaum. Pp. 55–88.

O'Sullivan, C. S., and F. T. Durso. 1984. "Effect of Schema-Incongruent Information on Memory for Stereotypical Attributes." *Journal of Personality and Social Psychology* 47:55–70.

Paul, T. V. 1994. *Asymmetric Conflicts: War Initiation by Weaker Powers*. Cambridge: Cambridge University.

Payne, J., J. Bettman, and E. Johnson. 1988. "Adaptive Strategy Selection in Decision Making." *Journal of Experimental Psychology* 14:534–552.

Payne, J., J. Bettman, and E. Johnson. 1993. *The Adaptive Decision Maker*. Cambridge: Cambridge University.

Peters, T., and R. H. Waterman. 1982. *In Search of Excellence*. New York: Harper & Row.

Powell, R. 1989. "Crisis Stability in the Nuclear Age." *American Political Science Review* 83:61–76.

Powell, R. 1990. *Nuclear Deterrence Theory: The Search for Credibility*. Cambridge: Cambridge University.

Pruitt, D. G. 1971. "Choice Shifts in Group Discussion: An Introductory Review." *Journal of Personality and Social Psychology* 20:339–360.

Pruitt, D. G. 1981. *Negotiation Behavior*. New York: Academic.

Pryor, J. B., and N. Kriss. 1977. "The Cognitive Dynamics of Salience in the Attribution Process." *Journal of Personality and Social Psychology* 35:49–55.

Putnam, R. D. 1988. "Diplomacy and Domestic Politics: The Logic of Two-Level Games." *International Organization* 42:427–460.

Pyszczynski, T. A., and J. Greenberg. 1981. "Role of Disconfirmed Expectancies in the Instigation of Attributional Processing." *Journal of Personality and Social Psychology* 40:31–38.

Quattrone, G. A., and A. Tversky. 1988. "Contrasting Rational and Psychological Analyses of Political Choice." *American Political Science Review* 82:719–736.

Quester, G. H. 1977. *Offense and Defense in the International System*. New York: John Wiley.

Rapoport, A., and M. J. Guyer. 1966. "A Taxonomy of 2 x 2 Games." *General Systems: Yearbook of the Society for General Systems Research* 11:203–214.

Raynor, J. O., and D. B. McFarlin. 1986. "Motivation and the Self-System." In *Handbook of Motivation and Cognition: Foundations of Social Behavior*, eds. R. M. Sorrentino and E. T. Higgins. New York: Guilford.

Reder, L. M., and J. R. Anderson. 1980. "A Partial Resolution of the Paradox of Inference: The Role of Integrating Knowledge." *Cognitive Psychology* 12:447–472.

Regan, D. T., E. Straus, and R. Fazio. 1974. "Liking and the Attributional Process." *Journal of Experimental Social Psychology* 10:385–397.

Reitman, W. 1965. *Cognition and Thought*. New York: John Wiley.

Richardson, L. 1992. "Avoiding and Incurring Losses: Decision-making in the Suez Crisis." *International Journal* 47:370–401.

Richardson, L. 1993. "Avoiding and Incurring Losses: Decision-making in the Suez Crisis." In *Choosing to Co-operate: How States Avoid Loss*, eds. J. G. Stein and L. W. Pauly. Baltimore: Johns Hopkins University.

Riker, W. H. 1995. "The Political Psychology of Rational Choice Theory." *Political Psychology* 16:23–44.

Rosenau, J. N. 1969. "Linkage Politics: Essays on the Convergence of National and International Systems." In *Linkage Politics*, ed. J. N. Rosenau. New York: Free Press. Pp. 44–63.

Rosenberg, S. W. 1995. "Against Neoclassical Political Economy: A Political Psychological Critique." *Political Psychology* 16:99–136.

Rosenthal, R. W. 1991. "A Note on Robustness of Equilibria with Respect to Commitment Opportunities." *Games and Economic Behavior* 3:237–243.

Ross, L. 1977. "The Intuitive Psychologist and His Shortcomings: Distortions in the Attribution Process." In *Advances in Experimental Social Psychology*, vol. 10, ed. L. Berkowitz. New York: Academic. Pp. 173–220.

Ross, L., and C. R. Anderson. 1982. "Shortcomings in the Attribution Process: On the Origins and Maintenance of Erroneous Social Assessments." In *Judgment Under Uncertainty: Heuristics and Biases*, eds. D. Kahneman, P. Slovic, and A. Tversky. Cambridge: Cambridge University.

Ross, L., M. R. Lepper, and M. Hubbard. 1975. "Perseverance in Self Perception and Social Perception: Biased Attributional Processes in the Debriefing Paradigm." *Journal of Personality and Social Psychology* 32:800–892.

Ross, M., and F. Sicoly. 1979. "Egocentric Biases in Availability and Attribution." *Journal of Personality and Social Psychology* 37:322–336.

Roth, A. E. 1995. "Introduction to Experimental Economics." In *The Handbook of Experimental Economics*, eds. J. H. Kagel and A. E. Roth. Princeton: Princeton University. Pp. 3–109.

Rubin, J. Z., and B. R. Brown. 1975. *The Social Psychology of Bargaining and Negotiation*. New York: Academic.

Runyan, W. M. 1984. *Life Histories and Psychobiography: Explorations in Theory and Method*. New York: Oxford University.

Runyan, W. M. 1988. "Progress in Psychobiography." *Journal of Personality* 56:295–323.

Russett, B. 1990a. *Controlling the Sword*. Cambridge: Harvard University.

Russett, B. 1990b. "Economic Decline, Electoral Pressure, and the Initiation of Interstate Conflict." In *Prisoners of War? Nation-States in the Modern Era*, eds. C. S. Gochman and A. N. Sabrosky. Lexington, Mass.: D. C. Heath. Pp. 123–140.

Russett, B. 1993. *Grasping the Democratic Peace*. Princeton: Princeton University.

Russett, B. 1995. "The Democratic Peace: 'And Yet It Moves.'" *International Security* 19:164–175.

Sadat, A. 1978. *In Search of Identity: An Autobiography*. New York: Harper & Row.

Sadat, A. 1984. *Those I Have Known*. New York: Continuum.

Sage, A. P. 1990. "Human Judgment and Decision Rules." In *Concise Encyclopedia of Information Processing in Systems and Organizations*, ed. A. P. Sage. New York: Pergamon. Pp. 232–244.

Salert, B., and J. Sprague. 1980. *Dynamics of Riots*. Ann Arbor, Mich.: Inter-University Consortium for Political and Social Research.

Samuelson, W., and R. Zeckhauser. 1988. "Status Quo Bias in Decision Making." *Journal of Risk and Uncertainty* 1:7–59.

Sargent, T. J. 1993. *Bounded Rationality in Macroeconomics*. Oxford: Clarendon.

Saris, W., and I. Gallhofer. 1984. "Formulations of Real-Life Decisions: A Study of Foreign Policy Decisions." *Acta Psychologica* 56:247–265.

Schank, R., and R. Abelson. 1977. *Scripts, Plans, Goals, and Understanding: An Inquiry into Human Knowledge Structures.* Hillsdale, N.J.: Lawrence Erlbaum.

Schelling, T. C. 1965. *Arms and Influence.* New Haven, Conn.: Yale University.

Schelling, T. C. 1978. *Micromotives and Macrobehavior.* New York: Norton.

Schelling, T. C. 1988. Foreword. to *Surprise Attack: The Victim's Perspective.* Cambridge: Harvard University. Pp. xiiv–xv.

Seligman, M. E. P. 1975. *Helplessness: On Depression, Development, and Death.* San Francisco: Freeman.

Semmel, A. K., and D. Minix. 1979. "Small-Group Dynamics and Foreign Policy Decision-Making: An Experimental Approach." In *Psychological Models in International Politics,* ed. L. S. Falkowski. Boulder, Colo.: Westview.

Shafir, E. 1992. "Prospect Theory and Political Analysis: A Psychological Perspective." *Political Psychology* 13:311–322.

Shefrin, H., and M. Statman. 1985. "The Disposition to Sell Winners Too Early and Ride Losers Too Long: Theory and Evidence." *Journal of Finance* 40:777–790.

Sicoly, F., and M. Ross. 1977. "Facilitation of Ego-Based Attributions by Means of Self-Serving Observer Feedback." *Journal of Personality and Social Psychology* 35:734–741.

Silver, E. 1984. *Begin: The Haunted Prophet.* New York: Random House.

Simon, H. 1957. *Models of Man.* New York: John Wiley.

Simon, H. 1959. "Theories of Decision-Making in Economics and Behavioral Science." *American Economic Review* 49:253–283.

Simon, H. 1973. "The Structure of Ill-Structured Problems." *Artificial Intelligence* 4:181–201.

Simon, H. 1976. "From Substantive to Procedural Rationality." In *Method and Appraisal in Economics,* ed. Spiro J. Latsis. Cambridge: Cambridge University. Pp. 129–148.

Simon, H. 1985. "Human Nature in Politics: The Dialogue of Psychology with Political Science." *American Political Science Review* 79:293–304.

Simon, H. 1986. "Rationality in Psychology and Economics." In *Rational Choice,* eds. R. M. Hogarth and M. W. Reder. Chicago: University of Chicago. Pp. 25–40.

Simon, H. 1995a. "The Information-Processing Theory of Mind." *American Psychologist* 50:507–508.

Simon, H. 1995b. "Rationality in Political Behavior." *Political Psychology* 16:45–61.

Simon, M. 1991. "A Dynamic Model of Civil Conflict: Implications for Intervention." Ph.D. dissertation, Department of Political Science, Indiana University.

Simon, M. 1994. "Hawks, Doves, and Civil Conflict Dynamics: A 'Strategic' Action-Reaction Model." *International Interactions* 19:213–239.

Simon, M. and H. Starr. 1995. "Two-Level Security Management and the Prospects for New Democracies: A Simulation Analysis." Paper presented at the annual meeting of the American Political Science Association, Chicago, August 31–September 3.

Simon, M., and H. Starr. 1996. "Extraction, Allocation, and the Rise and Decline of States: A Simulation Analysis of Two-Level Security Management." *Journal of Conflict Resolution* 40:272–297.

Sinden, J. L., and J. A. Sinden. 1984. "Willingness to Pay and Compensation Demanded: Experimental Evidence of an Unexpected Disparity in Measures of Value." *Quarterly Journal of Economics* 99:507–521.

Sitkin, S. B. 1992. "Learning Through Failure." *Research in Organizational Behavior* 14:231–266.

Slovic, P., and S. Lichtenstein. 1983. "Preference Reversals: A Broader Perspective." *American Economic Review* 73:596–605.

Slovic, P., B. Fischhoff, S. Lichtenstein, B. Corrigan, and B. Combs. 1977. "Preference for Insuring Against Probable Small Losses." *Journal of Risk and Insurance* 44:237–258.

Small, M., and J. D. Singer. 1976. "The War-Proneness of Democratic Regimes, 1816–1965." *Jerusalem Journal of International Relations* 1:50–69.

Small, M., and J. D. Singer. 1982. *Resort to Arms: International and Civil Wars, 1816–1980.* Beverly Hills: Sage.

Snidal, D. 1986. "The Game *Theory* of International Politics." In *Cooperation Under Anarchy*, ed. K. Oye. Princeton: Princeton University. Pp. 25–57.

Sniderman, P. M., R. A. Brody, and P. E. Tetlock. 1991. *Reasoning and Choice: Explorations in Political Psychology.* Cambridge: Cambridge University.

Snyder, G., and P. Diesing. 1977. *Conflict Among Nations: Bargaining, Decision Making and System Structure in International Crises.* Princeton: Princeton University.

Snyder, J. 1984. *The Ideology of the Offensive: Military Decision Making and the Disasters of 1914.* Ithaca, N.Y.: Cornell University.

Srull, T. K. 1981. "Person Memory: Some Tests of Associative Storage and Retrieval Models." *Journal of Experimental Psychology* 7:440–463.

Starr, H. 1990. "Modeling the Internal-External Linkage: Rethinking the Relationship Between Revolution, War and Change." Paper presented at the annual meeting of the American Political Science Association, San Francisco.

Starr, H. 1991a. "Opportunity and Willingness and the Nexus Between Internal and External Conflict." Paper presented at the annual meeting of the Western Political Science Association, Seattle.

Starr, H. 1991b. "The Relationship Between Revolution and War: A Theoretical Overview." Paper presented at the annual meeting of the International Studies Association, Vancouver, Canada, March 19–24.

Starr, H. 1994. "Revolution and War: Rethinking the Linkage Between Internal and External Conflict." *Political Research Quarterly* 47:481–507.

Starr, H., and M. D. McGinnis. 1992. "War, Revolution, and Two-Level Games: A Simple Choice-Theoretic Model." Paper presented at the North American meeting of the Peace Science Society (International), Pittsburgh.

Stein, A. A. 1976. "Conflict and Cohesion: A Review of the Literature." *Journal of Conflict Resolution* 20:143–172.

Stein, A. A. 1982. "When Misperception Matters." *World Politics* 34:505–526.

Stein, J. G. 1985a. "Calculation, Miscalculation, and Conventional Deterrence I: The View from Cairo." In *Psychology and Deterrence*, eds. R. Jervis, R. N. Lebow, and J. G. Stein. Baltimore: Johns Hopkins University. Pp. 34–59.

Stein, J. G. 1985b. "Calculation, Miscalculation, and Conventional Deterrence II: The View from Jerusalem." In *Psychology and Deterrence*, eds. R. Jervis, R. N. Lebow, and J. G. Stein. Baltimore: Johns Hopkins University. Pp. 60–88.

Stein, J. G. 1989. "Prenegotiation in the Arab-Israeli Conflict: The Paradoxes of Success and Failure." In *Getting to the Table: The Processes of International Prenegotiation*, ed. J. G. Stein. Baltimore: Johns Hopkins University. Pp. 174–206.

Stein, J. G. 1992a. "Deterrence and Compellence in the Gulf, 1990–91: A Failed or Impossible Task?" *International Security* 17:147–179.

Stein, J. G. 1992b. "International Cooperation and Loss Avoidance: Framing the Problem." *International Journal* 47:202–234.

Stein, J. G. 1994. "Political Learning by Doing: Gorbachev as Uncommitted Thinker and Motivated Learner." *International Organization* 48:155–183.

Stein, J. G., and L.W. Pauly, eds. 1993. *Choosing to Co-operate: How States Avoid Loss.* Baltimore: Johns Hopkins University.

Stein, J. G., and R. Tanter. 1980. *Rational Decision-Making: Israel's Security Choices, 1967.* Columbus: Ohio State University.

Steinbruner, J. D. 1974. *The Cybernetic Theory of Decision: New Dimensions of Political Analysis.* Princeton: Princeton University.

Stockholm International Peace Research Institute. 1995. *SIPRI Yearbook 1995: Armaments, Disarmament, and International Security.* Oxford: Oxford University.

Stohl, M. 1980. "The Nexus of Civil and International Conflict." In *Handbook of Political Conflict,* ed. T. R. Gurr. New York: Free Press. Pp. 297–330.

Strongman, K. T. 1978. *The Psychology of Emotion.* New York: John Wiley.

Suedfeld, P., and A. D. Rank. 1976. "Revolutionary Leaders: Long-Term Success as a Function of Changes in Conceptual Complexity." *Journal of Personality and Social Psychology* 34:169–178.

Suedfeld, P., and P. E. Tetlock. 1977. "Integrative Complexity of Communication in International Crisis." *Journal of Conflict Resolution* 21:168–184.

Suedfeld, P., and P. E. Tetlock. 1992. "Psychological Advice About Political Decision Making: Heuristics, Biases, and Cognitive Defects." In *Psychology and Social Policy,* eds. P. Suedfeld and P. E. Tetlock. New York: Hemisphere. Pp. 51–70.

Taber, C. S. 1989. "Power Capability Indexes in the Third World." In *Power in World Politics,* eds. R. J. Stoll and M. D. Ward. Boulder, Colo.: Lynne Rienner. Pp. 29–48.

Taber, C. S., and M. R. Steenbergen. 1995. "Computational Experiments in Electoral Behavior." In *Political Judgment,* eds. M. Lodge and K. M. McGraw. Ann Arbor: University of Michigan. Pp. 141–178.

Taliaferro, J. W. 1994. "Analogical Reasoning and Prospect Theory: Hypotheses on Framing." Paper presented at the annual meeting of the International Studies Association, Washington, D.C., March 29–April 2.

Taylor, S. E. 1982. "The Availability Bias in Social Perception and Interaction." In *Judgment Under Uncertainty: Heuristics and Biases,* eds. D. Kahneman, P. Slovic, and A. Tversky. Cambridge: Cambridge University.

Telhami, S. 1990. *Power and Leadership in International Bargaining: The Path to the Camp David Accords.* New York: Columbia University.

Temperley, H. 1964. *England and the Near East: The Crimea.* Hamden, Conn.: Archon Books.

Tesser, A. 1978. "Self-Generated Attitude Change." In *Advances in Experimental Social Psychology,* vol. 11, ed. L. Berkowitz. New York: Academic. Pp. 289–338.

Tesser, A. 1986. "Some Effects of Self-Evaluation Maintenance on Cognition and Action." In *Handbook of Motivation and Cognition: Foundations of Social Behavior,* eds. R. M. Sorrentino and E. T. Higgins. New York: Guilford.

Tetlock, P. E. 1980. "Explaining Teacher Explanations for Pupil Performance: An Examination of the Self-Presentation Interpretation." *Social Psychological Quarterly* 43:283–290.

Tetlock, P. E. 1985. "Integrative Complexity of American and Soviet Foreign Policy Rhetorics: A Time-Series Analysis." *Journal of Personality and Social Psychology* 49:1565–1585.

Tetlock, P. E. 1986. "Psychological Advice on Foreign Policy: What Do We Have to Contribute?" *American Psychologist* 41:557–567.

Tetlock, P. E. 1992. "The Impact of Accountability on Judgment and Choice: Toward a Social Contingency Model." In *Advances in Experimental Social Psychology,* vol. 25, ed. M. P. Zanna. San Diego, Calif.: Academic.

Tetlock, P. E., and R. Boettger. 1989. "Cognitive and Rhetorical Styles of Traditionalist and Reformist Soviet Politicians: A Content Analysis." *Political Psychology* 10:209–232.

Tetlock, P. E., and A. Levi. 1982. "Attribution Bias: On the Inconclusiveness of the Cognitive-Motivation Debate." *Journal of Experimental Social Psychology* 18:68–88.

Thaler, R. 1980. "Toward a Positive Theory of Consumer Choice." *Journal of Economic Behavior and Organization* 1:39–60.

Thorndyke, P. W., and B. Hayes-Roth. 1979. "The Use of Schemata in the Acquisition and Transfer of Knowledge." *Cognitive Psychology* 11:82–105.

Tilly, C. 1975. "Reflections on the History of European State-Making." In *The Formation of National States in Western Europe,* ed. C. Tilly. Princeton: Princeton University.

Tilly, C. 1978. *From Mobilization to Revolution.* Reading, Mass.: Addison-Wesley.

Tilly, C. 1985. "Connecting Domestic and International Conflicts, Past and Present." In *Dynamic Models of International Conflict.,* eds. U. Luterbacher and M. D. Ward. Boulder, Colo.: Lynne Rienner. Pp. 517–531.

Trope, Y. 1975. "Seeking Information About One's Own Ability as a Determinant of Choice Among Tasks." *Journal of Personality and Social Psychology* 32:1004–1013.

Trope, Y., and Z. Ginossar. 1988. "On the Use of Statistical and Nonstatistical Knowledge: A Problem-Solving Approach." In *The Social Psychology of Knowledge,* eds. D. Bar-Tal and A. W. Kruglanski. Cambridge: Cambridge University. Pp. 209–230.

Tsebelis, G. 1990. *Nested Games.* Berkeley: University of California.

Tversky, A., and D. Kahneman. 1973. "Availability: A Heuristic for Judging Frequency and Probability." *Cognitive Psychology* 5:207–232.

Tversky, A., and D. Kahneman. 1974. "Judgment Under Uncertainty: Heuristics and Biases." *Science* 185:1124–1131.

Tversky, A., and D. Kahneman. 1981. "The Framing of Decisions and the Psychology of Choice." *Science* 211:453–458.

Tversky, A., and D. Kahneman. 1982. "Judgments of and by Representativeness." In *Judgment Under Uncertainty: Heuristics and Biases,* eds. D. Kahneman, P. Slovic, and A. Tversky. Cambridge: Cambridge University.

Tversky, A., and D. Kahneman. 1986. "Rational Choice and the Framing of Decisions." *Journal of Business* 59:S251–S284.

Tversky, A., and D. Kahneman. 1991. "Loss Aversion in Riskless Choice: A Reference Dependent Model." *Quarterly Journal of Economics* 41:1039–1061.

Tversky, A., and D. Kahneman. 1992. "Advances in Prospect Theory: Cumulative Representation of Uncertainty." *Journal of Risk and Uncertainty* 5:297–323.

Tversky, A., P. Slovic, and D. Kahneman. 1990. "The Causes of Preference Reversal." *American Economic Review* 80:204–217.

Tversky, A., and P. Wakker. 1995. "Risk Attitudes and Decision Weights." *Econometrica* 63:1255–1280.

Uhlaner, C. J. 1993. "What the Downsian Voter Weighs: A Reassessment of the Costs and Benefits of Action." In *Information, Participation and Choice: An*

Economic Theory of Democracy in Perspective, ed. B. Grofman. Ann Arbor: University of Michigan. Pp. 67–79.

van Damme, E. 1991. *Stability and Perfection of Nash Equilibria.* Heidelberg, Germany: Springer.

van Damme, E., and S. Hurkens. 1993. "Commitment Robust Equilibria and Endogenous Timing." Discussion paper no. 9356, Center for Economic Research, Tilburg University, the Netherlands.

Vertzberger, Y. I. 1990. *The World in Their Minds: Information Processing, Cognition, and Perception in Foreign Policy Decisionmaking.* Stanford, Calif.: Stanford University.

Volkan, V. D., and N. Itzkowitz. 1984. *The Immortal Attaturk: A Psychobiography.* Chicago: University of Chicago.

Von Neumann, J., and O. Morgenstern. 1944. *Theory of Games and Economic Behavior.* New York: John Wiley.

Von Winterfeldt, D., and E. Edwards. 1986. *Decision Analysis and Behavioral Research.* New York: Cambridge University.

Voss, J. F., T. R. Greene, T. A. Post, and B. C. Penner. 1983. "Problem-Solving Skill in the Social Sciences." In *The Psychology of Learning and Motivation: Advances in Research and Theory,* vol. 17, ed. G. H. Bower. New York: Academic. Pp. 165–213.

Voss, J. F., and T. A. Post. 1988. "On the Solving of Ill-Structured Problems." In *The Nature of Expertise,* eds. M. T. H. Chi, R. Glaser, and M. J. Farr. Hillsdale, N.J.: Lawrence Erlbaum.

Voss, J. F., C. R. Wolfe, J. A. Lawrence, and R. A. Engle. 1991. "From Representation to Decision: An Analysis of Problem Solving in International Relations." In *Complex Problem Solving: Principles and Mechanisms,* eds. R. J. Sternberg and P. A. Frensch. Hillsdale, N.J.: Lawrence Erlbaum.

Walker, S. G. 1988. "The Impact of Personality Structure and Cognitive Processes Upon American Foreign Policy Decisions." Paper delivered at the annual meeting of the American Political Science Association, Washington, D.C.

Walt, S. M. 1987. *The Origins of Alliances.* Ithaca, N.Y.: Cornell University.

Waltz, K. N. 1964. "The Stability of a Bipolar World." *Daedalus* 93:881–909.

Waltz, K. N. 1979. *Theory of International Politics.* Reading, Mass.: Addison-Wesley.

Ward, M., D. Davis, and C. Lofdahl. 1995. "A Century of Tradeoffs: Defense and Growth in Japan and the United States." *International Studies Quarterly* 39:27–50.

Welch, D. A. 1993. *Justice and the Genesis of War.* Cambridge: Cambridge University.

Weyland, K. 1996. "Risk Taking in Latin American Economic Restructuring: Lessons from Prospect Theory." *International Studies Quarterly* 40: 185–208.

Wilkenfeld, J. 1972. "Model for the Analysis of Foreign Conflict Behavior of States." In *Peace, War and Numbers,* ed. B. Russett. Beverly Hills: Sage.

Williams, J. T., and M. McGinnis. 1991. "Bayesian Correlated Equilibria in Spatial Voting Games." Paper presented at the annual meeting of the American Political Science Association, Washington, D.C.

Winkler, R. L., and A. H. Murphy. 1973. "Experiments in the Laboratory and the Real World." *Organizational Behavior and Human Performance* 10:252–270.

Wintrobe, R. 1990. "The Tinpot and the Totalitarian: An Economic Theory of Dictatorship." *American Political Science Review* 84:849–872.

Wittman, D. 1991. "Contrasting Economic and Psychological Analyses of Political Choice: An Economist's Perspective on Why Cognitive Psychology Does Not

Explain Democratic Politics." In *The Economic Approach to Politics: A Critical Reassessment of the Theory of Rational Action,* ed. K. R. Monroe. New York: HarperCollins. Pp. 405–432.

Wohlstetter, R. 1962. *Pearl Harbor: Warning and Decision.* Stanford, Calif.: Stanford University.

Wu, S. S. G., and B. Bueno de Mesquita. 1994. "Assessing the Dispute in the South China Sea: A Model of China's Security Decision Making." *International Studies Quarterly* 38:379–403.

Wyer, R. S., Jr., and S. E. Gordon. 1982. "The Recall of Information About Persons and Groups." *Journal of Experimental Social Psychology* 18:128–164.

Young, H. P. 1993. "The Evolution of Conventions." *Econometrica* 61:57–84.

Young, O. R. 1975. "The Bargainer's Calculus." In *Bargaining: Formal Theories of Negotiation,* ed. O. R. Young. Urbana: University of Illinois. Pp. 364–387.

Zagare, F. 1977. "A Game-Theoretic Analysis of the Vietnam Negotiations: Preferences and Strategies, 1968–1973." *Journal of Conflict Resolution* 21:663–684.

Zagare, F. 1987. *The Dynamics of Deterrence.* Chicago: University of Chicago.

Zagare, F. 1990. "Rationality and Deterrence." *World Politics* 42:238–260.

Zagare, F., and M. Kilgour. 1993. "Modeling Massive Retaliation." *Conflict Management and Peace Science* 13:61–86.

Zajonc, R. B. 1980. "Feeling and Thinking: Preferences Need No Inferences." *American Psychologist* 35:151–175.

Zajonc, R. B., P. Pietromonaco, and J. Bargh. 1982. "Independence and Interaction of Affect and Cognition." In *Affect and Cognition: The 17th Annual Symposium on Cognition,* eds. M. S. Clark and S. T. Fiske. Hillsdale, N.J.: Lawrence Erlbaum.

Zey, M. 1992. *Decision Making: Alternatives to Rational Choice Models.* Newbury Park, Calif.: Sage.

Zukier, H. 1986. "The Paradigmatic and Narrative Modes in Goal-Guided Inference." In *Handbook of Motivation and Cognition: Foundations of Social Behavior,* eds. R. M. Sorrentino and E. T. Higgins. New York: Guilford.

Contributors

Steven J. Brams is professor of politics at New York University. He is the author or co-author of twelve books that involve applications of game theory and social choice theory to voting and elections, international relations, and the Bible and theology. His most recent books are *Theory of Moves* (Cambridge University Press, 1994) and, with Alan D. Taylor, *Fair Division: From Cake-Cutting to Dispute Resolution* (Cambridge University Press, 1996). He is a fellow of the American Association for the Advancement of Science, a Guggenheim fellow, and a past president of the Peace Science Society (International).

Nehemia Geva is assistant professor of political science at Texas A&M University. He is the author of articles on cognitive processes in decisionmaking, experimental analyses of choice and democratic peace. He is also a member of the program in Foreign Policy Decision Making in the Department of Political Science at the George Bush Presidential Library Complex at Texas A&M University.

Jack S. Levy is professor of political science at Rutgers University. He is the author of *War in the Modern Great Power System, 1495–1975,* and over forty article-length publications. His research interests include the causes of war and theories of decisionmaking.

Zeev Maoz is professor of political science and head of the Jaffee Center for Strategic Studies at Tel-Aviv University. His books include: *Domestic Sources of Global Change* (University of Michigan Press, 1996), *Paradoxes of War* (Unwin Hyman, 1990), *National Choices and International Processes* (Cambridge University Press, 1990), and *Paths to Conflict* (Westview Press, 1982). His articles are published in the *American Political Science Review, World Politics, Journal of Conflict Resolution, International Studies Quarterly,* and the *Journal of Strategic Studies,* among others. He is currently working on a project on enduring rivalries in world politics. The International Studies Association selected Professor Maoz for the Karl Deutsch Award in 1989.

Alex Mintz is the Cullen-McFadden Professor of political science and director of the program in Foreign Policy Decision Making in the Department

247

of Political Science at the George Bush Presidential Library Complex at Texas A&M University. He is the author of numerous books and articles on political decisionmaking, simulation and experimentation, and defense politics and economics. The International Studies Association selected Professor Mintz for the Karl Deutsch Award in 1993.

James D. Morrow is senior research fellow at the Hoover Institution and Professor, by Courtesy, of political science at Stanford University. His published research uses game theoretic models to explore issues in crisis bargaining, alliances, and international cooperation. The International Studies Association selected Dr. Morrow for the Karl Deutsch Award in 1994.

Robert G. Muncaster is associate professor of mathematics and political science at the University of Illinois at Urbana-Champaign, specializing in applied mathematics. His current research interests are split between theoretical mechanics and international relations. In the latter area he has focused on the development and study of models of international conflict, with recent work published in the *Journal of Conflict Resolution, Synthese,* and the *Journal of Theoretical Politics.*

Steven B. Redd is a Ph.D. candidate in the Department of Political Science at Texas A&M University. His research interests include decision theory and foreign policy decisionmaking.

Marc V. Simon is associate professor of political science at Bowling Green State University. His research interests include international and civil conflict and their linkages, conflict resolution, economic sanctions, and game theory. He has recently published articles in *Journal of Conflict Resolution* and *International Interactions.*

Harvey Starr is the Dag Hammarskjöld Professor in International Affairs at the University of South Carolina. He is the former president of the Conflict Processes Section of the American Political Science Association (1992–1995), and APSA vice president (1995–1996). The editor of *International Interactions* since 1991, he specializes in international relations theory and method, international conflict, and foreign policy analysis. His most recent book is *Anarchy, Order and Integration: How to Manage Interdependence* (University of Michigan Press).

Janice Gross Stein is the Harrowston Professor of Conflict Management and Negotiation in the Department of Political Science at the University of Toronto. She specializes in conflict management, Middle East politics and

Canadian foreign policy. Some of her recent publications include *We All Lost the Cold War* (with Richard Ned Lebow) and *Powder Keg in the Middle East: The Struggle for Gulf Security* (edited with Geoffrey Kemp). Professor Stein is currently chair of the Research Advisory Board to the Honorable Lloyd Axworthy, minister of foreign affairs, Ottawa, Canada.

David A. Welch is associate professor of political science at the University of Toronto. During the 1996–1997 academic year, he was visiting associate professor of international relations (research) at the Thomas J. Watson Jr. Institute for International Studies, Brown University, and visiting fellow at the Center for International Affairs, Harvard University.

Dina A. Zinnes is the Merriam Professor of Political Science, director of the Merriam Laboratory for Analytic Political Research and co-founder and co-director of Data Development for International Research (DDIR) at the University of Illinois at Urbana-Champaign. Her professional leadership includes past service as president of the International Studies Association, Midwest Political Science Association, and Peace Science Society (International), vice president of the American Political Science Association, and editor of *American Political Science Review.* An active scholar interested in the dynamics of inner-nation interaction, her current research focuses on those patterns of hostile activities which produce international crises and wars and the application of mathematical models to describe and study these and other social processes.

Index

Abelson, R. P., 98
Ad hoc decisionmaking style, 171
Affect, 60–61
Allais, M., 37
Alliances, 139, 147
Alternatives: in decision design, 216, 217; in poliheuristic theory, 82–83, 85, 86–87, 90–92, 94(table), 95, 96–97. *See also* Choice; Individual choice; Preferences
Ambiguity: in rational choice theory, 52–53; in TIP, 174, 175(table), 176–177(table)
Analytic decisionmaking behavior, 1; in TIP, 166, 167, 171–172, 173, 175, 176, 178. *See also* Rational choice theory
Anderson, 217
ANOVA, 96, 97, 98
Anticipation: games, 108(fig.), 111, 116, 125, 127(n17), 128(nn 20, 21), 129(n33); Pearl Harbor attack, 125, 128(nn 23, 24)
Arab-Israeli conflict (1970–1975), 171, 172, 173
Archimedean axiom, 13–14
Arrow, Kenneth, 3, 220
Astorino, A., 167
Attitude, 74(n10)
Attribution theory: in cognitive psychology, 54–55, 58, 60–61, 75(nn 15, 17, 20); and fundamental error, 54, 74(n8); in motivational psychology, 58, 74(n14)

Backward induction, 21–22, 31(n4); in TOM, 110, 112–113, 114, 115, 116, 127(nn 16, 18, 19)
Balance-of-power theory, 14, 139
Bargaining theory, 20, 47, 49
Barnet, R., 141
Bayesian equilibrium, 16, 22–24, 134
Beach, L. R., 215
Begin, Menachem, 122, 123, 125
Beliefs, 23; in cognitive psychology, 54, 55, 74(n8); in game theory, 21, 22, 23–24, 30

Biases, 35, 37, 59; cognitive and motivational factors, 54, 55, 57–58, 59, 60, 61, 75(nn 17, 18)
Billings, R. 97
Binmore, K., 24
Bipolar international system, 146–147, 156, 202, 204
Black, D., 68, 71
Bounded rationality, 16–17, 24–25, 57, 81, 87, 139
Brecher, M., 5, 176
Brody, R. A., 4
Bueno de Mesquita, B., 4, 163, 183; expected utility model, 68–72, 76(nn 29, 31, 32, 33, 34), 77(nn 35, 36)
Building capabilities. *See* Defense capabilities
Bureaucratic politics, 45–46, 48

Certainty effect, 38, 45
Change, in cognitive schemata, 55–56
Chicken (game), 103, 126(n3)
Choice, 41, 50(n11); in cognitive theory, 53, 58–61, 75(n20); in expected utility theory, 2, 14–15, 16, 30, 37, 48, 76(n24); in game theory, 18, 21, 22, 26; in poliheuristic theory, 82, 99; in prospect theory, 33, 36–37, 40, 43–46, 48, 62–64, 76(n24); in rational choice theory, 13, 26, 53, 64–65; theory of risky, 38, 40, 44; and uncertainty, 13, 31(n1). *See also* Alternatives; Expected utility theory; Individual choice; Preferences; Reference point framing; Theory of international processes
Civil conflict. *See* Domestic security; Opposition groups
Cognitive complexity, 56, 74(n11), 166, 167
Cognitive psychology, 1, 53–57, 72–73, 74(n8); decisionmaking model, 1, 2, 4, 5–6, 7(n1), 167, 173, 175, 176, 221. *See also under* Choice

Coleman, James, 3
Collective decisionmaking. *See under*
    Decisionmaking
Common knowledge, in game theory, 25
Common logic security model. *See* State
    security (common logic) model
Concession aversion. *See* Loss aversion
Conflict. *See* Opposition groups;
    Revolution; War
Conjectures, 20, 23; in game theory, 17, 18,
    19–20, 21, 24
Crimean War, 70
Cuban missile crisis, 41, 50(n11), 61–62,
    76(nn 26, 27)
Cybernetic decisionmaking behavior, 1, 81,
    173, 175, 176

De Bondt, W., 3
Decision board simulator, 89–93, 94–95, 97,
    99
Decisionmaking, 1, 3, 5–6, 74(n10),
    157(n7), 163, 179, 180, 180(n4); in Arab-
    Israeli conflict, 172–178; and cognitive
    complexity, 56, 74(n11), 166, 167;
    collective, 43–46, 48, 163, 167–168,
    171–172, 180(n5), 220–221; as dynamic,
    216, 218–220; individual, 163–164,
    171–174; matrices and design, 215–218;
    personality in, 165, 166, 177; problem
    representation, 67–68, 72, 73. *See also*
    Alternatives; Choice; Cognitive
    psychology; Game theory; Individual
    choice; Poliheuristic theory; Preferences;
    Rational choice theory; Stress; Theory of
    international processes; Time Pressure
Defense capabilities: in state security model,
    135(fig.), 136, 138(table), 144(fig.), 145,
    147, 148(fig.)
Deterrence processes, 139
Dictatorship, 150
Dispute initiation, 26–28
Dispute sequence model, 184–192, 210,
    210(n1); polarization in, 202–208,
    209(table), 211(nn 3, 4); simulations, 185,
    195–208, 209(table)
Domestic political behavior. *See* Political
    behavior
Domestic security: in state security model,
    131, 132, 135(fig.), 136, 138(table),
    144(fig.), 145–146, 147, 148(fig.), 149,
    153, 154(fig.), 155, 158(n18)

Doves, 141–142, 148(fig.), 149–150, 151,
    153, 154(fig.), 155–156, 159(nn 21, 24)
Dowty, A., 176

EBA. *See* Elimination By Aspect
Egypt, 121–123, 129(n31), 172, 173(table)
Elections, voter behavior, 3, 4, 68, 71, 219
Elimination By Aspect (EBA) rule, 5, 83,
    98, 100(n8)
Endowment effect, in prospect theory, 35,
    36–37, 40, 49(n5), 63
Equilibrium theory, 24–25; in belief, 21;
    mixed strategy, 20, 21, 29, 30. *See also*
    Bayesian equilibrium; Game theory; Nash
    equilibria; Nonmyopic equilibria;
    Strategy, game theory; Theory of moves
Etzioni, Amitai, 3
Expected utility theory, 2–3, 5, 6, 13–14, 17,
    48, 49(nn 3, 8); and dispute sequence
    model, 194, 195–197, 198, 201, 203(fig.),
    204, 205(fig.), 206, 207–208; and
    internation relations, 191–192;
    performance of, 68–72, 76(nn 29, 31, 32,
    33, 34), 77(nn 35, 36); and prospect
    theory, 34, 41–43, 48, 50(n13); utility
    function in, 197–198. *See also* Rational
    choice theory; *under* Choice; Individual
    choice

Familiarity, 82, 92, 94, 98, 99
Fearon, J. D., 28
Finite automata theory, 25
First strike, 27–28; Pearl Harbor attack, 118,
    128(n24)
Framing. *See* Reference point framing
Freedman, L., 85
Friedman, Milton, 2, 153

Gains and losses. *See* Loss aversion; Risk
    acceptance/aversion
Gambles, 13–14, 39, 121
Game theory, 17–26, 30, 104; termination,
    112, 114; in TIP, 169; two-level (nested),
    131, 133, 134, 135, 153; 2 x 2, 103, 110.
    See also Nash equilibria; Order of play;
    Peace initiative; Pearl Harbor attack;
    Prisoners' Dilemma; Strategy, game
    theory; Surprise Game; Theory of moves;
    under Choice; Outcomes
Geist, B., 176
George, A. L., 4

Geva, N., 15, 132, 219
Green, D., 4
Grofman, B., 2, 4
Groupthink, 44, 221. *See also* Decisionmaking
Gulf crisis, 85, 100(n6)

Harsanyi, J. C., 20
Hart, Thomas, 118
Hawks, 141–142, 147–150, 151, 153, 154(fig.), 156, 159(nn 21, 24)
Hegemons, 147, 148–149
Herek, G., 4
Heuristics: in cognitive psychology, 54–55, 58–60; in poliheuristic theory, 84–85, 88, 90, 92–93, 100(n5)
Historical study, 27, 28, 31(n9)
Huth, P., 4

Ikle, F. C., 141
Independence axiom, 14, 15, 21
Individual choice, 1, 14; and collective decisionmaking, 43–46, 167–168, 171–172, 220–221; in expected utility theory, 14, 15–16, 37; in prospect theory, 15–16, 43–46; in TIP, 166–167, 169, 170, 171, 179, 180(n5)
Information process, 1, 27–28, 217, 218, 219; and cognitive complexity, 56–57, 74(n11); in cognitive psychology, 53–54, 59, 75(n16), 221; in game theory, 18, 22; incomplete, 124, 169; motivational psychology, 57–58; in poliheuristic theory, 89, 92–93, 94, 95–98, 101(nn 9, 11); and schemata, 60
International conflict. *See* Revolution; War
International system, 193; evolution of relationships, 184–185. *See also* Dispute sequence model; Polarity; State security (common logic) model; Theory of international processes
Invariance assumption, 2, 3, 87
Israel, 121–123, 125, 172, 173(table)

Janis, I., 4, 44
Jervis, R., 4
Jordan, 153, 173(table)

Kahneman, D., 36, 38
Kaplan, Morton, 139
Karsh, E., 85
Kennedy, John F., 222

Khrushchev, Nikita, 41
Kilgour, M., 112
Kimmel, Husband, 118
Kissinger, Henry, 121
Klein, G. A., 217
Kugler, J., 28

Lakatos, I., 68, 69, 71, 76(n29)
Lalman, D., 4
Lau, R. R., 219
Lebow, R. N., 4
Legitimacy, 132, 138(table), 140, 142, 151, 152(fig.), 153, 154(fig.), 157, 159(nn 22, 23)
Levi, A., 98
Levy, J. S., 183, 195, 200, 218
Lichtenstein, S., 3
Loss aversion: in group decisionmaking, 44–45; and individual choice, 43; in poliheuristic theory, 83–84; in prospect theory, 33, 35–36, 40, 44–47, 75(n23); in rational choice theory, 48

Major powers, 138(table), 146(fig.), 147, 148(fig.), 149, 150(fig.), 152(figs.), 153, 154(fig.)
Maoz, Z., 167, 217, 220
McGinnis, M. D., 131, 134
Military expenditure, 150, 159(n21)
Minor powers, 138(table), 146(fig.), 147, 148(fig.), 149, 150(fig.), 151, 152(figs.), 153, 154(fig.), 159(n20)
Mintz, A., 8, 15, 83, 132, 219
Mitchell, T. R., 215
Mor, B. D., 180
Morgan, T. C., 89
Morgenstern, O., 2, 34
Most, B. A., 131, 133, 153
Motivational psychology, 57–58, 60–61, 72–73
Mueller, D. C., 83
Multipolar international system, 146–147

Nash equilibria, 25, 103–104, 124, 126(nn 3, 6); order of play, 105, 106(fig.), 107, 108, 109, 110; Pearl Harbor attack, 129(n32); stability, 110, 115, 116, 127(n9); in TOM, 113, 115, 117, 124, 128(nn 20, 21). *See also* Surprise Game
Network effect, in evolution of internation relations, 186

Niou, E. M. S., 14
Nisbett, R. E., 60, 220
NMEs. *See* Nonmyopic equilibria
Noise, in Pearl Harbor attack, 118,
  128(n23)
Noncompensatory process: in poliheuristic
  theory, 85–86, 93, 100(nn 3, 4), 132
Nonmyopic equilibria (NMEs), 104, 105,
  124, 126(nn 2, 6); in TOM, 116, 117,
  128(nn 19, 20)
Nuclear powers: and nonnuclear powers,
  28–29

Objective games, in TIP, 169, 170, 181(n7)
Objective reality, 168–169, 181(n6). *See
  also* True world
Opportunity perception, 164, 171, 174,
  175(table), 176–177(table)
Opposition groups, 151; mobilization, 142,
  149, 158(n12); and resource extraction,
  140, 141, 151, 153, 158(nn 8, 9); in state
  security model, 132–133, 135(fig.), 137,
  138(table)
Optimality assumption, 3
Order of play, 103, 126(n2); in Nash
  equilibria, 105, 106(fig.), 107, 108, 109,
  110; Pearl Harbor attack, 118, 128(n23);
  Surprise Game, 104, 109, 127(nn 10, 14);
  in TOM, 104, 105, 110, 111, 116, 117,
  124
Ordeshook, P. C., 14
*Organizational Behavior and Human
  Decision Making*, 2
Outcomes, 2, 6, 67, 163, 168, 220; in
  cognitive psychology, 60; and decision
  process, 26, 217, 220; and expected utility
  theory, 15; in game theory, 17, 18, 30,
  103, 105, 107, 109, 113, 168, 169; Pearl
  Harbor attack, 118–120; in poliheuristic
  theory, 87, 88; and probability, 37–38,
  49(n6); in prospect theory, 40, 42, 46–47,
  49(n4); Surprise Game, 105, 107; in TIP,
  163, 168–169, 170, 171–172, 178, 179,
  181(n8); in TOM, 104, 110, 111, 113,
  116, 124

Palestine Liberation Organization, (PLO),
  172, 173(table)
Payoffs, 103; in game theory, 18, 19, 20, 22,
  25, 31(n5); in Surprise Game, 104, 105,
  106, 107; in TOM, 110, 111, 116

Peace initiative (Sadat to Israel), 105,
  121–123, 129(nn 30, 31)
Pearl Harbor attack, 105, 117–121, 125,
  128(nn 22, 23, 25, 28), 129(nn 32, 34)
PLO. *See* Palestine Liberation Organization
Polarity, 146–147, 153, 154(fig.); in dispute
  sequence model, 202–208, 209(table),
  211(nn 3, 4)
Policy alternatives. *See* Alternatives
Policy choice. *See* Choice
Policy preferences. *See* Preferences
Poliheuristic theory, 14, 15, 23, 30–31,
  81–88; experimental demonstration,
  88–100, 100(nn 6, 8), 101(nn 12, 13). *See
  also under* Choice
Political behavior: in poliheuristic theory,
  83–84, 85, 86, 91, 93, 100(nn 2, 4); in
  prospect theory, 45–46, 48
Prediction: in expected utility theory, 71,
  77(n36)
Preemption game, 109–110
Preferences: in poliheuristic theory, 92; in
  rational choice theory, 12–14, 64–65,
  69–70; in TIP, 166, 167, 170. *See also*
  Alternatives; Choice; Individual choice
Prisoners' Dilemma, 67, 76(n27), 108, 168
Probability, 37–38; in dispute sequence
  model, 192, 200, 201(fig.); in group
  decisionmaking, 45; and outcome, 37–38,
  49(n6); in poliheuristic theory, 87; in
  prospect theory, 38–39, 42, 46–47
Prospect theory, 3, 14, 15–16, 23, 30–31,
  33–39, 41–47, 100(n1); and dispute
  sequence model, 183–184, 191–192,
  194–197, 198, 199–201, 203(fig.), 204,
  205(fig.), 206(fig.), 208; and expected
  utility theory, 41–43, 50(n13), 48;
  experimental research, 39–41;
  international conflict study, 62–64; and
  rational choice theory, 34, 44, 47–48;
  value function, 199– 200. *See also*
  Reference point framing; Risky choice
  theory; *under* Choice; Individual choice
Psychological study, 29–30; and
  international conflict study, 61–62, 67, 72,
  75(n22). *See also* Cognitive psychology;
  Motivational psychology
Push/pull models of behavior, 57–58
Putnam, R. D., 131, 134

Quattrone, G. A., 3

Rational choice theory, 1–2, 3, 4, 5–6, 7(n1), 12–14, 17, 26–30, 51–52, 221; and ambiguity, 52–53; and decision complexity, 52– 53, 73(n4); and international conflict, 23, 64–70, 73, 76(n26); and prospect theory, 34, 44, 47–48; and uncertainty, 13, 16, 31(n1). *See also* Analytic decisionmaking behavior; Bounded rationality; Expected utility theory; Game theory; *under* Choice

Rationality, 3, 166, 168, 180; in expected utility model, 69–70, 71–72; in game theory, 19, 103, 104, 108, 109, 112–113, 114, 124, 134, 168; Pearl Harbor attack, 120, 129(nn 28, 29); procedural/substantive, 42–43; Sadat peace initiative, 123; and surprise, 128(n23), 129(n29); in TOM, 111, 114, 116. *See also* Bounded rationality; Expected utility theory; Rational choice theory

Rational termination, 112, 114

Real world. *See* Objective reality; True world

Rebel groups. *See* Opposition groups

Redd, S. B., 219

Reference point framing: in Cuban missile crisis, 41, 50(n11); in prospect theory, 35, 36–37, 40, 42, 44–45, 46, 47, 49(n4), 63

Reflection effect, 35, 40, 45–47, 48

Relationship currency, 184–185, 193

Resolve, national, 27–28, 31(n7)

Resource allocation, 149, 156; domestic, 149, 159(nn 19, 23); in state security model, 141–142, 144(fig.), 145, 158(nn 10, 11); and system size, 145

Resource extraction, 135(fig.), 140–143, 148–149, 153, 156, 158(n13); international, 149, 159(n19); and legitimacy, 140, 151, 159(nn 22, 23); and rebel groups, 140–141, 158(nn 8, 9); in state security model, 135(fig.), 138(table), 142–143, 144(fig.), 154(fig.), 158(n11); and system size, 145. *See also* Hawks

Resources, societal. *See* Societal resources

Revolution, 134–135, 151, 157(n4), 159(n22). *See also* Opposition groups; War

Risk acceptance/aversion, 31(n1), 33, 43, 44–45; in dispute sequence model, 197, 200, 211(n2); in prospect theory, 33, 35,

36, 37, 38–39, 40, 41–42, 44, 49(n7), 63, 75(n23), 76(n24), 221; in state security model, 133, 135(fig.), 137–138, 145, 157(n6)

Risky choice theory, 38, 40, 44, 221

Roosevelt, Franklin, 118

Ross, L., 60, 220

Sadat, Anwar, 105, 121–123

Satisficing, 7, 57, 84, 86–87

Scapegoating, 138(table), 142

Schelling, T. C., 132

Schemata: in cognitive psychology, 54, 55–56, 60, 73(n6), 74(nn 7, 9)

Scherer, L., 97

Security. *See* State security (common logic) model

Security gains. *See under* State security (common logic) model Self-interest, political, 83

Shapiro, I., 4

Simon, Herbert, 42, 81, 141

Simplified representation, 67–68, 72–73

Situational ambiguity, in TIP, 174, 175(table), 176–177(table)

Slovic, P., 3

Sniderman, P. M., 4

Snyder, J., 26

Social cognition, 56–57, 101(n11)

Social conflict, common logic model, 132–134

Societal resources: in state security model, 135(fig.), 136, 138(table), 142, 144(fig.), 145, 148, 149, 150(fig.), 152(fig.), 153, 154(fig.), 155(fig.), 156, 157

Stark, Harold, 118

Starr, H., 131, 133, 134, 153

States (outcomes in game matrix), 104, 105, 126(n6); in TOM, 110–111, 112, 113, 116, 124, 127(nn 15, 17, 18), 128(n21)

State security model, 131–135; gains in state security system, 151, 152(figs.), 153, 154(fig.); simulation of capabilities, 135–143, 144(fig.), 145–156, 158(nn 14, 15, 16, 17), 159(n25); system size in, 143, 145–146, 154(fig.), 158(n18); willingness to act in, 27, 132, 136, 137, 138(table), 141, 144(fig.), 152(fig.), 153, 154(fig.), 156

State viability, 132–133, 142, 150, 155–156

Status quo, 141; bias, in prospect theory, 35, 37, 83; in state security model, 131, 134, 135(fig.), 141, 142, 157(nn 3, 4)
Steenbergen, M. R., 219
Stein, J. G., 4, 29, 173
Steinbruner, John, 81
Strategic decisionmaking style, in TIP, 171
Strategic interaction, 23, 25, 26, 46–47
Strategy, game theory, 18–19, 23–25, 26, 110, 127(n14); dominant, 18, 103, 105–106, 107, 109, 115, 123, 124, 126(n3), 128(nn 20, 21); dominated, 19, 103, 104, 105, 126(n5), 218; Pareto-superior/inferior, 107, 108, 127(nn 10, 19); pure/mixed, 20–21, 29; in TOM, 110, 127(n15). *See also* Equilibrium theory; Simplified representation
Stress, 164–166, 177; in TIP, 171, 174, 175(table), 176–177(table), 178–180
Subjective games: in TIP, 169–170
Suedfeld, P., 82, 87, 88
Surprise, 105, 126(n7), 171
Surprise attacks, 128(nn 23, 27), 129(n29); and TOM, 123–126, 128(n23). *See also* Pearl Harbor attack
Surprise Game, 103–110, 123–124, 126(n4); in TOM, 110–117, 124– 126
Syrian-Israeli disengagement agreements, 172, 173(table)

Taber, C. S., 219
Tanter, R., 173
Telhami, S., 122
Tetlock, P. E., 4, 82, 87, 88
Thaler, R., 3
Theory of international processes (TIP): decisionmaking model, 164, 166–172, 178–180, 180(n4); research design and findings, 172–178. *See also* International system; State security (common logic) model; Stress
Theory of moves (TOM), 104–105, 110–117, 124–125, 219. *See also* Pearl Harbor attack; Peace initiative
Threat perception, 165; minimizing

maximum, 139–140, 142, 157(n7); Pearl Harbor attack, 128(n23); in state security model, 133, 135(fig.), 137–139; in TIP, 171, 174, 175(table), 176–177(table)
Time pressure, 93, 164–165; in TIP, 171, 174, 175(table), 176–177(table)
TIP. *See* Theory of international processes
TOM. *See* Theory of moves
True world, 189, 190–191, 193, 197, 201; in dispute sequence model, 204, 206(fig.), 207(fig.), 208. *See also* Objective reality
Tsebelis, G., 131
Tversky, A., 3, 36, 38

Uncertainty, 13, 15, 16, 29, 30, 31(n1)
Unipolar international system, 146–147, 156, 202
Unitary actor model, 44, 131
United States: Arab-Israel conflict, 173(table); Pearl Harbor attack, 117–121, 125
Utility theory. *See* Expected utility theory

Value function, 199–200
Vertzberger, Y. I., 4
Von Neumann, J., 2, 34
Voter turnout, 3–4, 68, 71, 219

Walt, Stephen, 139
War, 26–27; frequency, 159(n25); initiation, in common logic model, 134–135, 157(n4); willingness to act, 27, 132, 137, 141, 142, 151, 152(fig.), 153, 156
Warning: Pearl Harbor attack, 128(n23)
War Trap (Bueno de Mesquita), 183
Welch, D., 29
Welch, D. A., 4
Wilson, R. K., 89
Wintrobe, R., 150
Wittman, D., 4

Yamamoto, Isoroku, 120
Yom Kippur War (1973), 122, 172

Zagare, F., 112

About the Book

Reviewing, comparing, and contrasting major models of foreign policy decisionmaking, contributors to this volume make a contribution to the substantial debate between cognitive and rational theories of decisionmaking.

The authors describe the leading cognitive and rational models and introduce alternative models of foreign policy choice (prospect theory, poliheuristic theory, theory of moves, and two-level games). They also identify conditions under which one strategy is more appropriate than another. Their collective work addresses the questions at the core of the debate about the actual decisionmaking behavior of political leaders.